THE HOMESTEAD STRIKE
OF 1892

THE

HOMESTEAD

STRIKE

OF 1892

ARTHUR G. BURGOYNE

With an Afterword by
DAVID P. DEMAREST, JR.

UNIVERSITY OF PITTSBURGH PRESS

Published by the University of Pittsburgh Press, Pittsburgh, Pa. 15260

Copyright © 1979, University of Pittsburgh Press

Feffer and Simons, Inc., London

Manufactured in the United States of America

Library of Congress Cataloging in Publication Data

Burgoyne, Arthur Gordon, d. 1914.
  The Homestead strike of 1892.

  Reprint of the 1893 ed. published by Rawsthorne Engraving and Printing
Co., Pittsburgh under title: Homestead.
  1. Homestead Strike, 1892.   I.   Title.
[HD5325.I5 1892.H42 1979]   331.89′287′1   79-4702
ISBN 0-8229-3405-1
ISBN 0-8229-5310-2 pbk.

CONTENTS

ILLUSTRATIONS

HOMESTEAD.

A Complete History of the Struggle of July, 1892, between
the Carnegie Steel Company, Limited, and the Amalgamated Association of Iron and Steel Workers.

BY

ARTHUR G. BURGOYNE.

ILLUSTRATED.

PITTSBURGH, PA.
1893.

PRESS OF
RAWSTHORNE ENGRAVING AND PRINTING CO.
PITTSBURGH.

INTRODUCTION.

THE demand voiced by representative working-men in the Pittsburgh district, not only on their own account but on that of their brethren the world over, for a correct and impartial history of the Homestead trouble, sufficiently explains the appearance of this volume.

The importance of the theme requires no demonstration. Since labor first organized for its own protection it has passed through no period more prolific in soul-stirring events and significant developments than that extending from July to November, 1892, and including the lock-out at the Carnegie mills, the battle with 300 Pinkerton guards, the military occupation of Homestead, the trial of labor leaders on capital charges and the ultimate collapse of the Amalgamated lodges for lack of funds to continue the struggle against non-unionism. This was a conflict of far more than local interest. It was watched with anxiety by both friends and foes of organized labor on both sides of the Atlantic; it claimed the attention of leaders of thought in all departments of human activity; it stirred up the British House of Parliament and the United States Congress, agitated the newspaper press of both continents, became an issue in the election for President and is said to have contributed more largely to the defeat of Benjamin Harrison by Grover Cleveland than any other influence.

The injection of partisan considerations into public discussion of the Homestead affair led naturally to a vast amount of misrepresentation, and even at this late day the causes and character of the struggle are widely misunderstood. It has been the mission of the author of this history to sift out the truth, to make clear the motives and methods of the disputants on both sides, and to recount in detail the events of the contest without sacrificing historic accuracy to romantic effect.

Personal observations in the course of visits to the "seat of war" while hostilities were in progress, and subsequent conversations with the leaders has made the task a comparatively easy one.

Little attempt is made to philosophize on the varying phases of the labor question as presented at Homestead. It is left largely to the reader to form his own deductions from the facts set forth and from the opinions of recognized authorities, not forgetting Mr. Carnegie himself, which are liberally cited.

That through the perusal of "Homestead" new light may be borne in upon some of the many who persist in regarding the American workingman as a mere piece of mechanism, deservedly at the mercy of his employer, is the earnest hope of   THE AUTHOR.

PITTSBURGH, November 22, 1893.

CONTENTS.

CHAPTER XVII. Capitulation.

CHAPTER XVIII. The First Trial.

CHAPTER XIX. Weaving New Toils.

CHAPTER XX. The Denouement.

HOMESTEAD.

CHAPTER I.

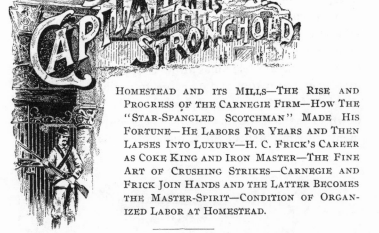

HOMESTEAD AND ITS MILLS—THE RISE AND
PROGRESS OF THE CARNEGIE FIRM—HOW THE
"STAR-SPANGLED SCOTCHMAN" MADE HIS
FORTUNE—HE LABORS FOR YEARS AND THEN
LAPSES INTO LUXURY—H. C. FRICK'S CAREER
AS COKE KING AND IRON MASTER—THE FINE
ART OF CRUSHING STRIKES—CARNEGIE AND
FRICK JOIN HANDS AND THE LATTER BECOMES
THE MASTER-SPIRIT—CONDITION OF ORGAN-
IZED LABOR AT HOMESTEAD.

IN a bend of the south bank of the Monongahela River,
eight miles from Pittsburgh, nestles the thriving
town of Homestead, a place of about 12,000 inhabitants, built up by the wealth and enterprise of the
Carnegie Steel Company and the thrift of the artisans employed by that great manufacturing corporation.

Without the Carnegie mills there would be no Homestead. Like the mushroom towns that sprang up along
the Northern Pacific Railroad while the line was in
process of construction and that died out as fast as the
base of operations was shifted, so Homestead sprang
into being when the site now occupied by the town was
picked out by Andrew Carnegie as a producing center,
and so, too, if the Carnegie firm were to move its works
to-morrow, would Homestead be blotted off the map,
or, at best, reduced to the rank of an insignificant village.

The interdependence of the works and the town is absolute.

The mill property covers 600 acres, bordering on the river, and includes thirty-seven acres under roof. The products comprise boiler and armor plates, beams and structural iron of various kinds. The manufacture of armor-plate for the United States Navy is conducted on a scale of unparalleled magnitude. From the huge hydraulic cranes lifting and carrying from place to place a weight of 200 tons, yet operated easily by one man, down to the delicate machinery in the finishing department, the equipment of the armor-plate mill is a marvel of

mechanical perfection. The great beam and structural mills, the Bessemer department and the bloom and billet mills are also magnificently equipped and are conducted on a mammoth scale, in comparison with which the operations of other American steel mills are almost insignificant.

Railroad tracks gridiron the yards and nineteen locomotives are required for the transportation of material. The repair shops cut an important figure and an army of blacksmiths, roll-turners, carpenters, tinners and other mechanics is employed to keep every detail of the working equipment in perfect order.

The plant is lighted throughout with electricity.

Within easy reach of the mills are the offices of the mill superintendent and his corps of clerks, draughtsmen and engineers. Eight handsome residences, farther back from the yard, are occupied by the assistant managers. There is also a club house for the use of guests and officers.

The foundation of this immense concern, representing a capital of many millions of dollars, and employing nearly 4,000 men, was laid in 1880, when, according to the census report, Homestead had a population of less than 600. The firm which has made all this possible, which, by virtue of intelligent effort and phenomenal accumulation and utilization of capital has called into being a full-fledged American town, with schools, churches, prosperous mercantile establishments, independent minor industries and a well-organized municipal government, is controlled by two men, whose names have, through the events to be recorded in this volume, been made familiar as household words the world over— Andrew Carnegie and Henry Clay Frick.

Andrew Carnegie is a self-made man, the son of a poor weaver of Dunfermline, Scotland. In 1845, the lad, then 12 years old, emigrated to the United States with his parents and settled in Pittsburgh. He was put to work tending a small stationary engine, and afterwards became a telegraph messenger boy and, in course of time, an operator. The Pennsylvania Railroad Company made him clerk to the superintendent of its Pittsburgh office and manager of its telegraph lines. About this time he met Woodruff, the inventor of the sleeping-car, and took a share in his venture. The enterprise was profitable and yielded what may be considered the nucleus of Mr. Carnegie's wealth. Again the young man was promoted, securing the superintendency of the Pittsburgh division of the Pennsylvania road. His future was now assured if he chose to continue in the railroad business; but his tastes, or rather his keen foresight led him in another direction. In company with his brother Thomas and others he purchased an established rolling mill, and from this grew the most extensive and profitable system of iron and steel industries in the world.

Mr. Carnegie has frequently challenged public notice by acts of philanthropy. He has given free baths and a free library to his native town of Dunfermline, a histological annex, known as the Carnegie laboratory to Bellevue Hospital, New York; a free library and music hall to Allegheny City; a free library and music hall, costing more than $1,000,000, to Pittsburgh; a free library to Edinburgh, Scotland, and similar donations to Braddock and other places where he has business interests. He has a fondness for literature, has written several books, of which "Triumphant Democracy; or Fifty Years' March of the Republic" is the most pretentious, and at one time controlled eighteen English newspapers in the Radical interest. Mr. Carnegie married late in life and has since maintained establishments in New York and at Cluny Castle, Scotland, rarely visiting his mills.

Estimates of Andrew Carnegie's character vary widely. To those associated with him in business he is known as a firm and considerate friend, quick to discern ability and generous in rewarding it. As an employer of labor he bore a high reputation for liberality and sympathetic regard for the well-being of his employees until the occurrence of the trouble at Homestead in 1892. How far he was personally chargeable with responsibility for Mr. Frick's iron-handed policy in that affair has never been positively determined; but it is certain that the relentless spirit shown by Mr. Frick cost Mr. Carnegie much of his popularity.

The connection of Henry Clay Frick with the Carnegie iron and steel industries, did not begin until Andrew Carnegie had reached the zenith of his success. Mr. Frick, however, had already carved his way to wealth along a different line, and was himself a millionaire. His success was gained in coke, and he came to be known as "the Coke King." Coke is indispensable to the manufacture of steel, but for a long time its production remained a separate industry. The Connellsville region, lying about fifty miles south of Pittsburgh, was occupied by a number of small producers, whose cut-throat mode of competition was highly advantageous to the steel men. Starting with small holdings, Mr. Frick gradually increased his territory and the number of his ovens until he obtained a practical monopoly of the Connellsville production and was able to dictate terms to consumers. He further strengthened his grip on the trade by investing heavily in coal lands and thus acquiring an unlimited source of supply for his ovens.

Mr. Carnegie perceived the rich possibilities of a union between the steel and coke industries, and, in 1882, bought a half interest in the Frick Coke Company for $1,500,000. Six years later, on the death of one of his partners, he induced the coke king to enter the Car-

negie Company, and the interests thus combined have
since been, to all intents and purposes, a unit.

The details of Mr. Frick's early career may be recited in very few words. He is the son of a farmer and
was born at West Overton, Pa., in 1850. After gaining
the rudiments of an education in the common schools
of Fayette County, he began business life as a dry
goods clerk in Mount Pleasant. Leaving the dry goods
business he became book-keeper in his grandfather's
distillery at Bradford. He lived economically and with
the money which he saved out of his salary he embarked in the coke business with A. O. Tintsman and
Joseph Rist. Although barely 21 years old, he was the
senior partner of the firm, which began with an equipment of 300 acres of land and 50 ovens. The opening
of the Mt. Pleasant and Broad Ford railroad imparted
new life to the coke trade about this period and young
Frick took advantage of the boom to add to his firm's
plant. The firm also built the Henry Clay works of one
hundred ovens on the Youghiogheny River near Broad
Ford.

In 1876 Mr. Frick bought out his partners and continued the business on his own account. In the following year a depression of trade placed the lease of the
Valley coke works at his disposal. The young operator
put Thomas Lynch in charge, and despite the dullness
of the market, kept the works going every day in the
year.

In the fall of 1877 Mr. Frick took into partnership
E. M. Ferguson, the owner of a plant of 70 ovens, and
the new firm operated as H. C. Frick & Co. A .year
later the firm leased the Anchor works and the Mullen

works near Mt. Pleasant and admitted Walton Ferguson as a partner.

In 1879 the coke trade revived amazingly, prices advancing from a maximum of $1.15 a ton to $4 and $5 a ton. The Frick Company continued to extend its business until, in 1882, it controlled 3,000 acres of coal land and 1,026 coke ovens. Meanwhile Mr. Frick organized the Morewood Coke Company, limited, and built the Morewood works of 470 ovens, the largest works in the region. Carnegie Bros. & Co., Limited, were admitted into the firm in January, 1882.

The Frick corporation now pushed its operations with such vigor that, in 1890, according to a semi-official statement, it "owned and controlled 35,000 acres of coal land and 42 of the 80 plants in the region, aggregating 10,046 ovens, three water plants with a pumping capacity of 5,000,000 gallons daily, and 35 miles of railroad track and 1,200 railroad cars. 11,000 men were then employed by the company, and for the equipment of its plants it had 23 locomotives, 72 pairs of stationary engines, 172 steam boilers and 816 horses and mules."

Mr. Frick had several serious strikes to contend with. His plan of campaign was always the same—to crush the strikers by main force and make no concessions. The Coal and Iron police, an organization of watchmen maintained under a state law, the drilled and armed watchmen of the Pinkerton detective agency, and the state militia were pressed into service as the occasion demanded, and the shedding of blood and sacrifice of human life resulted on more than one occasion.

Mr. Frick's character need not be analyzed at this

point. It will be illustrated clearly enough as our narrative progresses.

The Homestead mill and the Frick coke works, vast as they are, constitute merely a fraction of the Carnegie Company's interests. In addition to these the Company owns the Edgar Thompson furnaces and the Edgar Thompson steel works at Bessemer, eleven miles from Pittsburgh on the Pennsylvania railroad; the Duquesne steel works, on the same side of the Monongahela river as the Homestead works; the Lucy Furnaces, Pittsburgh; the Keystone Bridge Works, Pittsburgh; the Upper and Lower Union Mills, Pittsburgh; the Beaver Falls mills at Beaver Falls, 32 miles from Pittsburgh on the P. & L. E. railroad; the Carnegie Natural Gas Company; the Scotia ore mines in Center County, Pa.; the American Manganese Company, and interests in several large ore companies in the Lake Superior region. About 13,000 persons are employed in the various concerns operated by the firm, and of these about 3,800 are engaged in the works at Homestead.

In June 1892, Andrew Carnegie, while maintaining the controlling financial interest in the firm, transferred the managing authority to H. C. Frick. At that time the firm was reorganized, the separate enterprises which had previously been conducted under the names of Carnegie Bros. and Company, Carnegie, Phipps & Co., and other independent titles, being merged under the control of a single corporation known as the Carnegie Steel Company, Limited. H. C. Frick was made chairman, the other partners being Andrew Carnegie, Henry Phipps, Jr., George Lauder, H. M. Curry, W. L. Abbott, John G. A. Leishman, F. T. F. Lovejoy, Otis H. Childs and sundry minor stockholders whose interests were conferred upon them by Mr. Carnegie by way of promotion.

The power of the firm in the iron and steel industries was now dictatorial. On the fiat of the Carnegie Company depended almost entirely the price of steel in the market. Rivalry was dwarfed and competition nullified. Rarely in the industrial history of the world has a similarly powerful monopoly been built up on no other foundation than the combination of brains and capital, with such indirect aid as the protective tariff system affords.

Against this tremendous power,—a power equal to the control of 13,000 men and more than $25,000,000 of capital, the men of Homestead were destined to pit themselves in a life and death struggle; how destructive and hopeless a struggle will appear from the story told in these pages.

The men of Homestead, on their side, had comparatively limited resources to count upon in a battle against such fearful odds. They reckoned, to begin with, upon that species of *esprit de corps* which prevails among workingmen, especially those of the more intelligent class, and which is the solid ground under the feet of organized labor.

Not that the 3,800 workmen in the Homestead mills had a complete and comprehensive organization. On the contrary, out of this number, not more than one thousand were enrolled in the eight lodges of the Amalgamated Association of Iron and Steel Workers maintained in the town. These were the workers known as "tonnage men," because the nature of their employ-

ment permitted the graduation of their wages on a scale
determined by the price of billets per ton.　Outside the
lodges were the mechanics and laborers, working, for
the most part, for daily wages.　At the same time, the
joint influence of fraternity and of confidence in the
force of organization was deemed sufficient to inspire all
the Homestead workers, in and out of the lodges, to
make common cause in the event of a quarrel between
the lodges and the Carnegie firm.　Should this emergency arise, it was argued, the firm could not find
enough non-union steel-workers in the United States to
take the places of its army of employees, and as a consequence, if the men went out on strike, the mills
would have to be shut down and the heavy loss resulting
would force the firm to come to terms.

With this impression ingrained in their minds, the
men smiled confidently at the suggestion of a cut in
wages, and tacitly defied the new chairman, Mr. Frick,
to do his worst.

That the new chairman was liable to make some disagreeable departure had to be admitted by the most confident.　Dubious associations hung around the name of
this man H. C. Frick.　He had acquired unpleasant
notoriety by reducing wages in the coke regions, and by
crushing the labor insurrections which followed by the
employment of Pinkerton detectives and even by calling
in the state militia.　There was no dilettantism or lib-
erally-advertised philanthropy of the Carnegie stripe in
Frick's composition.　Everybody knew that.　He was
a man of blood and iron like Bismarck, so the workmen
said ; cared not a penny whether his underlings loved
or hated him, and rather preferred an opportunity to

crush—crush—crush intractable working folk under his heel than not.

Was this man placed in power by Andrew Carnegie in order to carry out at Homestead what he had carried out in the coke regions; to challenge organized labor by the submission of conditions which it could not accept and, on its refusal, try the old game of crushing the unions under foot? Did Carnegie shrink from the task himself and pick out Frick as a willing and capable instrument? Such were the questions discussed in the lodge-room and in the privacy of the domestic circle at Homestead during the time which intervened between the re-organization of the Carnegie interests and the next annual signing of the wage scale. Whatever conclusions might be reached, there was one thing certain at all events, in the not too penetrating judgment of the unionists: Frick might reduce wages, and Frick might fight, but Frick could not repeat in conflict with the 3,800 brawny and intelligent artisans at Homestead the comparatively easy victories which he had gained over his poor coke workers. So said they all, and they believed it, too, as firmly as if it were Holy Writ.

The feeling of ownership had a place in the reasoning of these simple people. Many of them had bought and paid for their homes and were pillars of the borough government. Some were still paying for their dwellings —paying off the mortgages held by the Carnegie Company, which had been in the habit of helping those who cared to build, and which even did a regular banking business for the advantage of its employees. It was clearly impossible that men of substance, heads of families, solid citizens of a prosperous municipality could be rooted up, as it were, out of the soil in which they were so firmly planted and beaten to earth by the creature of their labor—for without labor, it was argued, capital would be impotent and valueless.

In this mood, with suspicions as to the mission of Chairman Frick, but with impregnable confidence in themselves, the men prepared to settle the scale of wages, which was to be agreed upon in the spring of 1892 and to go into effect on July 1.

They sought no advance in wages, but it was a foregone conclusion that, if wages were to be depressed, they would offer implacable resistance.

There was calmness in all quarters at this time. No smoldering embers of dissatisfaction; no long nourished grievances were in existence to precipitate a sudden outbreak.

Mr. Potter, the superintendent of the Homestead mill, calmly discharged his daily round of duties.

Mr. Frick sat in his comfortable office in Pittsburgh, and calmly mapped out a plan of some, as yet, unheralded campaign.

Mr. Carnegie calmly continued to hob-nob with European celebrities and to indulge his *penchant* for the erection of free libraries.

There was not a cloud the size of a man's hand to mar the serenity of the horizon that bounded the little world of the Carnegie interests.

The gathering of the storm had not yet begun.

CHAPTER II.

THE GATHERING OF THE STORM

HISTORY AND METHODS OF
THE AMALGAMATED ASSOCIA-
TION—OPERATION OF THE SLIDING
SCALE AT HOMESTEAD — SUPERIN-
TENDENT POTTER MAKES AMICABLE
SUGGESTIONS *a la* CARNEGIE—AN ULTIMA-
TUM FROM FRICK—HE THREATENS NON-UNION-
ISM AND FORTIFIES THE MILLS—LODGES HOLD
A SUNDAY MORNING MEETING—BURGESS MCLUCKIE'S
BOLD SPEECH—"HIGH FENCES, PINKERTON DETECTIVES,
THUGS AND MILITIA"—POLITICAL EXIGENCIES GIVE HOPE
TO THE WORKMEN.

THE Amalgamated Association of Iron and Steel
Workers is, with the possible exception of the
Association of Window Glass Workers, the best
generaled and most substantially organized labor organization in the United States. One of the fundamental
principles in the doctrine of the association is to avoid
and discourage strikes; and so closely has this article of
faith been observed that the number of strikes officially
ordered in the iron and steel industries has been small
in comparison with the record of most other labor
unions.

The adjustment of wage scales by the association is
largely the affair of the lodges. The equipment and
requirements of different iron and steel mills vary con-

siderably, and hence, each mill or kindred group of
mills must have a separate scale, adjusted to its needs.
It is incumbent on the lodges to report their respective
scales to the association at large through the medium of
an annual delegate convention.   Should there be a dispute in any district, the convention passes upon the
merits of the case and decides whether or not it shall be
taken up by the association as a whole.   If not, the
usual mode of procedure is to notify the belligerent
lodge or lodges to yield the disputed points.   If, on the
other hand, the association decides to intervene, the
chief executive officers are authorized to act, and it
becomes their duty to exhaust all fair means of bringing
the recalcitrant mill-owners to terms, before counten-
ancing a strike.   An official order to strike commits the
association to the payment of weekly benefits to the
strikers.

The president of the Amalgamated Association is
always chosen with special reference to his capacity for
cool, stable, conservative leadership.   Mental brilliancy
is not so much sought after in the man who is called
upon to fill this responsible position, as level-headed-
ness and inflexible nerve.   William Weihe, who served
as president during the troublous days of 1892, fully
met these requirements.   A giant in stature, slow and
deliberate in speech and action, and never committing
himself without being perfectly sure of his ground,
Weihe was just the man to preserve the dignity and
influence of the association when the spectres of riot
and anarchy stalked abroad and organized labor, smarting from a thousand gaping wounds, threatened to break
down the bulwarks of law and order and to sacrifice the

good-will of its friends. At no time throughout a contest which set men's souls aflame from one end of the land to the other did President Weihe lose his self-possession or his ability to stand between the solid fabric of the association and those of its friends, who, in the rashness of the hour, would fain have involved it in the ruin which engulfed the lodges at Homestead.

The Homestead scale was prepared early in the spring. In January, the superintendent of the mill, Mr. Potter sent for the joint committee of the local lodges and requested that the men prepare a scale. It was not the policy of the Carnegie firm, Mr. Potter said, to leave the way open for a strike. If there were differences of opinion between employer and employees, the proper method of settlement was by arbitration, and it was, therefore, advisable that the scale should be presented early, so as to leave ample time for an amicable adjustment of disputed points.

For three years previous, the men had been working under what was known as a sliding scale, an expedient which at the time of its adoption was regarded as a sure preventive of strikes. This scale established as the basis on which wages were to be determined, the market price of steel billets, in the manufacture of which the Carnegie Company was extensively engaged. When the price of billets went up, wages were to go up correspondingly, and when the price of billets went down, wages were to be correspondingly lowered. $25 a ton was agreed upon as the minimum. If billets were quoted below that figure, there was to be no further depression of wages. In other words, the men and the firm were practically in partnership, increased profits to the latter meaning increased earnings to the former, unless the bottom fell out of the market, in which case it became the duty of the stronger partner to protect the weaker.

The circumstances under which this equitable compact was made are of interest in so far as they exhibit the very different temper of the Carnegie Company towards its men in the past from that which marked its line of conduct after Mr. Frick was placed at the helm. In January, 1889, the men, who had been working under a yearly scale, quarreled with the firm over the terms proposed for the ensuing year and a strike was declared. William L. Abbott, a man of comparatively mild and liberal disposition, was then serving as chairman. Mr. Abbott undertook to break the strike, and when the men resorted to riotous conduct, called upon the sheriff of the county for aid. The sheriff, Dr. Alexander McCandless, an official who enjoyed great popularity, and possessed the courage and tact essential in such an emergency, went promptly to the scene with a force of deputies recruited for the occasion. At the first encounter with the mob, the deputies let their courage ooze out at their fingers' ends and fled from the town.

The sheriff, nowise disheartened by the desertion of his forces, took the best possible means of ending the trouble by constituting himself a mediator between the Carnegie firm and the strikers. Through his efforts a conference was arranged, and peace was restored through the adoption of the famous sliding scale, with the understanding that it would hold good until June 30, 1892. Mr. Carnegie, then absent in Europe, professed to be much pleased with the amicable settlement arrived at and the incidental guarantee of peace for three years to come, and for the time being the names of Sheriff McCandless and William L. Abbott were surrounded with a halo of glory.

When Superintendent Potter, in January, 1892, spoke to the men about a new scale, he gave no hint of the prospect that the firm contemplated sweeping away the beneficial arrangement which had so long governed their earnings. As already noted, Mr. Potter touched upon the subject of possible differences of opinion and of the firm's desire that such differences should be settled in a friendly way.

The shadow of Mr. Frick loomed up gloomily in the background, it is true, but there was really no occasion to think of shadows when the genial Potter presented himself as the very embodiment of sunshine. The ideas put forth by this gentleman bore the special brand of Mr. Carnegie. Mr. Carnegie was on record as being opposed to the use of force in settling disputes between capital and labor. In 1886, he had written for the magazines on this question, and the liberality of his views had elicited general commendation. Thus he said in the *Forum:*

''Peaceful settlement of differences should be reached through arbitration. I would lay it down as a maxim that there is no excuse for a strike or a lock-out until arbitration of differences has been offered by one party and refused by the other.''

Mr. Carnegie declared further, that ''The right of the workingmen to combine and to form trades unions is no less sacred than the right of the manufacturer to enter into association and conference with his fellows, and it must sooner or later be conceded.'' Manufacturers should "meet the men *more than half way*," and "To expect that one dependent upon his daily wage for the necessaries of life will stand by peaceably and see a new man employed in his stead is to expect much."

This was the gospel of Carnegie in 1886, and, the shadow of Frick to the contrary, notwithstanding, it was not singular that it should have been the gospel of Potter in January, 1892.

It was, then, with a feeling of reasonable security that the men went to work upon their scale. This, when completed, differed little from that of the previous three years. It was presented to Mr. Potter in February, but, strange to say, did not seem to please that worthy exponent of the Carnegie idea of harmony. The joint committee of the lodges waited frequently upon the superintendent in the hope of reaching some definite conclusion, but the conferences were barren of results.

At length, to the amazement of the men, the Carnegie firm officially promulgated a new sliding scale, based on billets at $26.50 per ton as a standard, but fixing as the minimum basis of wages, $22 per ton, instead of $25 as formerly. As the billet market was now abnormally depressed—a condition which, it was claimed by many, had been designedly brought about in order to give the Carnegie Company a pretext for wage reductions—it was apparent that a serious reduction in many departments of the mill would follow the acceptance of the firm's propositions.

June 24 was fixed as the last day on which the men could accept as members of the Amalgamated Association. After that date, the firm would not consent to treat with them otherwise than as individuals. In short, Mr. Frick wanted it to be understood, definitely and finally, that, if his employees did not yield promptly and with a good grace, he would non-unionize the mill and abolish the right of self-protective organization, to which Mr. Carnegie, six years before, had feelingly referred as "sacred."

There was a flavor of coke region discipline about the Frick ultimatum which was not calculated to promote good feeling at Homestead. Nor did it. The men who drove the sheriff's deputies out of Homestead in 1889

might yield to milder measures, but the crack of the whip was irritating. "Are we to be lashed into Mr. Frick's way of thinking?" men asked one another, and the very thought bred insurrection.

If there was a calm now, it was the calm that preceded a hurricane.

As if to accentuate the sentiment of disaffection among the Homestead people, Mr. Frick accompanied the issuance of his ultimatum with preparations of a warlike character. A large force of men was employed upon the construction of a solid board fence, three miles in extent, surrounding the property of the firm between the Pittsburg, Virginia & Charleston railroad and the Monongahela river. All the workshops were included within this enclosure. The offices and stables, situated on the other side of the railroad, were similarly enclosed. An elevated wooden bridge connected the two enclosures. The fence was surmounted with strands of barbed wire, and perforated at intervals, as if for the convenience of sharpshooters stationed within, although Mr. Frick, in his testimony before a committee of Congress, averred that the holes were simply for the purpose of observation. High in the air, at the ends of the tall mill buildings, twelve-foot platforms were erected, on which were placed electric search-lights, designed to enable sentinels to keep watch at night over every part of the mill yard.

There was a cold and sanguinary determination about these provisions which boded ill for the workmen. Clearly, the redoubtable tamer of the coke-workers had made up his mind to force a bloody conflict with organized labor, and the wage ultimatum was his defi. One of King John's barons could not equip his feudal castle with more elaborate offensiveness than this nineteenth century ironmaster displayed in fortifying his mill, with the apparent intention of making war—actual war with arms upon the men of Homestead. So it was that the men viewed the preparations at the mill. The supposition that Mr. Frick might regard their disposition as one of invincible stubborness, sure to lead to deeds of violence, and that his fences, barbed wire, loopholes, platforms and search-lights might be pure measures of self-defense was not entertained for an instant.

The fortification of the mill was a huge threat—a challenge—an insult. With this exhibition of brute force held up before them, the workmen deemed their manhood, as well as the life of their organization to be at stake. Come what might, they must now burn their boats behind them, as the firm had done, and refuse to recede an inch from their demands.

While affairs were taking this ominous turn at Homestead, the annual convention of the Amalgamated Association met at Pittsburgh, the session opening on June 7. Of the stormy conditions under which the delegates came together and which caused their deliberations to be protracted for an unusual period, mention is reserved for another chapter. Suffice it to state here that the delegates from Homestead duly submitted their scale; that it received the indorsement of the association, and that the local lodges were empowered to persist in their demand for the retention of the rate of $25 a ton on billets as the minimum basis of tonnage men's wages. This made it optional with the local lodges to declare a strike, although it followed by implication only, and not of necessity, that the strike, if ordered, would receive the sanction and support of the association.

Excitement in Homestead mounted rapidly to fever heat.

The first concerted public demonstration on the part of the men was on Sunday, June 19, when the lodges held an open meeting in the opera house. Some of the leading officials of the association and many delegates to the Pittsburgh convention from other states were present. The gathering included almost the entire working force of the Homestead mill. William

A. Carney, First Vice-President of the association acted
as chairman. The speechmakers, for the most part,
while exhorting the men to stand firm, counseled moderation and respect for the law.

A young vice-president of the association, Jere
Doherty, touched upon the place of the wage-worker
in politics and the efficacy of the Homestead struggle as
a test of the protection guaranteed to labor by the
Republican party.

The crowning address of the day was made by John
McLuckie, the burgess of the town, a simple, earnest,
straightforward man, whose rugged eloquence told more
forcibly with the brawny multitude who heard him
than if it had been couched in the language of a Cicero
or a Demosthenes. Burgess McLuckie said:

"What brings you here this morning? Is it idle
curiosity, or is there a real, tangible reason beyond?
The cause of this wage trouble is not generally understood. We were persuaded to vote the Republican
ticket four years ago in order that our wages might be
maintained. As soon as the election was over a wide-
spread feeling on the part of the manufacturers towards
a reduction of wages was exhibited all over the land.
As soon as the McKinley bill was passed, the article in
the production of which we work was the only article
that suffered a reduction. It is Sunday morning, and
we ought to be in church, but we are here to-day to see
if we are going to live as white men in the future. The
constitution of this country guarantees all men the
right to live, but in order to live we must keep up a
continuous struggle. This is the effect of legislation
and nothing else. The McKinley bill reduced the tariff

on the four-inch billet, and the reduction of our wages is the result. You men who voted the Republican ticket voted for high tariff and you get high fences, Pinkerton detectives, thugs and militia!''

There was politics in this speech, but almost every member of a labor organization is a politician in a small way, and McLuckie's bill of indictment against the Republican party struck fairly home. It had been freely charged that, when the McKinley tariff bill was being prepared, Andrew Carnegie had waited on the conference committee which put the finishing touches to the measure and secured as a return for his generous contributions to the Republican campaign funds, a reduction in the duty on steel billets, this product being the single standard of wages in his Homestead works. As the Carnegie firm controlled the billet market, there was nothing to hinder a depression of prices, as a seeming consequence of a lower duty, and this was to serve as a cover for the new scale and the Frick ultimatum.

The plausibility of this story, and the bluntness with which McLuckie, himself a poorly paid workman of the Carnegie Company, put the political duplicity involved before his fellow workmen exercised a telling effect. Particularly did the pointed allusion to ''high fences, Pinkerton detectives, thugs and militia'' carry weight in the estimation of the workingmen present at that Sunday morning meeting. Nor did it stop there, for within the next twenty-four hours this, the first public arraignment of the Republican party and the Carnegie Company jointly was flashed over the telegraph wires to newspapers in all parts of the United States, and the country at large began to realize that there were two ways of looking at the doctrine of ''protection to American labor,'' and that the difference between them was on the eve of receiving an impressive demonstration.

The temper of the people of Homestead after the meeting of the lodges, was, in spite of the scarcely concealed militant resolution harbored in the breasts of the men as individuals, moderate and orderly. There was still time, they reasoned, for Mr. Frick to withdraw his defiant ultimatum. Nearly two weeks remained until the new wage scale would be enforced. In the mean time there would be conferences. Possibly Mr. Carnegie might be heard from over the cable. Perhaps even the great men who were interested in proving that protection protects would use their influence to obviate the astounding object lesson which would be presented to the world if the Carnegie firm, at the noontide of its prosperity, should reduce the wages of its employees. If there was hope in this way of looking at the prospect, it was a forlorn hope, and the most sanguine of the tonnage men, who were the first to be affected by a change in the scale, could not consider it otherwise.

The cloud was plain to be seen, but of the silver lining not a vestige was perceptible.

So the men went to bed on that Sunday night with McLuckie's bold words ringing in their ears, and a strong conviction deep down in their hearts that a crash was coming, that somebody was destined to go under, and that, come what might, the victors of 1889 would not show the white feather.

CHAPTER III.

LOCKED OUT!

ABOUT the time of the assembling of the delegates to the convention of the Amalgamated Association, the Pittsburgh *Post*, a Democratic newspaper, printed an article in which it was alleged that the impending conflict at Homestead was to be precipitated not in the interest of the Carnegie Company alone, but in that of all the iron and steel manufacturers of Western Pennsylvania and Eastern Ohio. Homestead, it was said, was chosen as a battle ground, (1) because of the ease with which the mill property could be equipped for offensive and defensive purposes; (2) because the ruin wrought in that town by a disastrous strike would be more sweeping and complete than could be effected anywhere else, and (3) because the Carnegie Company had the largest interests to serve and should, therefore, be willing to bear the brunt of the battle. If war was declared, and the lodges at Homestead were broken up, the other manufacturers were to follow the lead of the Carnegie Company, defy the Amalgamated Association and reduce the wages of their employes to an extent varying from 20 to 60 per cent.

The *Post's* story received little credence when it appeared, but later on the course of events gave it a strong coloring of probability. Mr. Frick proceeded to fortify the Homestead mills with every evidence of inviting a desperate conflict. At the same time, the other manufacturers commenced to show their hand, those of the Mahoning and Shenango Valley, a district located about fifty miles from Pittsburgh, taking the initiative by announcing a general reduction of wages ranging from 20 to 60 per cent. The Pittsburgh manufacturers avoided taking a distinctly aggressive stand, but gave out significant statements to the effect that the condition of the iron and steel market rendered it impossible for them to continue paying the rate of wages maintained during the previous year.

These symptoms of depression in one of the most generously protected industries within a short time after the passage of the McKinley tariff bill afforded a prolific subject of commentary to the opponents of the high tariff system. Both political parties made their nominations for the presidency in the month of June, when the labor trouble was waxing warm, and it became only too plainly perceptible that, since the Republican party took its stand mainly on the benefit resulting to American labor from the protective tariff, Republicanism would be held answerable by the working classes for the proposed wage reductions in Pennsylvania. As a matter of fact the efficacy of the tariff as a wage-maintaining agency had been grossly overdrawn by stump orators and over-zealous partisan newspapers. For years it had been dinned into the ears of the workingman that it was his duty to vote for Republican candidates because the Republicans in Congress maintained the high protective tariff and the high protective tariff meant high wages.

But now, at the opening of a presidential contest, the workingman was confronted with what seemed to be proof positive that the high tariff had lost its virtue, and when the Democratic press pointed to the astonishing spectacle of wage reductions ordered by the "pampered iron barons" of Pennsylvania, as illustrating that the protective system was a sham and a fraud, what wonder that organized labor was quick to accept the indictment as a just one!

The Democratic national convention did not lose sight of the opportunity thus offered, and in the platform on which Grover Cleveland was nominated at Chicago perhaps the most telling plank was that which denounced the protective system as fraudulent and referred to the strikes in the iron trade as an immediate attestation of the failure of "McKinleyism."

Meanwhile, newspapers friendly to President Harrison sought to dissuade the iron and steel manufacturers from making the threatened cut in wages and precipitating a general conflict with the operatives. In Pittsburgh, especially, a bitter discussion was carried on, the papers controlled by the manufacturers persistently asserting that the tariff has nothing to do with the making of

wage scales and that a general wage reduction and consequent strikes during a presidential campaign could
not be construed as reflecting upon the efficacy of the
McKinley bill and the Republican party's pledges to
American labor; while the Democratic and independent
press subjected the manufacturers to merciless criticism.

All this was full of encouragement to the workingmen. They felt that their cause was expanding from
the dimensions of a mere local trouble to those of an
affair of national importance, affecting the destinies of
the dominant political parties. At Homestead, which
had previously been a Republican stronghold, the Democratic propaganda found special favor. "If all else
should fail us," thought the men, "we can, at least,
have revenge at the polls in November."

And they kept their word.

It is not within the province of the writer of this narrative to analyze the peculiar aspect put upon the case
of the workingmen by political agitators for campaign
purposes. Merely the facts are stated here, leaving it
to the reader to make his own deductions as to the justice or injustice of the assaults on the American system
of protection to labor provoked by the seeming selfish-
ness of tariff-enriched manufacturers. Suffice it to state
that every shot told and that, if the whole truth were
known, it would be found that political considerations
went a long way to prevent the other manufacturers
from joining Mr. Frick in a body and using their combined resources to destroy the Amalgamated Association
and strip their employees of all means of self-defense.

It will be seen that the position of the Homestead
workers was greatly strengthened by the common

danger. Homestead was not to be alone in its fight. The entire Amalgamated Association was threatened, and the spirit of mutual helpfulness was, therefore, powerfully stimulated at all points. The good old unionist principle, "One for all, and all for one," was bound to receive a full and magnificent exemplification.

On June 15, the convention of the Amalgamated Association completed the general wage scale for iron mills and presented it to the manufacturers' committee. The manufacturers responded by producing a scale of their own, embodying extensive reductions. This was the beginning of a dispute, stubborn on both sides, which was kept up long after the final adjournment of the convention, that body assigning the duty of conferring with the manufacturers to a special wage committee.

The consideration of the scales for steel mills, including that prepared by the Homestead lodges, was not completed by the convention until June 23. On that day, a committee, headed by William Roberts, one of the most intelligent of the Homestead mill workers, appeared at the offices of the Carnegie Company, on Fifth Avenue, Pittsburgh, and was escorted to Mr. H. C. Frick's private room. Mr. Frick, General Manager Potter, H. L. Childs and F. T. F. Lovejoy acted for the company in the conference which followed. Mr. Roberts, acting as spokesman for his colleagues, presented the Homestead scale as approved by the convention, and explained that the employees were prepared to concede several points, admitting, however, of no reduction exceeding 15 per cent. in any department. The men were willing even to reduce the minimum selling price of billets on which the rate of wages should be estimated to $24 per ton, but the firm insisted upon the $23 rate, which, as previously explained, signified a serious depression in wages.

The conference, after a discussion lasting several hours, broke up without accomplishing anything.

The following day, June 24, had been fixed by Mr. Frick as the last on which the Carnegie firm would treat with its employees as members of the Amalgamated Association. The day passed without a conference. It was believed, however, that, in view of the concessions which the men had stated their willingness to make, even though they refused to make the complete surrender which Mr. Frick demanded, the firm would consent to fresh conferences with the committee. Yet the fact that the firm, which had sufficient orders on hand to keep the mill busy for many months, was canceling these orders, coupled with the extraordinary preparations for warfare which were being made at the mills, cast a damper on the hopes of the men. There was hardly a ray of sunshine to brighten the gloomy outlook.

On June 25, Mr. Lovejoy, secretary of the Carnegie Company, stated through the newspapers that the conferences were at an end, that the firm had decided to make the rate of $23 a ton on billets the basis of wages, and that this rate would be enforced without regard to the opinion of the Amalgamated Association. It was also the intention to change the time of fixing the wage schedule from June to January, so that if a strike or lock-out should occur, the hardships of the winter season would strengthen the company's hand. So, at least, the men interpreted the proposed change.

Mr. Lovejoy's statement, although given out in an informal way, was generally accepted as meaning that the ax was forthwith to be let fall upon the neck of organized labor at Homestead, and that no human power could stay the hand of the executioner.

Still all was quiet at Homestead. June 25 was Saturday and pay-day, but the day was marked by less activity and bustle than usual. The stores were not crowded, and little money was spent. In the face of trouble, the end of which it was impossible to foresee, men carefully put away the contents of their pay envelopes. The wolf might come to the door before long and resources had to be husbanded. Few cared for the little Saturday jollifications common at other times. Wherever a group of mill men came together, the one theme of discussion was the ultimatum of the firm, the prospect of a wholesale discharge of union men on July 1 and the meaning of the warlike equipment of the mill property.

A new and significant name was devised for the Carnegie enclosure, with its ramparts, watch towers, searchlights and other suggestions of war, and flew from mouth to mouth with the rapidity of lightning.

"FORT FRICK."

An ill-omened name it was, bristling with offensive associations; but its propriety as a descriptive epithet could not be questioned.

Who was to occupy the "fort?" Whose guns were to be used through those loop-holes?

"Pinkerton detectives," said some, and the rumor that an army of "Pinkertons" had been hired and might already be on its way to garrison the works and shed the blood of the men of Homestead found ready credence and deepened the feeling of resentment abroad in the town. Many were disposed to believe that Pinkerton scouts had arrived and were making things ready for the coming of the main guard.

On Tuesday, June 28, the company ordered the armor-plate mill and the open-hearth department shut down, throwing 800 men out of employment.

This was the beginning of the lock-out, for a lockout it was, and not a strike, as has been very generally represented.

A strike occurs when dissatisfied workingmen cease work of their own accord and refuse to return until the cause of dissatisfaction is removed.

A lock-out originates with the employing individual or corporation, and consists in the refusal to let the employees work until they come to terms with the employer.

As Mr. Frick took the initiative, the trouble at Homestead was distinctively a lock-out, although, if Mr. Frick had chosen, he could have permitted it to take the form of a strike.

It made little difference in the end which of the contestants took the first aggressive step. Once the Frick ultimatum was promulgated, a struggle was inevitable, and if the firm had not thrown down the gauntlet, the men most assuredly would have forced the fighting on their own account.

The night of June 28 witnessed strange scenes in Homestead. The pent-up feelings of the men now found vent unrestrainedly. Effigies of Frick and Potter were hung on telegraph poles. Denunciations of the firm and its policy were heard on every hand. Knots of angry men gathered outside the board fence that hedged the mill enclosure, peered through the loopholes at the watchmen on duty within and talked defiantly of what would happen if the methods that triumphed over the poor, disorganized serfs in the coke regions were to be tried upon four thousand sturdy and intelligent steel-workers. If an apostle of non-unionism had ventured upon the streets of Homestead that night he would have fared badly.

The next morning, at the call of the officers of the local lodges, 3,000 steel-workers met in the opera house. The chairman of the executive committee stated to the meeting that, at a conference of committeemen representing the eight lodges, held on the preceding evening, it had been decided to submit the question of shutting down the mechanical department of the mills to the steelworkers *en masse*, irrespective of affiliation with the lodges, and that the decision thus arrived at should be binding on all. This report was approved and a motion was made that a committee be appointed to request the mechanics and day laborers to quit work at once. A workman asked if the watch-

men were to be included, and another answered: "Three years ago the watchmen wanted to come out and now they *must* come."

The motion passed amid tremendous cheering.

The chairman of the executive committee, resuming his address, refuted the report spread through the newspapers that six or seven hundred mechanics and day laborers had signed a scale arranged by the firm. A committee of this class of workmen, he said, had waited on General Manager Potter and had been thrust aside pending the settlement of the tonnage men's wages. After this, the mechanics and laborers had resolved to cast their lot with the Amalgamated Association, and had signified their decision to the lodges.

William Roberts, chairman of the conference committee, which had waited on Mr. Frick by authority of the Amalgamated convention, took the platform and detailed the action of his committee. Mr. Roberts told of the committee's offer to concede a basis of $24 and of the firm's demand that the scale terminate on the last day of the year. "We wouldn't agree to this," he said, "and I now ask you had we any right to do so?"

"No! No! No!" shouted 3,000 voices.

The speaker described how, when the committee presented as its last and only demands that a $24 basis be adopted and that the scale expire on the last day of June, Mr. Frick jumped to his feet and exclaimed hotly: "Gentlemen, that ends all conferences between you and this firm." "So you see," Mr. Roberts went on to say, "This is not a strike. The firm put a snag in our road. . . . We filled our contract. Now the firm has laid the entire mill off one day ahead of time. Has it lived up to its contract?"

Again 3,000 voices shouted "No," and the action of the wage conference committee was ratified without a dissenting voice.

A resolution was offered providing that, in case any man left Homestead during the coming trouble without permission from the lodge officials, the men should refuse to work with him on his return. The chairman asked all who were in favor of the resolution to rise. Instantly every man in the hall sprang to his feet and the resolution was adopted with three cheers and a tiger, followed with hisses for H. C. Frick.

A motion to appoint a press committee, consisting of one member from each of the eight lodges, was carried after a discussion as to unreliable reports. The membership of this committee was kept secret for the time being.

A whirlwind of excitement was roused when a speaker told of a report that 200 non-union workmen were coming to Homestead disguised in the blue uniform of Pinkerton detectives. "Watch the depots," was the unanimous cry that followed this alarmist statement.

When, after a session of two hours, the meeting adjourned, there remained not the least doubt as to the unity of feeling among all classes of workers in the town. Every man was ready to enter upon relentless strife, and if there was a coward or malingerer in any quarter, he wisely held his peace.

After the general meeting, the eight lodges held a secret session, at which an advisory committee was appointed, with full power to direct the workmen's campaign. This body, which played the most important part in the tragic drama soon afterwards enacted, was composed of the following members: David H. Shannon, John McLuckie, David Lynch, Thomas J. Crawford, Hugh O'Donnell, Harry Bayne, Elmer E. Ball, Isaac Byers, Henry Bayard, T. W. Brown, George W. Champene, Isaac Critchlow, Miller Colgan, John Coyle, Jack Clifford, Dennis M. Cush, William McConeghy, Michael Cummings, William Combs, John Durkes, Patrick Fagan, W. S. Gaches, Nathan Harris, Reid Kennedy, John Miller, O. O. Searight, John Murray, M. H. Thompson, Martin Murray, Hugh Ross, William T. Roberts, George Rylands and George W. Sarver.

Special committees were appointed to patrol the river stations and all entrances to the town. The patrols were directed to cover their beats night and day and report to the advisory committee. Arrangements were also made to have the river patrolled in skiffs, and the steamboat "Edna" was secured to aid in this service.

Headquarters were established in a commodious public hall, with accommodations for telegraph operators, the committee being expected to maintain communication with all parts of the country, so as to obtain instant information of any movement of non-union men designed for service at Homestead. The liquor saloons were visited and the proprietors requested to use special precautions against the promotion of drunkenness and disorderly gatherings, under pain of being required to close their establishments.

Eight effigies of Carnegie officials were cut down by the committee, and notice was given that persons outraging decency in this manner in the future would be disciplined.

The burgess of the town, John McLuckie, was

Workers in the rail mill of the Homestead Works during the 1880s, many holding a turning wrench, the tool of their trade (Bill Gaughan)

Hugh O'Donnell

John McLuckie

Henry Clay Frick several years after the strike (The Bettmann Archive)

Andrew Carnegie (Carnegie-Mellon University)

Mill retirees during the nonunion era, photographed on the steps of the Homestead Works General Office Building (Randy Harris)

informed that he might call upon the Amalgamated Association for whatever number of men he might deem necessary to assist him in preserving the peace.

In short, the govenment of Homestead had now passed absolutely into the hands of the advisory committee of the Amalgamated lodges, and the committee was determined to use its arbitrary authority for the preservation of order and decency and the protection of life and property as well as the exclusion from Homestead of non-union men, better known to the unionist as "scabs" or "black sheep."

On July 2 the entire force of employees at the Carnegie mills was paid off and served with notices of discharge.

With the exception of a slight altercation between General Manager Potter and some of the men who were guarding one of the gates of the mill there was no disorder.

Secretary Lovejoy now made his final statement on behalf of the firm declaring the mill to be permanently non-unionized. "Hereafter," he said, "the Homestead steel works will be operated as a non-union mill. We shall not recognize the Amalgamated Association of Iron and Steel Workers in our dealings with the men. The mill will be an open one where all men may work regardless of their affiliation with a labor organization. There will be, no doubt, a scale of wages; but we shall deal with the men individually; not with any organization. Such a thing as a union will not be recognized. There will be no further conerences with the Amalgamated Association."

The mammoth steel plant was now deserted, except

by a few watchmen and the government steel inspectors, with whom the advisory committee did not interfere.

The locked-out men were perfectly organized and ready to fight against any odds at a moment's notice. A report that strangers were on the way to Homestead along either of the railroads brought a battalion of stalwart fellows to the stations on the outskirts.

Mr. Frick might as well have undertaken to storm Gibraltar as to introduce a force of non-unionists into the town.

Meanwhile the convention of the Amalgamated Association had finished its business, elected new officers, including a successor to President Weihe in the person of Mahlon M. Garland, and left it to a committee to fight it out with the manufacturers. This the committee was doing with considerable success. The ominous turn which affairs were taking at Homestead, together with the endless reproaches heaped upon the graceless beneficiaries of the protective tariff by Mr. Harrison's campaign managers had a most discouraging effect on the manufacturers' committee and it was plain to be seen that the "fight all along the line," inaugurated a month before, was to end in a compromise favorable to the Amalgamated Association.

Mr. Frick was left to do his own fighting, single-handed and alone.

CHAPTER IV.

THE PINKERTON GUARDS.

WHILE Mr. Frick's men were busily engaged in
perfecting a martial organization and putting
the government of the town of Homestead on a
war footing, Mr. Frick himself was not idle. He did
not waste any time in considering projects for immediately introducing non-union men into the mills, being
well aware that, if men foolhardy enough to take the
risk of "blacksheeping" at Homestead could be found,
it would still be impracticable to get them past the
picket lines of the locked-out steelworkers, and that,
even if a force of non-unionists could be piloted into the
mill their presence would be the signal for an attack by
the union men and possibly for the destruction of the
firm's property.

Mr. Frick had another plan—a plan suggested by his
successful encounters with the Connellsville coke-
workers. He conceived the idea of garrisoning "Fort
Frick" with a sufficient number of armed and disciplined Pinkerton guards to hold any attacking force at

bay and later on to bring in non-union workmen under cover of the Pinkerton men's rifles.

How long this project had been maturing in the mind of the Carnegie Company's chairman cannot be told. Certain it is that he had made up his mind to carry it out long before he met the wage conference committee for the last time, and that when, on June 23, he went through the form of a discussion with Mr. Roberts and Mr. Roberts' confreres, he had not the least notion of coming to any kind of an understanding other than that which might be brought about by force.

Mr. Frick was too well acquainted with the estimation in which the Pinkerton men are held by the labor unions to underrate the import of his action, and can hardly have been ignorant of the fact that in bringing on these myrmidons, he was making doubly sure of sanguinary times at Homestead.

A sketch of the personnel and methods of the "Pinkerton National Detective Agency," as it is styled by its chiefs, will make clear to the reader the reasons for the hatred and contempt entertained for this body by workingmen everywhere.

The agency was founded in 1850 by Allan Pinkerton, a young Scotchman, who had been brought into public notice at Elgin, Ill., by his success in ferreting out a counterfeiter. Allan Pinkerton's fame as a detective became national. He organized a war secret service, was trusted by Lincoln, whose life he once saved; by Grant and other national leaders in war times, and aroused continual interest by his strokes of skill and daring. The enterprise from which sprang the Pinkerton "standing army" of to-day was set on foot in a shabby little office in La Salle Street, Chicago, and there the headquarters of the agency still remain.

Pinkerton detectives came into great request and were soon engaged in the unraveling of crimes and the hunting down of criminals all over the continent. Allan Pinkerton meanwhile discerned a fresh source of profit and turned it to account by hiring out his men as watchmen for banks and great commercial houses. The "Pinkerton Preventive Watch," composed of trained men, uniformed and armed, and acting independently of the municipal police, was established.

The emblem adopted by the agency was a suggestive one. It consisted of an eye and the motto, "We never sleep."

As old age came on Allan Pinkerton and his business kept growing, he turned over the work of supervision to his sons, William A. and Robert A. Robert was placed in charge of a branch bureau in New York and William remained in Chicago. Agencies with regular forces of men were established in Philadelphia, Boston, St. Paul, Kansas City and Denver. By communication with these centres, the chiefs could control, at a few days' notice, a force of 2,000 drilled men, and this could be expanded by drawing on the reserves registered on the books of the agency for service on demand, to 30,000, if necessary,—more men than are enrolled in the standing army of the United States.

When a large number of recruits is needed, the Pinkertons usually advertise in the newspapers asking for able-bodied men of courage, but without stating for whose service. In New York, prospective recruits are brought to a building on lower Broadway where the

Pinkertons have an armory, stocked with Winchester rifles, revolvers, policemen's clubs and uniforms. After the number of men needed is secured, the addresses of the eligible applicants for whom there are no places are taken and they are notified to hold themselves in readiness for a future call.. Men who have served in the army or as policemen receive the preference.

Pinkerton detectives have no real authority to make arrests. They are rarely sworn in as special constables or as deputy sheriffs and the uniform which they wear is merely for show.

Of late years they have been employed very frequently to protect the property of great manufacturing corporations during strikes or lock-outs. This is, without exception, the most trying and perilous service which they have to undergo. The pay is good, however, the rate agreed upon for duty at Homestead, for example, being $5 a day for each man.

In the great strike on the New York Central railroad, which cost the Vanderbilt corporation $2,000,000, the item for Pinkerton service was about $15,000. The guards were posted at danger points all along the line. Conflicts with the strikers were frequent, and, in many cases, the guards used their rifles with deadly effect. On August 17, 1890, they killed five persons, one a woman. So freely were the Pinkerton rifles brought into play during this trouble that the people of New York state became thoroughly aroused and forced the legislature to pass an anti-Pinkerton bill.

The agency was responsible for the killing of a boy during a longshoremen's strike in Jersey and at Chicago during the Lake Shore railroad strike a man named

Bagley fell a victim to Pinkerton lead. The guard who shot Bagley was spirited away and never brought to justice.

Pinkerton guards have done duty in the miners' strikes in the Hocking Valley, at the H. C. Frick Company's mines in the Connellsville region and at Braidwood, Ill,, as well as in all the great railroad strikes since 1877.

In recent years, the conversion of the guards into an irresponsible military organization, with self-constituted authority to overawe striking workmen has provoked a feeling of intense hatred on the part of organized labor towards these soldier-policemen. Attempts to abolish the Pinkerton system by legislation have succeeded in only a few states, New York and New Jersey among the number, for the reason that the corporations which find use for armed mercenaries have sufficient wealth and influence to control legislative action.

Congressman Thomas Watson, of Alabama, a representative of the Farmers' Alliance, introduced a bill in Congress making it illegal for private persons to maintain a "standing army" to usurp the police powers of the states, and made a strong plea for its passage, but the measure failed. The great industrial corporations have a hold upon the federal legislature too strong to be broken by the insistence of common people.

As has already been told, the men of Homestead entertained a profound abhorrence of the Pinkertons and were resolved to push resistance to any extreme rather than permit themselves to be whipped into submission by armed hirelings. They had no knowledge of Mr. Frick's dealings with the agency, although their familiarity with the Frick policy in the coke regions, coupled with the equipment of the mill property for occupation by a garrison excited a well-defined suspicion of what was coming.

Mr. Frick gave the final order for a supply of guards in a letter written to Robert A. Pinkerton, of New York, on June 25, the day after his meeting with the wage committee from the Amalgamated convention. The order was given in as matter-of-fact a manner as if the Carnegie chairman were bespeaking a supply of coke or pig-iron.

"We will want 300 guards," he wrote, "for service at our Homestead mills as a measure of precaution against interference with our plan to start the operation of the works again on July 6, 1892."

"These guards," Mr. Frick went on to direct, "should be assembled at Ashtabula, O., not later than the morning of July 5, when they may be taken by train to McKees Rocks, or some other point on the Ohio River below Pittsburgh, where they can be transferred to boats and landed within the enclosures of our premises at Homestead. We think absolute secresy essential in the movement of these men, so that no demonstration can be made while they are en route."

As Mr. Frick acknowledged in his letter the receipt of "your favor of the 22d," it was evident that the negotiations with the Pinkerton agency had been pending for some time.

Immediately after having despatched his order for a Pinkerton battalion, Mr. Frick sent for Captain Rodgers, of the towboat Little Bill, and directed him to fit up two barges with sleeping accommodations and provisions for 300 men, who were to be taken on board at some point not then determined, brought to the works at Homestead, and subsequently lodged and boarded on the barges.

He also notified the sheriff of Allegheny county, William H. McCleary, through Messrs. Knox & Reed, attorneys for the Carnegie Company, that there would be a strike at Homestead and that 300 Pinkerton watchmen had been engaged, and requested the sheriff to deputize the entire force; that is to say, to appoint them police agents of the county. The sheriff maintained afterwards that, on the advice of his attorney, he had declined to deputize the Pinkerton men until they should be installed in the mill and had reserved the right to act at his discretion when that time came. Mr. Frick, on the other hand, declared on the witness stand that the sheriff consented to deputize the men and assigned his chief deputy to swear them in.

The train was now laid; the fuse was lit, and all that remained to be done in the Carnegie camp was to wait for the explosion.

To disarm suspicion on the other side, however, Mr. Frick, as the crisis approached, gave out information leading the public in general and the locked-out men in particular to believe that he meant to rely on the ordinary processes of law to protect him in the non-unionizing of his works. On the evening of July 4, after a conference with the other chief officers of the firm, he furnished a statement to the newspapers alleging that there was no trouble to be feared, that the men were weakening, a large number of them being anxious to get back to work, and that the plant would be placed in the hands of the county, the sheriff being requested to furnish enough deputies to ensure adequate protection.

With all his firmness, the doughty chairman of the Carnegie Company dared not make a clean breast of his program. The way for the *coup de grace* had to be cleared by strategy and dissimulation.

The locked-out men celebrated Independence Day with due patriotic fervor. The force of guards was increased from 350 to 1,000, the picket system being expanded so as to form an outline five miles in extent, covering both sides of the river.

In the afternoon an alarm was sent in to headquarters. Two men had been seen landing from a boat near the works and were taken for spies. Quick as a flash a thousand men rushed to the river bank and inclosed within a semi-circle of stalwart forms the place where the suspects had landed. It proved that the latter were merely honest citizens of the town returning from a picnic across the river, but the incident showed how effectually the men kept themselves on the *qui vive*, precluding the entry of an enemy at any point.

When Sheriff McCleary reached his office in the Allegheny County court-house, on the morning of July 5, he found awaiting him a formal application from the Carnegie Company for the services of one hundred deputies at Homestead. The Sheriff was discomfited by the demand. His predecessor in office, Dr. Mc-Candless, had been forced to engage in a long and irksome legal battle in order to recover from the Carnegie Company the money due for the service of deputies at Homestead in 1889, and the prospect of a fresh dispute over the pay of special officers was not inviting. So Mr. McCleary, who was gifted by nature with a strong tendency to evasiveness, returned an evasive answer, and conceived the idea of going to Homestead with his own office force of twelve men and making some sort of dignified showing pending the arrival of that army of Pinkertons, which he already knew to be moving on the devoted town.

The Sheriff and his little posse proceeded accordingly to Homestead and were received by the men, if not with cordiality, at all events with decent consideration. A proclamation was issued embodying the usual warning against breaches of the peace. Then a phalanx of strong-limbed steelworkers escorted the officers to the mill and pointed out that nobody was trespassing upon or damaging the Carnegie Company's fortified territory.

The sheriff stated that, under the law, the company should be permitted to bring in whatever men it chose and to operate its own works.

The men responded that neither the county authorities nor anyone else would be permitted to bring non-union men into the mill, and, having thus emphatically signified their purposes, escorted the sheriff and his followers—all of them more or less afflicted with nervousness—to the railroad station and saw the little party safely out of town.

Had the sheriff been less evasive, less nervous, less of a politician and more of a man, there was still time for him to avert disaster. He, as chief police officer of the county, had been informed of the coming of Mr. Frick's hired army. He could not fail to be aware that a collision between the Pinkerton men and the 4,000 steelworkers was bound to come, that blood would run like water at Homestead, that demoralization and disgrace, and perhaps even heavy financial loss to the county would follow, and that, therefore, to remain supine in the face of all this, to let the crash come and not lift a finger to prevent it was literally a dereliction of duty.

There was no obligation resting on this official to keep Mr. Frick's operations secret. On the contrary, he was under a strong moral obligation to prevent the execution of those operations at all hazards by giving them prompt publicity and enabling the exhaustion of all available legal means of stopping an invasion of the county by armed mercenaries of a class condemned by law in two neighboring states and bitterly hated by workingmen in every state of the Union.

It did not appear to occur to the sheriff that the hiring of Pinkerton detectives was an offensive arraignment of himself as the county's chief executive officer. The one idea uppermost in his mind seemed to be to steer clear of the whole unpleasant business as far as he conveniently could and to trust to luck and the Pinkertons to pull Frick through somehow.

Decidedly a weak and inefficient man, this sheriff. For the time being, he had abdicated in favor of Frick and the Pinkertons and it would not be his fault if the devil were not unchained.

And now from a score of cities came the Pinkerton myrmidons to the headquarters at Chicago, few among them knowing or caring on what mission they were bound, as long as they got their daily rations and their daily pay, but all comprehending that blind obedience was the watchword. Captain F. H. Heinde had been detailed to take charge of the expedition, and under his guidance the men proceeded from Chicago to Youngstown, and thence to Bellevue, on the Fort Wayne railroad, opposite the Davis Island dam, arriving at this point at 10:30 o'clock on the evening of July 5.

Early in the day, Mr. Frick had issued final orders to Captain Rodgers, directing him to tow his two barges down the Ohio River to the dam in time to meet the battalion of Pinkerton guards. Captain Rodgers duly carried out his orders. With the boats Little Bill and Tide, each having a barge in tow, he arrived at the dam at 10 P. M. There he was met by Colonel Joseph H. Gray, Sheriff McCleary's chief deputy, who had been dispatched by the sheriff to "keep the peace," if his own testimony and that of the sheriff are to be accepted, whereas, according to Mr. Frick's story, his real mission was to deputize the Pinkerton guards and thus render the county liable for the acts of these strangers.

At 10:30 P. M., the trainload of guards arrived; the men embarked in the barges; the Little Bill and the Tide puffed away as cheerfully as if they were towing a pleasure party, and in the stillness of the beautiful July night the expedition moved slowly in the direction of Homestead.

CHAPTER V.

THE FIRST SHOT

ON BOARD THE BARGES—FLOATING
BARRACKS EQUIPPED FOR BLOODY
WARFARE—UP THE MONONGAHELA
AT MIDNIGHT—HOMESTEAD GETS
WARNING—DEFENDERS AT THE MILL
LANDING—FRICK'S ARMY REPULSED
WITH HEAVY LOSS—HUGH O'DONNEL
TAKES COMMAND OF THE WORK-
MEN—SHERIFF MCCLEARY'S APPEAL TO THE GOVERNOR—FRICK
REFUSES TO INTERFERE.

THE barges on which Captain Heinde and his 300
men embarked were primitive specimens of the
boat builders' art, previously used for the transportation of freight. Unlike the ordinary coal barge,
these were roofed in, and, were it not for the flat roof,
would have exactly resembled Noah's ark. They measured 125 feet long and 20 feet wide. One was known
as the Iron Mountain; the other as the Monongahela.
These floating barracks had been purchased a week
before the time of the Pinkerton expedition by an agent
of Mr. Frick's, and quietly fitted up at the landing-place

of the Tide Coal Company, in Allegheny City. The
Iron Mountain was equipped as a dormitory, several
tiers of berths being constructed on both sides and furnished with bed clothes. Two rows of cots occupied
the middle of the floor. The Monongahela was converted into a vast dining-room. Two rows of tables
were placed in the middle and board seats were provided.
In the stern was a commodious kitchen, with a full out-
fit of stoves and cooking utensils. An experienced
steward and a corps of twenty waiters were employed.
At the last moment a number of mysterious looking
cases were put on board. These contained Winchester
rifles and had been forwarded to the Carnegie Company
by Adams Express. Watchmen at the landing met all
inquiries with the explanation that the barges were
intended for the transportation of laborers to the Beaver
dam on the Ohio River.

It has been said that most of the Pinkerton men had
no idea of the nature of their mission. The fact is that
only the officers of the expedition comprehended the
gravity of the work in hand. However, when the men
found themselves being conveyed up the river in the
close quarters which the barges afforded to so large a
number, many of them became uneasy, and, weary as
they were after their long trip by rail, but few were able
to close an eye.

As the barges approached the mouth of the Monongahela River, the lights of the two great cities of Pittsburgh and Allegheny illuminated the surface of the
waters; but no midnight wayfarer who saw the Little
Bill and the Tide, with their odd-looking tows, dreamt
for an instant that within those coffin-like craft was the

Frick army of invasion and that, within a few hours, those same craft would harbor terror, bloodshed and death. The two cities slept on, unconscious of the thunderbolt that was to fall at the dawning of the day.

When the boats drew near the Smithfield Street bridge, which connects South Pittsburgh with the city proper, there were, however, keen eyes to note their coming. A scout from Homestead, who was one of a detail appointed to look out for suspicious movements along the Pittsburgh wharves under the cover of night, detected the ominous procession and, hurrying to a telegraph office, wired the warning to Homestead: "Watch the river. Steamer with barges left here." On receipt of this news, the advisory committee prepared to issue a general alarm at five minutes' notice. The belief at headquarters was that 100 special deputies were on the way to take charge of the mill under orders from the sheriff.

With the exception of the disabling of the Tide, nothing occurred to mar the serenity of the invading force until near daylight. Up the Monongahela steamed the little tugs, the barges gliding stealthily in their wake. Captain Rodgers, somewhat inflated with the idea of his dignity as commodore of a war fleet, stood on the deck of the Little Bill and chatted with Pinkerton Detective J. H. Robinson, of Chicago. The Tide being disabled, the Little Bill had to "lock" both barges through at Lock No. 1, where a dam crosses the river.

At 3 A. M. the barges reached the B. & O. railroad bridge at Glenwood. Day was breaking, but a heavy fog overhung the water, so that the barges were not visible from the shore; nor could the watchers on deck perceive what was going on a few hundred yards away on the Homestead side of the river.

Yet, while the signs of danger were hidden from the eye, there were manifestations, the significance of which could not be misunderstood.

The voices of men, women and children were heard breaking in harshly upon the stillness of the early morning. Scout called to scout almost loudly enough for their words to be caught by the listeners on the water.

Captain Heinde, although a brave man, and used to dangerous situations, felt a sinking of the heart at this unmistakable proof that the secret of the expedition was no longer a secret and that if a landing was to be made at Homestead, it would have to be gained by fighting for it.

A feeling of alarm seized upon the green hands among the guards. There was danger in the air, and numerous as they were, what chance was there for self-defense as long as they were cooped up within four walls? It took the utmost tact and firmness on the part of the experienced guards, who served as officers, to calm the anxious ones and lead them to believe that they would soon reach safe quarters on *terra firma.*

About this time, a horseman riding at breakneck speed, dashed into the streets of Homestead giving the alarm as he sped along. In a few minutes the news that barges, supposed to be filled with deputies, were nearing the town had spread far and near and, with one accord, the people rushed to the river bank. Here, for two hours that seemed like weeks, thousands of men and women waited for the arrival of the enemy—a dangerous enemy, they felt sure, judging by the manner of his coming.

As the barges drew nearer to Homestead, the noise on the shore grew louder and louder and soon the sharp crack of rifles rang out, giving a foretaste of what was in store for the unwelcome visitors. Whether these shots, which were fired before the Pinkertons attempted to land, were intended as signals or were aimed, in a random way, at the barges has never been determined. There is no doubt, however, that the firing from the bank stopped as soon as the Little Bill and its tow drew up opposite the mill landing.

This landing was on the beach within the mill enclosure, Mr. Frick having had the wire-topped fence carried down to low-water mark, so as to shut off all access by land. Above the landing-place frowned a steep eminence largely composed of slag and other refuse from the mill. At this point, also, rise the piers of an iron bridge, over which the P., McK. & Y. railroad runs into the mill yard. This bridge is familiarly known at Homestead as the "Pemickey."

No sooner did the waiting multitude on the river bank perceive that the occupants of the barges meant to put in at the Carnegie Company's landing-place than, with a roar of anger, strong men tore down the fence that barred their path, and ran to the spot where, had they delayed five minutes longer, the Pinkerton men would have disembarked in safety.

Prior to this time the workmen had religiously refrained from trespassing upon the company's property. It had been their set purpose to avoid the odium which would attach to any act suggesting vandalism or arbitrary assaults upon property rights.

But now was not the time to think of conservative

methods. Who could tell what kind of invaders were
in those ugly-looking barges?

Were they deputies whom the sheriff sought to bring
in like a thief in the night? Were they—and at this
thought every man's blood boiled—a regiment of Pinkertons brought there to repeat the Pinkerton exploits of
a few years before in the coke regions?

What were the odds, one way or the other? Whoever
the visitors were, they came with every manifestation of

RIVER ENTRANCE TO THE WORKS.

an evil purpose, and was not self-preservation the first
law of nature, applying as such to a Homestead steelworker in danger of losing his job and, perhaps, his home?

So the fence went down, and the straight road from
the river to the mill was blockaded by a band of resolute
fellows that neither Pinkerton men nor sheriff's deputies
could hope to overcome.

The scene at this time within the barge Iron Mountain, which had been towed close to the shore, was one

of wild confusion. The plan of a secret landing had been frustrated, and there was nothing for it now but a hand-to-hand conflict against terrible odds.

The cases of rifles were broken open and these weapons and revolvers were hastily distributed among the men. About fifty men were armed with clubs. Captain John W. Cooper, of the New York and Philadelphia division, Captain Charles Norton, of the Chicago division, and Captain Heinde, who had general charge of the expedition, supervised these arrangements. When all were in readiness for battle, a gang-plank was shoved out and the three captains stepped forward, with Heinde in the van. Twenty of the rank and file appeared behind them on the bow of the boat.

At this offensive move, the Homestead men, most of whom were armed, shouted a fierce warning.

"Go back," they cried, "go back, or we'll not answer for your lives."

There were blue uniforms among the group on the bow of the Iron Mountain, and these told their own story to the excited people on the shore.

For a moment the Pinkerton men stood at bay. The scene before them was one to appal the bravest. On the beach several hundred men and women—for mothers, wives and sisters had joined in the mad rush to the landing-place—some of them half dressed, some carrying loaded guns, some with stones or clubs in their hands; in the distance hundreds more rushing to the defense; in the background a huge embankment intercepting the passage to the mills; behind them the river and the chance of saving themselves by flight. Retreat, however, would have been ruinous to the prestige of the Pinkerton agency besides resulting probably in throwing upon the agency the entire cost of the fruitless expedition, for Mr. Frick would hardly be willing to pay for services not even fairly begun.

So the warning of the workmen was disregarded, and, with a word of command to his men, Captain Heinde pressed forward.

Suddenly a shot was fired—whether from the barges or from the shore has always been a mystery.

Captain Cooper turned instantly towards the barges and in a loud voice gave the order: "Fire!"

A score of Winchester rifles were discharged into the crowd on the bank with deadly effect. Several of the workmen were seen to fall. The first blood had been shed and now the one thought of the men of Homestead was *vengeance*, merciless and complete, on the strangers who had come to shoot them down.

The volley fired from the barges was repaid with interest, and when the smoke from the answering discharge cleared away it was seen that havoc had been wrought on the barges. Captain Heinde had been shot through the leg; J. W. Kline and another detective were mortally wounded and perhaps a dozen others on the Pinkerton side were wounded more or less severely. The Little Bill was fairly riddled with bullets, and Captain Rodgers, having taken the injured men off the barges, lost no time in steaming away from his uncomfortable quarters, leaving the Pinkertons to land, if they could, and if not, to remain where they were and make the best of a desperate situation.

Both sides now withdrew, the workmen abandoning their exposed position, where they offered an easy target to the marksmen on the barges, and establishing themselves on the heights, while the Pinkertons retired into the barges and proceeded to prepare for renewed action by cutting loopholes in the sides of the craft. It would have been suicidal to attempt another sally.

One of the last of the workingmen to leave was an intrepid fellow who had thrown himself, face down, upon the gang-plank just as Captain Heinde came out, and waited, with revolver cocked for the advance of the enemy. If the guards had landed, they would have done so over his body.

The leadership of the Homestead defenders in this crisis devolved, by common consent, upon Hugh O'Donnell, a man who, in outward appearance, showed none of the customary attributes of a labor leader. A young, handsome individual he was, pale-faced and black-moustached, and rather slight of build. His attire suggested rather the man of fashion than the horny-handed individual generally accepted as the correct type of millworker. O'Donnell, however, was one of the superior class of workmen; enjoyed a comfortable income, and owned his own well-appointed residence, over which one of the plumpest and prettiest little wives in Homestead presided. Of the great influence exercised by this man over his fellow-workmen there could be no question. "Hughey," as they called him, was admired and looked up to. Fluent of speech and quick of action, he was the right man to take control on an occasion such as this. Associated with him in the government of the crowd that had come together haphazard to repel the

Pinkertons were Hugh Ross and Jack Clifford, both pugnacious and the latter with a strong trace of the daredevil in his disposition.

O'Donnell's first design was to drive the Pinkertons away without firing a shot, and if the latter had heeded his advice and desisted from the attempt to land, there would have been no sacrifice of life and limb. But once the attack was made, the young leader saw that it was useless to plead for peace, and devoted himself accordingly to the task of getting the women and children out of the way and removing the wounded, among whom were William Foy, Michael Murray, Andrew Soulier, John Kane and Harry Hughes.

The workmen now occupied themselves with the construction of ramparts out of pig and scrap iron. Enough of these were piled up to accommodate scores of sharpshooters. Men armed with rifles also took positions at various points of vantage in the mill buildings and a desultory fire was kept up. At the same time armed men appeared on the other side of the river and began a fusilade on the barges. The non-combatants—men, women and children to the number of about 5,000—thronged the steep hills which rise above Homestead, whence they had an unobstructed view of what was taking place in the mill yard and on the river.

A few venturesome spirits pulled out in skiffs and fired into the barges at close quarters.

The Little Bill crossed to Port Perry, opposite Homestead, without further mishap. There is a B. & O. railroad station at that place, and there Captain Rodgers and Deputy Sheriff Gray put Captain Heinde and five other wounded Pinkertons on a city-bound train with instructions to have them taken to the West Penn and Homeopathic hospitals.

The burgess of Homestead, honest John McLuckie, issued a proclamation ordering the liquor saloons to be closed and calling upon all good citizens to help him in preserving the peace. As the burgess was a staunch Amalgamated man and himself a sharer in the common tribulation, everybody understood, as a matter of course, that the preservation of the peace, from his point of view, consisted in a united effort to make short work of the Pinkertons.

While these events were transpiring at the scene of action, the telegraph wires were carrying the news of the battle to all parts of the country. In Pittsburgh excitement rose to fever heat. Sheriff McCleary reached his office early and, having come to the conclusion that, where 300 Pinkerton men were worse than powerless, it was useless for him to think of interposing, sent a message to Governor Pattison, briefly detailing the situation at Homestead and the inability of the civil authorities to cope with it, and soliciting "instructions at once." The governor promptly answered as follows:

"Local authorities must exhaust every means at their command for preservation of peace."

The sheriff, who had been hoping that the militia would be ordered to his relief, was much discomfited by this plain intimation that, as chief peace officer of the county, he was expected to be up and doing instead of collapsing under fire. Being a prudent man, however, he took no risks, but remained in the safe seclusion of his office.

At the Carnegie offices there were no signs of perturbation, although Mr. Frick and his associates were early informed of the bloody outcome of their scheme of invasion. President Weihe, of the Amalgamated Association, urged a conference with the men as the only expedient which might be successfully employed to stop the shedding of blood.

The answer to this humane suggestion was characteristic. It was a flat refusal. "Our works are now in the hands of the sheriff," said Secretary Lovejoy, "and it is his official duty to protect the property from destruction or damage. If it is necessary in his judgment to call out troops, he is the proper authority to do so. Everything is in his hands."

This, at a time when the sheriff was publicly announcing that he was powerless, and when the chances were a hundred to one that the entire force of Pinkertons would be destroyed like rats in a trap, betokened very clearly that the sacrifice of life was a trifle in the eyes of the Carnegie officials compared with the sacrifice of the non-unionist policy to which the firm had tied itself down. The Pinkertons might be killed to the last man, but the Frick ultimatum must stand. No doubt, the firm also considered that the worse the turn taken by affairs at Homestead, the stronger the probability that the militia would be ordered out, and that, with soldiers on the ground, there would be no trouble about bringing in non-unionists.

There was, then, nothing to be looked for in the way of humane mediation at the hands of the firm, and nothing in the way of masterful intervention at the hands of the sheriff.

Four thousand infuriated steelworkers and three

hundred caged Pinkertons were to be left to fight out their deadly quarrel without let or hindrance.

The dictates of law and humanity were alike suspended upon that July day—the most unfortunate day in the history of organized labor in the United States.

CHAPTER VI.

WHILE the heroes of the battle at the landing
were building breastworks in the mill-yards and
keeping up an intermittent fire on the enemy,
a busy scene was in progress at the telegraph office in
the advisory committee's headquarters. Here a temporary arsenal was established and rifles, shot guns and
ammunition were distributed to volunteers eager to take
a hand against Mr. Frick's emissaries.

Soon a new terror was added to those already men-
acing the Pinkertons. The dull roar of a cannon was
heard proceeding from the heights across the river,
and, at the first shot, a huge gap was torn in the
roof of the outer barge. Another shot flew wide of the
barges and struck Silas Wain, a young steelworker who
was standing in an exposed part of the mill yard, killing
him instantly. Wain's sweetheart, a young English
girl named Mary Jones, to whom he was to have been
married in a few weeks, almost lost her reason when

the news of her lover's death reached her, and was delirious for hours. In consequence of this unfortunate occurence, the cannon that did the mischief—a twenty-pounder—was subsequently shipped across to the Homestead side. Another piece of ordnance, of smaller calibre, was taken from the quarters of the Homestead Grand Army post and mounted at the pump-house of the county poor farm, adjoining the mill-yard. Owing to the elevation of the position, however, and the inexperience of the men who were handling the guns, it was found impossible to get the range of the barges and both pieces were ultimately abandoned.

BEHIND THE BARRICADES.

As the morning advanced, the workmen began to realize that some more effective means than rifle bullets must be resorted to in order to dispose of the barges and their obnoxious freight. The Pinkertons took care not to expose themselves, unless when one more venturesome than the rest undertook to make a reconnoissance and emerged on the bow of either barge. As this exploit invariably attracted a hail of bullets it was not frequently attempted. About 50 of the guards, all of them old hands in the Pinkerton service, kept up a regular fire through the loopholes cut in the sides of the barges, rendering it unsafe for a workman to show himself outside the furnace-stacks and piles of metal used as ramparts. George Rutter, an old and respected Amalgamated man and a member of the Grand Army, forfeited his life by taking chances on the accuracy of the Pinkerton men's marksmanship. He was shot in the thigh and died from the wound a few days later. John Morris, another millworker, and Henry Striegel, a young man who was on the field merely as a sympathizer, met the same fate. Striegel accidentally shot himself with his own gun, and was struck by shots from the barges after he fell.

Shortly after 11 o'clock, the Little Bill steamed back towards the landing-place flying the Stars and Stripes, Captain Rodgers having conceived the idea that the mill men would not dare to fire on the national flag, despite its being hoisted above a hostile craft. The captain's mind was speedily disabused of this idea. Volley after volley was poured into the little steamer, smashing the glass in the pilot-house and making the splinters fly in all directions. The man at the wheel, Alexander McMichaels, had to abandon his post and rush below. John T. McCurry, who had been hired the day before as watchman on the boat, without being informed of the kind of service in prospect, was shot in the groin, and Captain Rodgers only saved his life by throwing himself on his face on the deck. According to the story told afterwards, the Captain had purposed connecting with the barges and releasing them from their perilous position, but was glad enough to run the gauntlet with his own boat without attempting to relieve others.

The Little Bill arrived at a moment when the escape of the Pinkertons seemed hopeless. A body of desperate men had formed the design of burning the barges, and commenced by setting fire to a raft composed of timbers soaked with oil and floating it down the river.

A groan of agony was sent forth from the unhappy wretches in the barges when this messenger of death was seen drifting towards them. Some of the men, driven to the verge of insanity by the suspense of the morning and the dread of death at any moment, proposed to desert the barges and try to swim to a place of safety. One of the captains put a quietus on the plan by threatening to blow out the brains of the first man who endeavored to desert his fellows in the face of danger which menaced all equally.

The burning raft failed to accomplish its mission. The flames which shot up from it when it was launched were gradually extinguished by the water and, by the time it reached the barges, it was only a charred and blackened mass.

Nowise discouraged by their failure, the men on shore turned their hand to a new plan of incendiarism. From the converting department of the mill down to the water's edge where the barges were moored runs a railroad switch, forming a steep incline. A car was run on to this switch and loaded with barrels of oil, lumber, waste and other combustibles. A torch was applied to the inflammable pile, and the car of fire, from which the flames mounted high in the air, was sent whirling down the incline. Thousands of eyes were fixed upon this

spectacle. The Pinkertons gazed with blanched faces
and trembling limbs, confident that their last hour had
come. Far back on the hills, women and children
watched what was being done and shouted their approval. The sharpshooters dropped their guns and looked
on with bated breath.

Surely that fiery monster, looking like a thing of life
as it sped downward, would crash into the barges and do
its work with infernal effectiveness.

But no. Great as was the momentum of the car, it

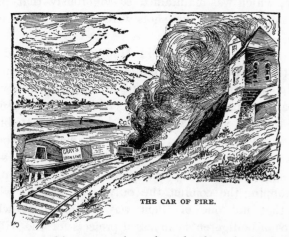

THE CAR OF FIRE.

came to a sudden stop when the wheels embedded themselves in the soft soil at the water's edge, and the workmen were again baffled.

The Little Bill, which, in the absence of the
wheelman, had been knocking about aimlessly between
the barges and the shore, was the only sufferer. The
little tug was badly scorched, and those on board had to
labor like Trojans to preserve her from total destruction.

After this crowning stroke of misfortune, Captain Rodgers decamped with all possible celerity, and went on down the river to Pittsburgh. His departure was a blow to the Pinkertons, who were hoping that the Little Bill might tow them out of danger. Now that the tug was gone, the last ray of hope vanished, and it seemed to be a question of only a short time until the expedition, already badly shattered, would be burnt up or blown up.

The Little Bill's departure was the signal for renewed firing, which was maintained so vigorously that probably not less than 1,000 shots were fired within ten minutes.

At this time the scenes in Homestead beggared description. The streets were filled with women, weeping, wailing and wringing their hands and begging for news of husbands, sons and brothers. Females were excluded from the mill yard, and very wisely, for if admitted they would only have hampered the fighting men and exposed their own lives without benefit to anyone. In some places, substantial citizens gathered and discussed plans for stopping the conflict, the only drawback to which was that not one of them was feasible. Elsewhere groups of belligerents canvassed projects for the killing of the Pinkertons in a body. And all this amid the crackling of rifle-shots and the din of a legion of angry voices.

President-elect Garland and Vice-President Carney, of the Amalgamated Association, arrived early on the ground and were met with due honors by the local committee. Mr. Garland's well-known figure was recognized at once by the men. He was deeply affected by

the gravity of the occasion and expressed regret that
things had reached such a lamentable extremity. One
of the leaders escorted the visiting officials to the front
and let them ascertain, by personal observation, how
little use there was in striving to mediate between the
workmen and the Pinkertons, since every shot fired by
the former was meant to avenge the death of their comrades. Vice-President Carney said openly that if Mr.
Frick had consented to waive the demand to have the
scale expire on the last day of the year, instead of the
last day of June, the wage question might have been
amicably settled and the present carnage avoided.

At noon a telegram was received at the headquarters
of the advisory board stating that the governor had
refused to call out the militia and that the sheriff had
started up the river with a squad of deputies. The gratification of the people over the governor's attitude was
not a whit keener than their resolve to send the sheriff
and his deputies to the right-about if it was proposed to
clear the way for the introduction of the Pinkertons into
the mill.

However, nothing was further from Sheriff McCleary's
mind than a visit to Homestead while the bullets were
flying. The sheriff held a consultation with Judge
Ewing, of the quarter sessions court, and with other
gentlemen learned in the law, but without results other
than those exhibited in an order to close the saloons in
Homestead and Mifflin township, which was sent out at
noon, and in a second message to the governor. The latter
communication embodied an urgent plea for aid, recited
the episodes of the early morning at Homestead, declared
that there were "no means at my command to meet the

emergency," and that any delay in ordering out troops might lead to further bloodshed and destruction of property.

The governor made no response to this appeal.

By noon, the men who were posted behind the ramparts in the yard of the Homestead mill were almost worn out with fatigue and hunger. Most of them had been up all night without tasting food, and the strain upon them had been enough to tax sorely the most robust physique. At 1 o'clock a relief expedition was organized and a squad of men carrying baskets of provisions made their way into the yard and by dodging behind furnace stacks and piles of iron managed to reach their suffering comrades without exposing themselves to the fire of the enemy. Cheers from the throng on the hills behind greeted this successful maneuver. The men on guard, after eating a hasty meal, tired and begrimed as they were, announced their intention of staying at their posts to the end.

From time to time, the Pinkertons waved a flag of truce, but it was not respected any more than was the national flag hoisted on the Little Bill. Sentiment had no place in the calculations of the men who formed the garrison in the mill yard. The Pinkertons had made the attack; they had been warned off and refused to go when they had the chance, and they had fired upon the workmen and taken many lives. Therefore, they need expect no quarter. So the flags of truce were shot down one after another and as the display of these symbols made it necessary for one of the Pinkertons to expose himself in every instance, and exposure invariably meant being wounded, this recourse was soon dropped altogether. The horrors of the position of these men increased every hour. The atmosphere of the barges was stifling. The relentless rays of the July sun beat down upon the roofs of the craft and raised the temperature within beyond the limit of endurance. There was scarcely a breath of air to carry away the noxious exhalations from the lungs of the 300 men within and the fumes of smoke and powder. Bullets, bolts, scrap metal and other missiles struck the frail structures on every side and gave promise of demolishing them piecemeal before sunset. Occasionally a missile found its way through a loophole and brought down one of the guards. It was in this way that Thomas J. Connors, of New York, was killed. Connors was sitting under cover in the outer barge, with his head buried in his hands, when a rifle bullet whizzed through the open doorway of the barge and struck him in the right arm, severing the main artery. He died in a few hours. This man's death is a matter of special interest, since it was afterwards made the basis of indictments for murder lodged against several of the Homestead leaders.

The wounded Pinkertons were waited upon and helped as far as the limited resources of the barges permitted by A. L. Wells, a young student of Bennett Medical College, Chicago. Wells had joined the expedition for the purpose of earning enough money during the vacation months to help him comfortably through his next year's course. He was a stout-hearted fellow and did his best to alleviate the sufferings of the unfortunates around him, many of whom lay groaning in agony on the floor, amid pools of blood. The young man fortunately escaped injury and stuck to his suffering companions to the last, unmindful of his own comfort. Even in that Pinkerton barge there was room for genuine heroism.

Shortly after one o'clock, a council of war was held among the men behind the barricades, and a new plan was agreed upon for the quick destruction of the barges.

Dynamite.

Here was a sure destroyer; one that could be trusted to do the work which the burning raft and the car of fire

THROWING DYNAMITE BOMBS.

had failed to do. A supply of stick dynamite was obtained and a dozen of the most reckless men in the yard opened up a bombardment of the barges with the deadly explosive. But somehow the sticks of dynamite proved little more effective than the means previously utilized. Most of them fell wide of the mark and the few which struck the barges did slight damage. Guardsman Wells, in telling the story of the fight afterwards, held that the first stick thrown tore a hole in the side of the barge Iron Mountain as easily as if the barge were made of paper. If so, this was the only instance in which the dynamite was really effective. The workmen, who felt confident that it would be easy to blow the barges to pieces, were greatly disappointed. It looked as if they might keep on firing lead and iron into the vessels forever without wiping out the enemy, while the importance of ending the battle before night-fall was plain to all of them.

About this time, it is said, some of the Pinkertons, unable to endure the agony and suspense any longer, eluded the vigilance of their officers and committed suicide by drowning. Detective Atkinson, of New York City, made this statement in a Pittsburgh newspaper on the day after the battle: "When we saw that preparations were being made to burn the barges, I loaded my revolver and made up my mind to blow out my brains should the boat be set on fire. I am just as positive that not less than a dozen of our men committed suicide during the day as I am that I am standing here. I saw four jump into the water and sink and I have been told that several others made away with themselves in the same way." The proprietors of the Pinkerton agency professed subsequently to have examined their roster and accounted for all the missing men, and that, with one exception, there were no cases of suicide. Atkinson's story, however, was corroborated by others, and is given here as having, at least, a semblance of truth.

The news received over the telegraph wires at the

advisory committee's headquarters was not of a character to dampen the ardor of the Homestead defenders or lead them to dread the accounting to which somebody must be held after the score which they had to settle with the Pinkertons would be wiped out in blood. First came the information that the sheriff had thrown up his hands and that the governor declined to call out the militia. Then messages of sympathy and encouragement began pouring in, and, as these multiplied, the conviction impressed itself upon the men that they were fighting not only their own battle, for the salvation of themselves and their families, but the battle of organized labor as a whole, and that the eyes of workingmen all over the continent were upon them. Perhaps this was an extravagant conception, but it was substantially justified by the tone of the telegrams sent in from far and near, proffering aid and bidding the men of Homestead stand to their guns. Even from far-away Texas came the news that artillery would be shipped to Homestead to help the cause of labor. To many rough fellows, heroic in their way and easily misled by circumstances, it appeared more likely than not, that the killing of those two barge-loads of Pinkerton guards was but the first step in a conflict of national extent, which would wind up in the coming of an industrial millennium. Hardly a man among them imagined that the law would seek atonement for the death of Mr. Frick's hired invaders.

One of the most significant bits of news that reached the men was that conveyed in a dispatch from Washington, D. C., to the effect that Representative Caminetti, of California, had introduced in Congress a resolution reciting the benefits conferred upon Andrew Carnegie by protective tariff legislation and calling for the appointment of a committee to investigate and report upon the cause of the Homestead lock-out and its sanguinary consequences.

There were some cool-headed and conservative people in Homestead who tried to assemble a mass meeting for the purpose of taking measures to stop the shedding of blood and to have the Pinkerton barges removed and sent down the river. The pleas of these would-be peacemakers fell upon deaf ears. In fact, it became dangerous to suggest a cessation of hostilities within the hearing of those who had experienced their baptism of fire and felt that lust of bloodshed which is said to be latent in the breasts of most men. He who talked of meeting the "Pinkerton butchers" half way challenged suspicion as a coward or a traitor.

CHAPTER VII.

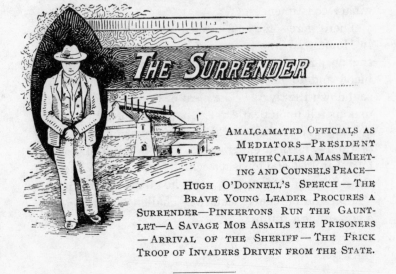

THE SURRENDER

AMALGAMATED OFFICIALS AS
MEDIATORS—PRESIDENT
WEIHE CALLS A MASS MEET-
ING AND COUNSELS PEACE—
HUGH O'DONNELL'S SPEECH — THE
BRAVE YOUNG LEADER PROCURES A
SURRENDER—PINKERTONS RUN THE GAUNT-
LET—A SAVAGE MOB ASSAILS THE PRISONERS
— ARRIVAL OF THE SHERIFF — THE FRICK
TROOP OF INVADERS DRIVEN FROM THE STATE.

AT three o'clock President William Weihe, of the
Amalgamated Association, came up from Pittsburgh, bearing a commission from the Sheriff.
He was accompanied by Assistant President-elect
C. H. McEvay, of Youngstown, Ohio; Secretary Shaw,
Charles Johns and other prominent officials and members
of the association. President-elect Garland joined the
party. The visitors, whose mission was one of mediation,
arrived none too soon. The same indefatigable individuals who had experimented with the burning raft and
the car of fire, had just turned their attention to pumping oil into the water and throwing heaps of burning
waste upon it, expecting to set fire to the barges by this

means. It was also determined to pump streams of oil upon the barges with the aid of the borough fire-engines and, having once thoroughly soaked the craft with the inflammable fluid, dynamite, the men thought, ought to do the rest.

There was a lull in these proceedings when word was passed along the line that the Amalgamated officials desired to address the men. The mass-meeting, which a few citizens of the town had unsuccessfully sought to bring about was now gotten together in a short space of time and with no appreciable difficulty, for the men entertained a high regard for President Weihe and were anxious at heart to hear what advice he might have to tender them. The meeting was held in one of the mill buildings. Mr. Weihe addressed the crowd, explaining that he came by virtue of an agreement with the sheriff to propose that the Pinkertons be allowed to depart with the guarantee that they would not return. The barbarity of continuing the battle until it ended in an absolute massacre was enlarged upon, and it was pointed out that the workmen were already victorious and could afford to rest on their laurels and to avoid tarnishing the good name of Homestead by committing what the world would regard as an outrage upon humanity.

Mr. Garland, who had mounted on a boiler as a rostrum, followed in an earnest appeal to the manhood of his hearers. "For God's sake, brethren, be reasonable" he cried. "These men have killed your comrades, but it can do no good to kill more of them. You have doubtless had two lives for one already."

A roar of disapproval greeted this deliverance. "We'll

have the lives of the rest of the villains," shouted a
chorus of angry voices. "Let us blow them out of the
water or burn them alive." "Order, order!" cried others,
and the rebuke was reinforced by a display of clubs and
brawny fists which had the effect of silencing the turbulent element for the time being.

"If you permit these men to depart," Mr. Garland
continued, "You will show to the world that you desire
to maintain peace and good order along with your rights.
Public opinion will still uphold you in your struggle."

Again clamorous disapproval greeted the speaker.
Cries of "Kill them!" "Burn them!" were heard on all
sides, but there were also a few who shouted "Let them
go!"

Mr. McEvay spoke next. "This day," he said, "You
have won a victory such as was never before known in
the history of struggles between capital and labor."
Tremendous cheering followed this diplomatic exordium.
"But," the speaker resumed, "If you do not let these
men go, the military will be sent here and you will lose
all you have gained. We have no assurances, but we
hope for a conference if peace is established. It is certain that, after this lesson, Pinkerton detectives will
never come here again." Cheering was renewed when
Mr. McEvay finished and the cries of "Let them go" increased in volume.

Mr. Weihe seized this opportunity to suggest that a
steamer be allowed to come up the river and tow away
the barges. "Will the Little Bill come after them?"
somebody howled, and once more pandemonium broke
loose. Mr. Weihe's promise that an unobjectionable
boat would be secured had, however, a quieting effect,

and the meeting dispersed leaving the impression in the minds of the officials that the Pinkertons could be released.

The news of what had taken place in the meeting traveled quickly through the mill yard, reaching even the tireless laborers who had been throwing oil on the barges and who were now engaged in bombarding them with Roman candles, sky-rockets and other fireworks—surplus Fourth of July stock obtained from the stores.

Hugh O'Donnell seized this opportunity to make another plea for peace. Grasping a small American flag, the intrepid young leader sprang upon a pile of iron and commanded the attention of perhaps a thousand men, who gathered eagerly around him. O'Donnell began his speech cautiously, discussing the situation in such a manner as to feel the pulse of his auditory and make sure that he had their sympathy. After having assured himself of his ground, he unfolded a plan for a pacific settlement, suggesting that a truce be arranged, and that the workmen take the initiative by displaying a white flag.

"Show the white flag? Never," was the unanimous response. "If there is any white flag to be shown, it must fly from the boats."

This brought O'Donnell to the point he wished to reach, "What will we do then?" he asked.

"We will hold them in the boats until the Sheriff comes and we will have warrants sworn out for every man for murder. The Sheriff will then have to take them in charge," said one man, and, singularly enough, considering the mood in which the men had been a few minutes before, this comparatively mild proposal evoked a general shout of approval.

O'Donnell, satisfied that a peaceable adjustment could now be effected, stepped down and went among the men strengthening the resolution which had just been taken. In the meantime the Pinkertons had been holding a final conference among themselves. A majority favored surrender and forced the captains, who were still doggedly bent upon holding out, to give in. Once more a white flag was hoisted on the Iron Mountain, and this time it was not shot down.

At the sight of the flag, the workmen cheered and cries of "Victory!" "We have them now," "They surrender," rent the air.

O'Donnell, accompanied by two other members of the advisory committee, ran down to the river bank and received the message of the detective who acted as spokesman. The purport of it was that the Pinkertons would surrender if protection from violence were assured to them. After a short parley, this was agreed to, although the howls and imprecations of an unruly mob which had thronged into the mill-yard boded ill for the fulfilment of the guarantee. O'Donnell had more than his own comrades to answer for. Throughout the afternoon thousands of outsiders—some of them millmen from South Pittsburgh, some roughs and toughs who relished the prospect of taking a hand in a fight of any kind, some Anarchists, aching for a chance to strike a blow at "Capital" and its representatives—had walked into Homestead over the railroad tracks and were now mingled with the steelworkers. These strangers, of course, were careless of consequences and indifferent to the restraining influence of O'Donnell and those associated with O'Donnell in ending the conflict. The women,

too, were not to be relied upon. After being shut out
of the battle-ground all day, it was questionable whether
or not they could be held in check when the Pinkertons
were placed at their mercy. It is well to bear these facts
in mind in connection with the painful scene which is
now to be depicted.

The Pinkertons, despite O'Donnell's pledge of protection, seemed to lose all heart when the moment came
to leave the barges. Nobody was willing to be the first
to go on shore, and, as if seized by a panic, the helpless
wretches huddled together behind benches and boxes
and waited, in fear and trembling, for a summons from
the other side. The workmen, however, were not slow
to make themselves masters of the situation. Hundreds
of them rushed down the bank, crossed the gang-plank
and clambered into the barges. On the shore a tremendous crowd gathered, hooting and yelling, most of them
carrying weapons of some kind. No wonder the Pinkertons blenched. They had to run the gauntlet, and if
the experience before them was not destined to be almost
as trying as that attributed to the victims of the gauntlet
torture in tales of Indian life, it was not because the
mob did not show all signs of thirsting for a fierce carnival of revenge.

The crowd on the shore formed itself, as if by a pre-
concerted plan, into two lines, 600 yards long, between
which the men from the barges had to pass. As the
first of the Pinkertons emerged from the barge Iron
Mountain, it was seen that he carried his Winchester
rifle. "Disarm him," yelled the crowd, and directly
every one of the guards was forced to lay down his arms.

Then the Pinkertons came out, in a dilapidated looking string, walking, running or crawling as best they could. The first few passed through the lines without molestation beyond hoots, jeers and imprecations. Suddenly the fury of the mob broke out. A man struck a detective with his open hand. The example was contagious. Clubs and stones were used with demoniacal ferocity. Women, converted for the nonce into veritable furies, belabored Mr. Frick's janizaries with bludgeons, stoned them, kicked them and spat upon them. The hated Pinkerton uniforms were torn off and cast into the river. Cries for mercy were treated with derision.

As a means of identification the Pinkertons had been compelled to uncover their heads, and thus offered an easy mark to their half-crazed assailants.

"Men, for the love of God, have mercy on me." shrieked a gray-headed man, wounded and bleeding. Mercy! The time for that weakness had gone by. The suppliant was an accursed Pinkerton and again and again he was struck down and beaten before he reached the end of those terrible lines.

One young fellow, on leaving the gang-plank, threw himself on his knees, burst into tears and begged to be spared. Kicks brought him to his feet again, and he had hardly risen when he was felled to the earth by a blood-stained club.

The satchels and other small articles that the Pinkertons carried were snatched from them and destroyed.

Only those who were seriously wounded were permitted to pass without being attacked.

While this exhibition of barbarism was in progress, Hugh O'Donnell and a corps of aids, representing the advisory committee, made frantic efforts to shield the prisoners ; but the mob, for the most part, owed no allegiance to the Amalgamated lodges, and set the officials at defiance. In fact, several of the men who made up the hastily-formed escort were themselves struck and reviled for their humanity.

The Pinkertons were led through the streets to the rink, or opera-house, suffering indignities all the way. Even children threw mud and stones at them. Arrived at the rink, the entire posse was driven in like a herd of sheep. Guards were placed and members of the Amalgamated Association, assisted by physicians of the town, attended to the wounded. Entrance to the rink was not secured without serious trouble. A crowd of Hungarians gathered here to take vengeance for the death of one of their countrymen who had fallen in the early morning skirmish. Women were among them and incited the men to mischief. When the Pinkertons appeared, a brawny Hungarian seized one of them by the throat and struck him in the face, while a stoutly-built woman belabored him with a club. A guard, placed there by the advisory committee, leveled his gun at the Huns, and shouted "Stand back, or by——I'll shoot the next man or woman that raises a hand against them. We have promised to protect them and we'll do it, even if we have to use our guns." This declaration provoked a howl of rage and cries of "Kill the murderers." Instantly a dozen guns were leveled at the mob, and disaster might have followed, had not Burgess McLuckie come forward, commanded peace and assured the crowd that the Pinkertons would be locked up and held for murder. No further trouble was experienced in getting the bruised and battered prisoners into their temporary quarters.

A sorrier sight than these men presented when they were assembled after the horrors of the day's fighting in the barges and of the march to the rink could not well be imagined. By actual count, one hundred and forty-three of the survivors were suffering from painful wounds or contusions, and those who had by extraordinary good luck, escaped with a whole skin, were half dead from fear and exhaustion.

They were kept in the rink under guard until near midnight. In the interim a conference was held between the borough council and the workmen's committee, at which it was agreed to let the Sheriff come to Homestead and remove the Pinkertons, whose presence in the town was a standing incentive to disorder. The Sheriff was sent for accordingly and arrived on a special train at eleven o'clock in company with the chief executive officers of the Amalgamated Association and W. J. Brennen, solicitor for the association. The Pinkertons were hurried into the Sheriff's train as quickly as their condition would permit, locked securely in the cars, and brought to Pittsburgh, where, after a score of the most dangerously wounded men had been removed to the hospital, the train was switched quietly to a side-track in the Pennsylvania Railroad yards, there to remain until the authorities decided what should be done with the Carnegie Company's troublesome agents. An hour or two later, it was decided, after a consultation held by the Sheriff with his bondsman, Chris L. Magee, a gentleman prominent in Republican politics, and the railroad officials, that the men should be sent east, and they were accordingly taken out of town, without considering the demand for their arrest and indictment.

This was, no doubt, the best thing that could be done under the circumstances, in view of the strong feeling against the Pinkertons among the working people of Pittsburgh.

When the Pinkertons had been driven from the barges, both vessels were subjected to a thorough search. Among the articles brought to light was a roster containing 266 names, divided into squads of 20, each in command of a lieutenant. Notes in the book showed that some of the men had been on duty at Walston, Pa., at Cleveland and other points where strikes had occurred.

The barges were for a time thronged with curious men, women and children. Somebody said "Burn them." Then the sight-seers fell back ; a few stout fellows carried out the last boxes of Winchesters and amunition ; oil was thrown upon the boats ; a torch was applied to each ; and, in a few minutes, the Iron Mountain and the Monongahela were enveloped in flames. The delight of the onlookers at this finale to the tragic events of the day knew no bounds. They cheered, clapped their hands and even danced with glee while the dry wood blazed and crackled, and two huge columns of smoke rose lazily towards the sky and formed clouds overhead. Not until the vessels had burned to the surface of the water and the last hissing embers disappeared beneath the placid bosom of the Monongahela did the enthusiasm abate.

The removal of the Pinkertons allowed the men of Homestead to rest for the first time in forty-eight hours, and the town now lapsed into its normal condition of quietude. Pickets were posted as usual to guard against surprise, but, aside from these watchers, the whole population sought repose, and by dint of sheer exhaustion, slept as soundly as if, a few hours before, carnage had not reigned supreme.

Whether the sheriff of Allegheny county slept or not is an open question. His last act before going to Homestead to remove the Pinkertons was to set his clerks at work making out notices to leading residents of Pittsburgh and Allegheny City, calling upon them, as loyal citizens of the commonwealth, to report next morning for service as special deputies at Homestead. The list was made up largely of editors, bankers, wealthy merchants and others of a class not likely to respond with alacrity. The outlook for a campaign against the fighting men of Homestead with such an army was hardly of a kind to promote wholesome slumber.

Mr. Frick, on whom the responsibility for the slaughter at Homestead was generally supposed to devolve, spent the night at his palatial residence in the East End, under the guardianship of private detectives.

Late at night, Secretary Lovejoy furnished a statement to the press. The Carnegie Company, he claimed, had offered $10,000 to any steamboat captain or owner who would go up the river and tow the barges down, but could find no one willing to take the risk. The company now left everything to the sheriff, with whom, quoth the secretary, "we cannot interfere in the discharge of his duty."

CHAPTER VIII.

CARNEGIE'S PROPERTY PROTECTED—CONFIDENCE STILL STRONG
AMONG THE MEN—HOMESTEAD AS A NEWS CENTER—THE DEATH-
ROLL—BURIAL OF THE DEAD—ANARCHISTS GET A SHORT SHRIFT
—THE SHERIFF FAILS AGAIN—INTERVIEWING THE GOVERNOR—
MARTIAL LAW IN SIGHT—PROCEEDINGS IN CONGRESS—OPINIONS
OF NEWSPAPESS AND PUBLICISTS—A PRESS CENSORSHIP ESTAB-
LISHED AT HOMESTEAD.

AT three o'clock on the morning of July 7, a committee of picked men made a search of the Homestead works, keeping a sharp look-out for stray
Pinkertons, spies or other interlopers. Nothing was
discovered. Even the rats were scared away from the
place, where empty cartridge shells, wadding and dis-
carded weapons—mute evidences of the bloody work
that had been done the day before—were scattered
around in profusion. Having completed its round, the

committee retired to headquarters and prepared an order requiring the watchmen, who had deserted their posts when the battle with the Pinkertons began, to resume the guardianship of the Carnegie Company's property. The men had guaranteed protection to the plant and showed by this step that they meant to keep their word.

At an early hour all Homestead was stirring, and anxious crowds assembled at headquarters and other distributing centers of information to ascertain what the new day was likely to bring forth. For the most part, the feeling of self-confidence which had inspired the locked-out men was as strong now, when a reaction might have been expected to set in, as it was at any time previously. Rumors of the coming of a fresh detachment of Pinkertons put the men on their mettle, and it was apparent that a repetition of Mr. Frick's experiment would be worse than futile.

Nobody gave serious thought to the likelihood of prosecutions to follow. The Pinkertons were invaders, whose purpose was to murder, and the workmen were legally justified in repelling them *vi et armis*. So the people reasoned, and this line of argument seemed, in their judgment, to be the only one that could present itself to any fair-minded and intelligent person. Even if it was wrong to kill and wound armed invaders, they believed it would be preposterous to think of arresting and imprisoning several thousand citizens.

The extraordinary interest taken in affairs at Homestead by the world without was demonstrated by the fact that, within the twenty-four hours elapsing after the firing of the first shot on July 6, this usually quiet little town was transformed into the busiest and most prolific

news center in the United States. An army of newspaper correspondents from all parts of the country found
quarters in the hotels and took possession of the telegraph offices. The ten daily papers of Pittsburgh had
variously from two to ten men on the ground. The
New York *World* headed the list of outsiders with five
correspondents and a special artist. The New York
Herald, *Sun* and *Mail and Express;* the Chicago
Tribune and *Herald;* the Philadelphia *Press* and *Times;*
the Cleveland *Leader* and *Press*, and the Baltimore *Sun*
and *World* all dispatched bright, able "specials" to the
scene of disturbance with that admirable promptitude
which makes American journalism a world's wonder.
The Postal and Western Union Telegraph Companies
also proved fully equal to the emergency. The Postal
Company placed a corps of operators in a large room in
the building where the Amalgamated Association held
its meetings, and the Western Union, in addition to its
regular office, established an annex in a restaurant,
where two expert operators were kept busy handling
huge masses of "copy," intended to be put in type,
perhaps a thousand miles away. The excellence and
magnitude of the work done by the newspaper men and
telegraph operators at Homestead from this time on were
unprecedented. Reporters from Pittsburgh were on
hand to meet the Pinkertons when a landing was
attempted, fraternized with the firing parties behind the
barricades while the battle was in progress, interviewed
the Pinkertons as they emerged from the barges after
the surrender, and withal seemed to lead a charmed life,
for there is no record of injury to any of the "gentlemen of the press." The latitude enjoyed by the jour-

nalistic fraternity was owing chiefly to the influence of Hugh O'Donnell, who had himself been a newspaper correspondent in a small way and who realized besides the advisability of aiding the press to secure accurate details of the struggle, so that the motives and actions of the workmen should not be injuriously represented. The gallant young leader had his reward. In a single day, the newspapers made him world-famous.

The making up of a list of the killed and wounded turned out to be a difficult matter. The Pinkertons had been hurried away, carrying many of their wounded with them and leaving not more than a dozen of their number in the Pittsburgh hospitals. At Homestead, there was a tendency to conceal the losses of the workingmen. How many of the latter were badly wounded has never been definitely ascertained. The official list of the dead, on both sides, as it appears on the books of the coroner of Allegheny County, is as follows:

Detectives—J. W. Klein, Edward A. R. Speer and T. J. Connors.

Workmen—Joseph Sotak, John E. Morris, Silas Wain, Thomas Weldon, Henry Striegel, George W. Rutter and Peter Farris.

Speer, who was a Pinkerton lieutenant in Chicago, was shot in the leg and lingered at the Homeopathic Hospital, in Pittsburgh, until July 17, when death ended his sufferings.

Rutter also survived until July 17. He fell at the first volley, having been shot in the thigh and abdomen. This man was a veteran of the Union army and one of the most respected millworkers in Homestead. He possessed courage above the ordinary and died rejoicing that he had been able to lay down his life for his fellow workmen.

At two o'clock in the afternoon of July 7, the members of the Amalgamated lodges and of the various other local societies were marshaled in attendance at the funeral services of their dead brethren—John E. Morris, Silas Wain and Peter Farris. The funeral of Morris was under the supervision of the order of Odd Fellows, of which he was a valued member. Rev. J. J. McIlyar conducted services at the Fourth Avenue M. E. Church, and delivered an impassioned oration, embodying a recital of the untoward events which had made Homestead a place of mourning. "The millmen," he said, "were organized in an association that enabled them to obtain just and adequate remuneration for their services. The existence of this union of the men was threatened by a body of Pinkertons, employed by somebody for the purpose. This is what has put this blessed man in his coffin to-day ; a perfect citizen ; an intelligent man ; a good husband who was never lacking in his duty ; a brother who was devoted and loyal and who will surely find his reward."

Rev. Mr. McIlyar told how easily the difficulty between the Carnegie firm and its employees might have been adjusted had arbitration been resorted to. "But," he added, "this town is bathed in tears to-day and it is all brought about by one man, who is less respected by the laboring people than any other employer in the country. There is no more sensibility in that man than in a toad." While the minister was speaking the sobs of Morris's broken-hearted widow interrupted his address, and her grief found a sympathetic echo in the hearts of all present.

Crowds lined the route to the cemetery and watched with tear-dimmed eyes the passage of the funeral cortege. On the way the hearse that bore the remains of Peter Farris fell into line. After the last sad rites had been performed over the graves of Morris and Farris, another procession was formed and all that was mortal of Silas Wain was removed to its resting-place.

Towards evening a stir was created by the appearance on the streets of a little band of anarchists from Allegheny City, who, like vultures attracted by the scent of prey, were drawn to the scene of trouble by the hope of fomenting still greater disorders. The unbidden guests proceeded to distribute incendiary circulars, setting forth that the mills were the rightful property of the working-men and should be seized as such, and calling on the good people of Homestead to become anarchists and strike for liberty hand-in-hand with their "brothers." Two of the agitators were placed under arrest and confined in the lock-up. The rest were promptly shipped out of town with an admonition not to return. It caused the workmen much concern to suppose that they might be credited with anarchistic tendencies; and, as a consequence, a species of censorship was established over the newspaper correspondents, with a view to preventing the publication of reports describing the Homestead defenders as a set of cut-throats and desperadoes, whereas, they wished the whole world to know that they were honest men, fighting for bread for themselves and their wives and children.

On the night of July 6, as has been told in the preceding chapter, Sheriff McCleary set his clerks to work on the issuing of notices to prominent citizens to report for service as deputies. The papers were delivered early in the morning, but the results were far from satisfactory. Some of the editors, bankers, merchants, manufacturers and political leaders addressed were too far advanced in years to be physically fit for active service, at least one of the number being over 80 years of age. Others had too wholesome a regard for their own safety to risk doing duty at Homestead and preferred being arrested and fined, if a penalty should be required. Only thirty-two men reported at the sheriff's office, and these were unarmed. The sheriff dismissed them with the remark that it was useless to go to Homestead with so small a force. Governor Pattison, however, was not moved by the representation that an appeal directed to persons who were not likely to undertake police duty under any circumstances exhausted the powers of the county government. He had already taxed the sheriff with shirking his duty and the course of events after the battle did not seem to have altered his opinion on this head. But the sheriff had made up his mind to incur no danger that he could avoid, and, therefore, remained all day in his office, leaving the local authorities of Homestead to preserve the peace if they could or would. The only important move which he made looking to the restoration of order was to call a conference in the evening to consider a proposition to introduce deputies into the Homestead works. At this meeting, C. L. Magee, John F. Cox, a Homestead attorney, Burgess John McLuckie, Hugh O'Donnell, President Weihe and President-elect Garland, of the Amalgamated Association, David Lynch, William Roberts, Jerry Doherty and James McCrory, also of the Amalgamated Association, were in attend-

ance. As might have been expected no definite conclusion
was reached, beyond what was embodied in the assurances
tendered by the Amalgamated men that they would do
their utmost in the interest of peace. The persistent
refusal of the Carnegie Company to lift a hand for the
prevention of another outbreak or to exhibit any trace of
friendly consideration for its locked-out employees was
an obstacle in the path of the peacemakers that could
not well be overcome.

A conference of militia officers at the Seventh Avenue
Hotel, in which the sheriff was also a participant, excited
considerable interest. The purpose of this consultation,
it was understood, was to consider the facilities for getting the citizen-soldiery into the field on short notice, in
case the governor should finally decide to order them
out.

Much uneasiness was felt in Homestead concerning
the chances of military interference. The citizens were
naturally averse to the quartering of troops in the town
for an indefinite period. It was apparent that this was
what Mr. Frick was aiming at. His own hired troop
having failed, it was his desire, with the aid of Sheriff
McCleary, to force the governor to call out the troops of
the state and place them indirectly at the disposal of the
Carnegie firm. With the militia at his back, the Carnegie Company's chairman counted on easily filling the
mill with non-union men and breaking up the Amalgamated lodges.

In order to prevent the execution of this design and to
offset the sheriff's representations, leading citizens of
Homestead telegraphed the governor requesting him to
take no action until he had conferred with a committee

which would immediately wait upon him at Harrisburg. The committee, which consisted of Attorney John F. Cox, Hugh O'Donnell, J. H. Williams, Dr. John Purman and G. W. Sarver, reached the executive chamber at 10:20 P. M. on July 8 and remained in conference with the governor until midnight. Messrs. Cox and O'Donnell made strong arguments against the calling out of the military, assuring the governor that order was restored in Homestead and that the sheriff would be allowed to take peaceable possession of the Carnegie property. Governor Pattison's reply was to the effect that insubordination would be checked if it took the whole military power of the state and of the nation; but, he added, the rights of all parties to the struggle would be maintained without regard to the merits or demerits of the business differences between them, and the military would be subordinated to the civil power. In short, without stating positively that he would call out the military, the governor sent the committee home with a pretty firm conviction that Sheriff McCleary's supineness had done its work and that, unless conditions altered amazingly, the troops would soon be on the ground. It was learned afterwards that the governor had sent an officer of the national guard to examine into the condition of things at Homestead and make an accurate report. The experiences of this individual, who, being a stranger, fell under suspicion and had some disagreeable encounters with the pickets and workmen's committees, were, no doubt, the real occasion of the governor's action; for it is certain that Sheriff McCleary's pleading telegrams had little weight at Harrisburg.

In the meantime, the aspect of affairs at Homestead became, if anything, more warlike. After the burial of their dead comrades had been attended to, the men set about strengthening their defenses, so as to guard against any attack, whether from Pinkertons or others. The fence around the mill-yard was repaired ; the picket lines were restored and reinforced and arms and ammunition were freely distributed. Scouts were sent out with instructions to post themselves in the railroad yards around Pittsburgh and at points along the river and to give the alarm at the approach of an invading party of any description. The military organization of the men was well-nigh perfect, and it was manifestly impossible that they could be surprised.

But one alarm was given during the night. At I A. M. the ringing of bells and the blowing of whistles aroused the town, and the works were quickly surrounded by men carrying loaded rifles. When it was ascertained that the alarm was a false one, the crowd just as quickly dispersed and from a state of wild excitement the town lapsed back into peace and quietude.

Much encouragement was given to the men by the interest taken in their cause not only by organized labor throughout the land but by some of the most noted men in public life. Congress entered into the discussion of the Homestead struggle with extraordinary zest. Representative Camminetti opened the ball in the lower house on July 6, and on the following day Mr. Palmer, of Illinois, made a fiery speech in the senate, declaring the Pinkerton invasion to be an insult to the commonwealth of Pennsylvania, and that the coercion of wage-workers by an armed force was reprehensible and called for the sternest condemnation. Mr. Palmer maintained further that the workmen of Homestead, having built up the mills by their labor, had a right to insist upon permanency of employment and reasonable compensation. Mr. Voorhees, of Indiana, argued that the Homestead troubles were the direct result of the Republican tariff system, by which the iron barons of Pennsylvania were heavily protected with a pretended understanding that the workingman would get his share of the benefits conferred. Mr. Carnegie, the speaker said, had done his part by sending an armed mob to shoot down his employees if they refused to serve for reduced wages or to abandon their jobs to others whose services could be had for less money. The Pinkertons had been killed by men acting in self-defense, and it was his only regret that Carnegie himself had not been at the head of that squad "instead of skulking in his castle in Scotland." Republican senators responded to these speeches, defending the protective tariff, but emphatically repudiating Pinkertonism. While these proceedings were going on in the senate, the house busied itself with arrangements to send a committee to Homestead, and several speakers also took occasion to denounce the employment of Pinkerton trained bands as contrary to the spirit of American institutions.

The press of the country was almost a unit in deploring the harsh methods employed by the Carnegie Company and in demanding legislation prohibiting the maintainence of a Pinkerton "standing army" and its utilization in labor troubles. The New York *World* suggested that the dispute at Homestead be settled by referring it to a board of arbitration, to be composed of

Governor McKinley, of Ohio; Governor Pattison, of Pennsylvania, and Terence V. Powderly, Grand Master Workman of the Knights of Labor. The New York *Sun* stood alone among the Democratic papers in upholding Mr. Frick and the Pinkertons.

General B. F. Butler, whose reputation as a constitutional lawyer gave special significance to his remarks, expressed the opinion that the Carnegie Company should be held legally responsible for the provocation of bloodshed, since it had prepared for riot and sent an armed expedition to precipitate it. In his judgment, the government should cause the Pinkerton forces to be disbanded.

General Weaver, the nominee of the People's Party for president, pronounced the outbreak an illustration of the subjugation of the Republic to corporate despotism. "When Rome was near her fall," he said, "the wealthy barons had their braves. Our corporate barons have their Pinkertons. . . . The frightful condition of affairs in Pennsylvania will strike the whole country like an alarm bell at midnight."

The newspapers containing these expressions were scanned with avidity by the locked-out men, and, at the same time the scrutiny exercised over the reporters was made all the more vigorous as it became apparent even to those of limited intelligence that Homestead was now the focus of world-wide observation, and that the judgment formed abroad depended entirely on the carefulness and veracity of the correspondents. Some of the latter protested hotly against what they regarded as unwarrantable interference with their work, but protests counted for nothing. Spies and impostors had slipped into town in the guise of newspaper men and the committeemen of the lodges deemed it necessary to supervise with the utmost vigor the work of those whose credentials were accepted, especially since the reporters were necessarily aware of the identity of the most active combatants and were in a position to betray secrets which might be used afterwards with fatal effect. Several correspondents who were suspected of making a questionable use of their opportunities were arrested and driven out of town, and those who were allowed to remain, had to wear badges provided for them by the committeemen. That there was reasonable foundation for these precautions was attested later on when it turned out that a few men who professed to represent reputable journals were in the pay of the Carnegie Company. One of these spies held credentials from a well known Chicago newspaper.

CHAPTER IX.

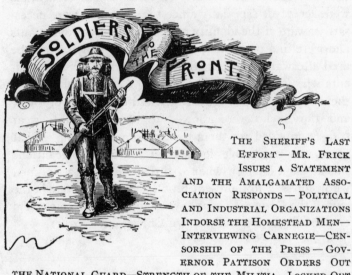

SOLDIERS THE FRONT.

THE SHERIFF'S LAST EFFORT — MR. FRICK ISSUES A STATEMENT AND THE AMALGAMATED ASSOCIATION RESPONDS — POLITICAL AND INDUSTRIAL ORGANIZATIONS INDORSE THE HOMESTEAD MEN— INTERVIEWING CARNEGIE—CENSORSHIP OF THE PRESS — GOVERNOR PATTISON ORDERS OUT THE NATIONAL GUARD—STRENGTH OF THE MILITIA—LOCKED-OUT MEN PREPARE TO WELCOME THE BLUE-COATS—A SPEECH THAT BURGESS McLUCKIE NEVER DELIVERED.

WITH the exception of alarms caused by rumors that Pinkertons were coming in force, Friday, Saturday and Sunday, July 8, 9 and 10, were comparatively uneventful days at Homestead.

On Friday morning Harris Striegel, a lad of 19, who had been among the first to fall, was buried with solemn ceremonies. In the afternoon a mass meeting was held at the rink, under the auspices of President Weihe and other officers of the Amalgamated Association. William J. Brennen, attorney for the Association, addressed the men, advising them to let the sheriff take possession of the works. If they refused to do this, he said, the militia would be ordered out, and then, if resistance should be offered, the troops would undoubtedly fire upon the citizens at a fearful cost of human life. Other speakers took the same ground as Mr. Brennen, and the disposition of the men seemed favorable to the admission of the sheriff and a posse of unarmed deputies. Nevertheless, the meeting adjourned without taking definite action.

Sheriff McCleary arrived in the town shortly after the adjournment of the meeting and was met by Dr. Gladden and five business men. The sheriff said that at the conference held in his office the night before he had received from attorney Cox and Dr. Gladden a list of twenty business men of Homestead who would serve as deputies. Only six out of the twenty were on hand to serve. What was there for him to do but to go home again? A large crowd surrounded the speaker, listening to his remarks, and followed him wherever he went. One of the locked-out men, a turbulent individual, named Burke, accused the sheriff of double-dealing and abused him roundly. Mr. McCleary hastened to get out of his uncomfortable quarters and boarded the first train for Pittsburgh.

The Amalgamated leaders devoted considerable time to the discussion among themselves of an interview given by Mr. Frick to the Philadelphia *Press* and published simultaneously in the Pittsburgh morning papers. This deliverance conveyed a carefully prepared history of the trouble between the Carnegie firm and its workmen, justified every act of the former, condemned every act of the latter, and declared that the firm would never again recognize trades unions. The principal points in Mr. Frick's defense were these:

1.—That $23 a ton for billets was a reasonable minimum on which to base wages, and that its acceptance should follow from the fact that the introduction of new machinery into the mills, at great expense, had enabled the men to increase their output and consequently to increase their earnings.

2.—That the expiration of the sliding scale on June 30 was embarrassing, because, in order to make contracts for the year, the firm should be informed on January 1 of the rates of wages to be paid.

3.—That the improvements already referred to warranted a decrease in tonnage rates, and that, even allowing for this decrease, the tonnage men would make more money than they did when the sliding scale went into effect in 1889.

4.—That there was no question of starvation wages, since the reductions proposed would affect only 325 men out of 3,800*, and would merely bring the wages of these men to an equality with those paid in other mills operated with union labor but not possessing the improved appliances of the Carnegie plant.

5.—That in the non-union mills operated by the Carnegie Company, good wages were paid and the employees were contented.

An answer to Mr. Frick's statement was drawn up by

---

*The event shows that Mr. Frick cannot have been sincere in this statement. Wages have been seriously depressed in almost all departments of the Homestead mill.

the workmen and published on the following day. The arguments in rebuttal were briefly as follows :

1.—That, as the workingmen do not sell the product of their labor, they must, under a sliding scale, protect themselves by requiring a minimum basis of wage-rates, which should not fall so low as to involve the payment of extremely low wages.

2.—That the enjoyment of fair rates of wages by the non-union workmen at Braddock and Duquesne was due to the fixing of a standard by the Amalgamated Association, below which the wages of non-unionists could not decently be permitted to fall.

3.—That, in preparing the scale, the workmen had made full allowance for improved machinery, not forgetting that the improvements had displaced many men, and thus, in a manner, repaid the cost of the investment. If there had been a misunderstanding on this head, it could have been adjusted by fair discussion, but fair discussion was impossible with an employer who declined to confer.

4.—That, of the 3,800 men employed, all or nearly all were affected by one or the other of the changes proposed, to-wit: a reduction in the minimum, another reduction in the proportionate rate of pay (thus making a double reduction) and the termination of the scale on December 31, 1893, instead of June 30, 1894.

In concluding their answer, the workmen said, "If argument and honest reasoning were substituted for the reserve and coldness of manner seen in the company's present attitude, there might be reason to expect an end of this deplorable state of affairs."

On Saturday, the Democratic Committee of Alle-

gheny County met in Pittsburgh at the call of its
chairman, William J. Brennen, Esq., the attorney for
the Amalgamated Association, and, after the completion
of routine business, adopted, by an unanimous vote,
resolutions sympathizing with the men of Homestead
in their efforts to "maintain American and resist European pauper wages," condoling with the friends of
those who had been "shot down by the hirelings of a
greedy and arbitrary combination of capital" and
denouncing Pinkertonism. These resolutions were presented by Jere Dougherty, of the Amalgamated Association.

Resolutions of similar tenor were adopted by all the
labor unions in Allegheny County, and thousands of
lodges in other localities placed themselves on record
to the same purpose and, in most cases, coupled their
expressions of sympathy and endorsement with offers of
financial support. The South Side Glassworkers' Union,
of Pittsburgh, demanded that the city councils reject
Andrew Carnegie's gift of $1,000,000 for a free library,
since the library would be paid for by the reduction of
workingmen's earnings. This home-thrust was repeated
by scores of other unions in and around Pittsburgh, and,
as a consequence, the councils let public business go to
the wall and avoided holding a meeting until the excitement had simmered down. The fact is that, since the
gift had been accepted, the money received and depos-
ited to the order of a special commission, and some of it
already spent, there was no way of returning it; but
anyhow the councils did not venture on a discussion of
the question, which must have led to a division on pro-
Carnegie and anti-Carnegie lines.

At Columbus, O., 2,000 workmen met in the state-house yard and passed resolutions calling upon the Pennsylvania authorities and the United States Congress to exterminate the Pinkerton system.

At Chicago, representatives of 20,000 men engaged in the building trades discussed the propriety of taking up arms and marching to the relief of Homestead.

Even in England, the trades unions entered protest against the Carnegie methods and called upon Kier Hardie, a workingmen's representative in Parliament, to whose election expenses Andrew Carnegie had contributed £100, to return the amount forthwith. Mr. Hardie very promptly forwarded the money, not to Mr. Carnegie, but to the people of Homestead, who, he held, had a valid title to receive and use it.

Three days elapsed after the battle at Homestead, before the English agents of the American press associations, who had been ordered to follow him up, were able to locate Mr. Carnegie and obtain an interview. Although regularly advised by cable of the progress of the troubles at his mills, he did not let the news interfere with his pleasures, but spent those three days on a coaching tour from Edinburgh to Kinloch, in Scotland. At Kinloch, he rented a shooting-box for eight weeks at a cost of $10,000. Here an American interviewer found him. According to the correspondent's statement, he was received by Mr. Carnegie in a "contemptuous and insulting" manner, as if the "intrusion upon his ducal magnificence" were a thing to be resented with the hauteur distinctively belonging to an American iron baron, who can afford to have castles and shooting-boxes in Europe. In response to a request for his opinion on the occurrences at Homestead, Mr. Carnegie said : "I am not willing to express an opinion. The men have chosen their course and I am powerless to change it. The handling of the case on the part of the company has my full approval and sanction. Further than this, I have no disposition to say anything."

Possibly this brusque statement may have been prompted in a measure by the irritation resulting from the use of the deadly parallels at the little millionaire's expense in the *Pall Mall Gazette*, a marked copy of which lay upon a table in the reception hall of the lodge. On one side appeared a report of Mr. Carnegie's philantrophic talk at the opening of the free library at Aberdeen, where he was seconded by the Earl and Countess of Aberdeen, and on the other a tell-tale table of reduced wages at Homestead.

The report of this interview with the high-priest of arbitration supplied a rich theme of comment to the locked-out men and it was well for Mr. Carnegie's dignity, that, just at this time, 3,000 miles separated him from his employees. Even at that distance, his ears must have tingled.

On Saturday evening, the press committee of the Amalgamated lodges, of which Hugh O'Donnell was chairman, distributed official press badges to the newspaper correspondents whose credentials were approved, and the committee signified its purpose of keeping close watch on the work of these gentlemen and of expelling from the town anyone of the number who, either by a violation of confidence or by sending out false statements proved himself unworthy of toleration. The reporters proposed the appointment of a committee composed of two newspaper men, two workmen and a fifth member, selected by these four, to pass upon disputes as to news matter, but this proposition was dropped on the receipt of a guarantee from Hugh O'Donnell that the rights of the press would be respected.

Throughout all these proceedings, the men acted in the belief that they were doing their best to maintain good order, and, although the committee which had been sent to Harrisburg returned without genuinely reassuring news, no one seemed to have the least idea that the military would be called out.

However, the visit of the governor's agent, previously referred to, had already borne fruit when, on the morning of Sunday, July 10, Sheriff McCleary forwarded his final appeal for military aid. In this communication, the sheriff once more averred that his powers were exhausted, and that the civil authorities could not raise a force of deputies large enough to cope with the locked-out men, "Only a large military force," he added, "will enable me to control matters."

At 10 o'clock on Sunday night the governor issued the following order:

George R. Snowden, Major-General Commanding N. G. P.:

Put the division under arms and move at once, with ammunition, to the support of the sheriff of Allegheny County, at Homestead. Maintain the peace, protect all persons in their rights under the constitution and laws of the state. Communicate with me.

ROBERT E. PATTISON, *Governor.*

Sheriff McCleary was informed of this order and directed to communicate with General Snowden.

Immediately on receipt of his instructions, General Snowden issued orders to the brigade commanders.

General Robert P. Dechert, in command of the First Brigade, with headquarters at Philadelphia, was directed to concentrate his brigade in camp at Mt. Gretna, near Lebanon, in the eastern part of the state, by Monday afternoon, battery horsed, and taking three days' rations. General J. P. S. Gobin, of the Second Brigade, was ordered to concentrate his command at Lewiston, moving west. General John A. Wiley, of the Third Brigade, composed of regiments from Western Pennsylvania, was ordered to proceed with his command to a point on the Pennsylvania Railroad within easy reach of the Monongahela River.

Within twelve hours from the time when Major General Snowden received the Governor's order the entire National Guard of Pennsylvania was on the march, fully equipped and ready for any kind of service.

It was no makeshift army that thus took the field on a few hours' notice. General Sherman said at the Garfield inauguration that the Pennsylvania Militia were the best body of troops in the National Guard of the country and, if confirmation of the accuracy of his judgment were needed, the Homestead "campaign" furnished it in amplest measure. The Guard underwent a signal transformation after the Pittsburg railroad riot of 1877. Prior to that time it was a loosely constituted, loosely governed organization, wholly unfitted for service in an emergency and serving principally as an agency for the distribution of military titles. The disastrous consequences of the movement against the Pittsburgh rioters, in which ignorance, incompetency and lack of concrete organization, in addition to causing the destruction of millions of dollars' worth of property came near bringing about the loss of many lives, opened the eyes of Major General Hartranft, then Governor of the state, and led him to formulate and carry into execution a plan of reorganization the success of which is seen to-day in the superiority of the Pennsylvania militia to any other body of troops in the United States outside the regular army. Under Governor Hartranft's direction the several divisions of the guard existing under the old order of things were merged in a single division of three brigades, composed of eighteen regiments of infantry, three troops of cavalry and three batteries of artillery. The maximum enrollment was limited to 8000 men. The regiments are recruited from all parts of the state and include all classes of citizens—farmers, mechanics, clerks, merchants and gentlemen of leisure.

The mobilization of this great body of men was accomplished with a degree of celerity and effectiveness unknown since the civil war. When the regiments advanced on the morning of July 11, all had nearly their full complement of officers and men. In a single night, preparations for service, the duration and hardship of which could not be estimated, were completed, and 8000 soldiers stood unreservedly at the disposal of the commonwealth.

The news that the soldiers were coming was received in Homestead without any perceptible feeling of alarm. It was understood by every one in the town that resistance to the power of the commonwealth was out of the question, and at the same time the idea went abroad that General Snowden and his men would confine themselves to the preservation of the peace and not aid Mr. Frick in the manning of the mill with non-unionists or the landing of another force of Pinkertons. There were, it is true, some hot-heads who disputed the justice of the Governor's action and canvassed the possibility of resisting the militia or of inducing the workingmen who bore arms for the state to make common cause with their brethren in the beleaguered town. The advisory committeemen, however, aided by other influential and intelligent citizens, were quick to suppress these disorderly symptoms and to emphasize the necessity of giving the soldiers a cordial and patriotic reception.

At two o'clock on Tuesday afternoon a mass meeting of workingmen was held in the rink, with Hugh O'Donnell in the chair. Burgess McLuckie made a fervent address, counseling a friendly demeanor towards the soldiers and eulogizing the Governor. "This man Pattison," said the sturdy Burgess, "Is acting quietly and rightly. He understands our position. He does not cater to monopolies. . . . Your friends are about to come; the safest, the best people that can come. We dont want Pinkertons here. We want the militia. . . . I stand here to say that any man who insults the militia shall be taken to the river and ducked." Cheers and laughter followed this sally and a motion in favor of ducking in the river any man who insulted the militia was carried unanimously.

John M. Carter, of the Baltimore *News*, who was fresh from an interview with the Governor, delivered a cheering speech, and other addresses of a prudent, common-sense tenor were made by members of the Amalgamated Association.

The feeling of friendship for the militia became contagious. It was decided that the blue-coated visitors should be received in state. All the brass bands in town took to rehearsing music of a triumphal character, to the inspiring strains of which Homestead was to be amicably turned over to its "protectors." In one band room, when the question of appropriate tunes came up, the exhilaration of the hour brought forth some odd suggestions. A young man who proposed "See the Conquering Hero Comes" was summarily suppressed, and a like fate befel an individual who thought the "Rogues' March" might fit the occasion. "Hold the Fort." "Comrades," "Johnny Get Your Gun" and "The Bogie Man" were canvassed, but a compromise was not reached until some gentleman of equal tact and discretion suggested "Ta Ra Ra, Boom De Ay," which was accepted without a dissenting voice as the correct thing to express Homestead's new-born sentiments of hope and contentment.

A reception committee, headed by Burgess McLuckie aud Hugh O'Donnell, was designated to welcome the representatives of the state and it remained only for the latter to reciprocate in kind to convert the military occupation of the town into a love-feast.

The Burgess issued a proclamation warning strangers to get out of town, directing the closing of drinking-places and enjoining women and children to keep off the streets. This duty performed, Honest John McLuckie immersed himself in the study of a speech, of specially artistic construction, intended for the edification of Major General Snowden and his staff on their entrance into Homestead, and warranted to inspire those dignitaries with a profound sense of the good-will and law-abiding spirit of the people of the town and their cheerful readiness to fraternize with the troops.

Unfortunately this little *chef d'oeuvre* was never delivered.

Like the flower in Gray's "Elegy," it was "born to blush unseen and waste its sweetness," if not on desert air, at all events on the cold and irresponsive dead wall of military discipline

All other themes of interest had now sunk out of sight in the face of the great event of the hour—the converging of the militia regiments upon Homestead. Even the Pinkertons, the fear of whose return with reinforcements had endured over Sunday, were forgotten, and the entire community was on the tip-toe of expectation, not knowing at what moment the glitter of swords and bayonets and the clatter of horses' hoofs would herald the advent of the advance guard.

Night fell and still no soldiers. General Snowden had taken care not to advertise the route of the troops nor the time of their arrival. It was his purpose to take the town by surprise and to occupy the positions selected in advance by an officer detailed to make a reconnoissance, before the people could be apprised of the nature and scope of his movements.

The maneuvers were carried out with the desired secrecy, the newspaper men and telegraph operators along the lines of march being kept in the dark, despite their habitual alertness.

So the Homestead folk went to bed without the opportunity of looking down the muzzles of any guns except their own and even these, together with the Winchesters taken from the Pinkertons as the lawful spoils of war, had been hidden from view, the occasion for their use having now finally departed.

While the good people on the banks of the Monongahela slept the sleep of contentment, the soldiers of the

First Brigade were stretched shivering on the open ground at Mt. Gretna, and General Snowden, with all of the Second and Third Brigades, except the regiments of the extreme West, was traveling as fast as the Pennsylvania Railroad Company could carry him towards the scene of disturbance.

CHAPTER X.

CAMP McCLELLAN

SNOWDEN'S SHARP TAC-
TICS—THE TAKING OF
HOMESTEAD — TROOPS
IN POSSESSION — SOL-
DIERS REPEL ADVANCES AND THE FRATERNAL RECEPTION IS
DECLARED OFF—O'DONNELL'S COMMITTEE AT HEADQUARTERS—
SUSPICION AND RESENTMENT ABROAD—THE LITTLE BILL RE-
TURNS—CONGRESSMEN HOLD AN INVESTIGATION—CAPITAL AND
LABOR IN CONFLICT ON THE WITNESS STAND—THE COST OF
PRODUCING STEEL REMAINS A RIDDLE.

IN pursuance of Gen. Snowden's plan to take Homestead by surprise, the Second and Third Brigades,
instead of being massed as announced in the newspapers, at Brinton, a station on the Pennsylvania R. R.
nearly opposite Homestead, came together at Radebaugh,
a mile and a half west of Greensburg, and 28½ miles distant from Pittsburgh. By 2.30 A. M. all the regiments had
reached the rendezvous, and at 5 A. M. the order to advance was given and the troops moved towards Homestead, crossing the Monongahela river over the P. V. &

C. bridge near Braddock. The Tenth and Fourteenth regiments, and a battery, were left on the Braddock side of the river with orders to occupy the hills above Port Perry, from which the guns would sweep the mill yards and the Homestead river front.

The early morning hours were full of surprise for the people of Homestead. Look-outs were posted at all avenues of approach and anxious crowds hung around the telegraph offices. As it drew on towards 9 o'clock, a report was circulated that the troops were at Greensburg. Telegraphic inquiries dispatched to that place brought the response that they were not there. At 9.25 the operator at Greensburg sent this message: "No. 23 was wrecked above this place last night; tracks are blocked and troops are delayed." A bulletin conveying the news was pasted on the window of the telegraph office and elicited faint cheers from the crowd. Evidently several hours must yet elapse before the soldiers would arrive, and the interval was ample to rest and eat breakfast.

But at the very moment when the Greensburg operator was ticking his message over the wires, a train pulled into Munhall station at the eastern end of the town, and from a parlor car in front a tall, distinguished-looking man, wearing the stars of a major-general, alighted, followed by six others in uniform and an individual in civilian's clothing. It was Major General Snowden, accompanied by his staff and Sheriff McCleary. Behind the general officers' train, which was made up of two cars, came another train of ten cars, from the windows of which bayonets and muzzles of guns protruded. Then came another train and another and still others, until 95 cars were drawn up in line, all bearing the same freight of guns and bayonets and lusty-looking fellows in the blue uniform of the National Guard.

There were, perhaps, 200 men and boys at Munhall when the military trains came in. Some of them had been up all night and were but half awake. None of them had expected the soldiers to arrive at that depot. After the first surprise was over, half a dozen scouts, who had been posted by the advisory committee, ran towards the town shouting : "The troops ! the troops !" The rest of the crowd pressed in around the staff officers' train and looked on with curious interest.

General Snowden, fearing that there was trouble brewing, held a hasty consultation with his staff, and had the troops drawn up in line without a minute's loss of time. Company E of the Eighteenth regiment was selected for skirmish duty and marched along the tracks, clearing the crowd away. Then the whole regiment advanced, throwing out detachments of skirmishers as it went, and taking a straight course to the place of encampment.

Shanty Hill, the position selected, lies north of the town and forms part of the Pittsburgh Poor Farm, which had been purchased by the Carnegie Company, but was still held by the city under a special arrangement. The hill slopes gently towards the base but develops midway into a rather steep ascent. A broad plateau extends back from the summit. A better position for military purposes could not have been found. The town and the mill yards stretched out below, covered within easy range by batteries on the heights, and no movement could occur on the streets without being detected from above.

Before the scouts who ran to give warning of the presence of the soldiers had fairly begun to spread the alarm, the Eighteenth regiment had gained the summit of the hill and formed a line of battle. The Fifteenth regiment followed and formed a line of battle to the right of the Eighteenth, then came the Thirteenth, Twelfth, Fifth, Ninth and Seventh regiments, and within half an hour 4,000 men were drawn up in parallel lines of battle, overlooking the town, and ready, at the word of command, to turn 4,000 rifles on the crowds that, by this time had massed below.

Meanwhile the surprised citizens of Homestead perceived another force of soldiers marching and countermarching on the hill tops on the other side of the river, their bayonets and field pieces glittering in the morning sunlight.

Homestead was beleaguered at all points. Without the firing of a shot or the semblance of a parley, the town, which a week before had been the scene of carnage, was captured, and its guardians were taken so completely by surprise that they scarcely realized what was occurring until the troops were in possession.

General Snowden had proved himself an admirable tactician, and the swiftness and unerring precision with which he handled the large body of men under his control were universally applauded.

The unexpected fashion in which

the soldiers entered broke up all the plans that had been arranged for their reception. The Homestead bands remained mute; Burgess McLuckie's speech was relegated to oblivion, and the reception committee was nonplussed by the circumstance that the guests had made themselves at home without waiting for a formal reception. It appeared, in short, that the soldiers were so intent upon business that they had no time for sentiment and that the process of fraternizing was not to be so easy as the people had expected.

If there was any doubt on this head it vanished when some of the workmen endeavored to make their way up Shanty Hill in order to mingle with the "boys in blue." Sentinels barred the way and informed those who sought to pass, that until further orders, no civilian would be allowed to go through the lines. So the townsfolk, including the committeemen of the Amalgamated lodges, had to content themselves with clustering at the foot of the hill and watching the manœuvres of the troops from a distance.

Shortly before noon a number of prominent citizens and leaders of the Amalgamated Association held a conference and appointed a committee to wait upon General Wiley (General Snowden's presence on the ground was not yet known), to tender the good wishes and co-operation of the Amalgamated Association and the people of Homestead, and to request that the military receive the workingmen in a body, accompanied by brass bands.

The committeemen obtained access to the headquarters of the Third Brigade, but, on stating the nature of their mission to General Wiley, were referred by him to General Snowden, who had established his division

The Homestead Works, circa 1890. The barges carrying the Pinkertons from Pittsburgh passed under the railway bridge in the upper center and attempted their landing some one hundred yards farther along, near open hearth #1 (the large shed in the right center). In the background, across the river, are the hills of Swissvale. (Randy Harris)

Workers cannonading the barges (Bill Gaughan)

The riverfront scene as the workers tried to burn the Pinkertons' barges (*Harper's Weekly*, July 16, 1892)

The surrender of the Pinkertons (Bill Gaughan)

The Pinkertons leaving the barges after the surrender (*Harper's Weekly,* July 16, 1892)

The Pennsylvania National Guard entering Homestead. The General Office Building of Carnegie Steel and "Frick's Fence" are in the background. (*Harper's Weekly*, July 23, 1892)

A smoke-free mill guarded by the military encamped along the hill above (Bill Gaughan)

A present-day view of the mill (David P. Demarest, Jr.)

headquarters at the Carnegie school house on Shanty Hill.

Sheriff McCleary was found in conference with General Snowden.

Captain Coon, an ex-militia officer and a representative citizen, spoke for the committee, informing the General of the desire of the Amalgamated Association and of the citizens generally to co-operate with the state authority in maintaining order. General Snowden checked the speaker with the statement that he did not recognize the Amalgamated Association or any authority other than that of the Governor of Pennsylvania and the Sheriff of Allegheny County. The best way in which the people of Homestead could co-operate with the state troops was, he said, by behaving themselves. Captain Coon undertook to renew the offer of assistance, but was cut short with the assurance that such offers could not be accepted.

At this point, Hugh O'Donnell stepped forward and explained that what the people desired was to attest their cheerful submission to legal authority in contrast to their refusal to submit to illegal authority as represented by Mr. Frick's troop of Pinkertons.

"The gentleman behind you is the one to whom you should submit," said General Snowden, with a wave of the hand towards Sheriff McCleary.

"We have always submitted to his authority," said O'Donnell.

"I beg your pardon," rejoined the General, "but you did not do so at the mill."

O'Donnell made a gesture of dissent. "I leave it to the Sheriff if we have not submitted," he retorted.

"No ; you did not," replied the Sheriff. "You didn't allow my deputies to take charge of the works."

Some further parley ensued, O'Donnell asserting that the committee represented, not the Amalgamated Association, but a citizens' mass meeting and General Snowden responding that he recognized no citizens but those of Allegheny County.

"Then," said the former, "as citizens of Allegheny County we come to see you."

"Then I'm glad to see you, gentlemen," was the General's rejoinder, "I am glad that our position here is welcomed by the citizens of Allegheny County."

O'Donnell now proposed that the men of Homestead, with four brass bands, be permitted to pass in review before the troops, but met with a flat refusal, General Snowden stating that he was there on the business of the state and not to indulge in formalities.

This concluded the interview and the committee withdrew in anything but a comfortable frame of mind.

It was useless to talk now of welcoming the soldiers as friends any more than of resisting them as foes. They had come to do the duty imposed on them by the state with mechanical precision and indifference to the human conditions around them. As well think of fraternizing with the pieces of ordnance that glistened ominously on the hill top as with the icy Snowden and Snowden's 4,000 subordinates. This tall, courtly gentleman with the huge moustache and gold-rimmed glasses perched upon his classic nose, seemed to have not a grain of sentiment in his composition. He was the visible incarnation of the state's police powers, stern and inflexible, and it is not overstating the case to say that, before night, all Homestead secretly detested him.

Sheriff McCleary, after quaking in his shoes for a week, fairly reveled in the sunshine of General Snowden's presence. With cannon to right of him, cannon to left of him, cannon in front of him and soldiers on all sides, the Sheriff became a new man and began to talk in a tone of authority which he had not previously ventured to assume. One remark attributed to him was that the men who took part in the fight with the Pinkertons would be prosecuted for riot and murder. When this ominous threat was bruited abroad, it created a sensation among the workmen. Most of the men, however, affected to regard it as mere buncombe. The participants in the affray were pledged to secresy, and, it was contended, if suits were to be entered at all, the whole population of Homestead would have to be made defendants. Still there was a growing feeling of uneasiness, especially since it was suspected, with good reason, as it proved afterward, that there were Pinkerton spies in town for the purpose of collecting evidence to be used in criminal prosecutions.

The immediate result of the disquietude thus developed was to put a keener edge on the discontent inspired by the uncongenial behavior of the military. Men gathered in groups on the streets and indulged in bitter murmurings. "We have been deceived," they said, "deceived by the Governor; deceived unwittingly, but none the less effectually, by our own advisers. We have stood idly by and let the town be occupied by soldiers who come here, not as our protectors, but as the protectors of non-union men, for whom Frick is now scouring the country and who will be brought into the mill and

installed in our places with the aid of the commonwealth. Then, if we undertake to resist the seizure of
our jobs, we will be shot down like dogs. It is the story
of the coke regions over again.''

As if to add fuel to the fire, the ''Little Bill,'' the
very name of which could not be mentioned by a Homesteader without a profane accompaniment, steamed up to
the landing place adjoining the mill yard in all the glory
of an official dispatch boat. One of General Snowden's
first acts had been to charter the detested little tug for
the use of the state, and Captain Rodgers, still smarting
from the effects of his experience on July 6, was only
too glad to obtain the chance of confronting his old enemies under circumstances which insured his safety.
The return of the Little Bill had upon the locked-out
men the effect that a red rag has upon a bull.

Whatever hopes were based by the men of Homestead
on the presence of sympathizers, workmen like themselves, in the ranks of the militia were quickly counter-
acted. It having come to the ears of Colonel Kreps, of
the Fifteenth regiment, that some of his men had promised to hand over their guns to the steelworkers in the
event of trouble caused by an attempt of the Carnegie
Company to operate the mill, the Colonel caused the
regiment to be drawn up in line, mentioned the report
which he had heard and closed with the words—''Let
any man be foolish enough to attempt anything of the
kind and I will shoot him down in his tracks.'' After
this, the militiamen put a bridle on their tongues and
disaffection was not hinted at.

Although martial law, in the strict sense of the term,
was not declared at Homestead, General Snowden took

the precaution of establishing a provost guard which made the rounds of the town and fulfilled the dual function of bringing disorderly stragglers into camp and repressing dangerous demonstrations among the townspeople. Burgess McLuckie's police were of little use and the saloonkeepers had disregarded the order to close their establishments, so that a close watch had to be kept to prevent drunkenness and disorder, particularly among the soldiery.

Nothing was left undone to make Camp McClellan, as it was called, a model of disciplinary perfection.

Just about the time when the National Guard was taking possession of Homestead, a special committee detailed by the National House of Representatives to investigate the trouble between the Carnegie Company and its employees, arrived in Pittsburgh. The committee consisted of W. C. Oates, of Alabama, chairman; W. H. Bynum, of Indiana; C. J. Boatner, of Louisiana; E. B. Taylor, of Ohio, and Case Broderick, of Kansas. Messrs. Taylor and Broderick were the only Republican members.

The committee visited Homestead in the afternoon, and at 7.30 P. M. began the hearing of testimony.

H. C. Frick was the first witness. In answer to leading questions he detailed the membership, resources and operations of the Carnegie Company, the wages paid at Homestead, the nature of the sliding scale and the events leading up to the lock-out.

Judge Oates asked: "Not counting anything by way of interest on investment, what is the cost per ton of billets?"

MR. FRICK.—I hardly think that is a fair question.

I do not think you ought to ask me to go into that.

Col. Taylor.—Would you object to informing us of the cost per ton of steel?

Mr. Frick answered that he would.

Mr. Boatner.—Don't feel disposed to give away the secrets of the trade, eh?

To this the witness responded that the matter in question was a trade secret and must be respected as such.

Mr. Frick was then questioned concerning his enlistment of Pinkerton guards. He had acted, he said, on the conviction, gathered from prior experience, that the sheriff was powerless. After June 24, the firm had decided to hire the guards at $5 a day per man, and to put new workmen into the mill. The witness read a copy of a letter which he had sent to Robert A. Pinkerton under date of June 25. The communication called for 300 guards to be used in enabling the starting of the Homestead mill on July 6, directed the massing of the force at Ashtabula, O. and advised "absolute secresy in the movement of these men, so that no demonstration can be made while they are in route." It concluded as follows: "As soon as your men are upon the premises, we will notify the sheriff and ask that they be deputized either at once or immediately upon an outbreak of such a character as to render such a step desirable."

Mr. Frick was plied with interrogations concerning the Little Bill, the barges and the famous fence topped with barbed-wire, and Mr. Boatner asked particularly as to the "port-holes" in the latter. "They were made," the witness replied gravely, "for the purpose of looking out to see who might be on the outside."

The examination of the Carnegie chairman was not

completed when the committee adjourned, after a two hours' session, and on the resumption of the hearing next morning, he was again placed on the stand. Congressman Boatner opened the ball by endeavoring to ascertain whether or not there had been an agreement between Mr. Frick and the Pinkerton agency prior to June 25, a point on which it appeared, Mr. Frick's memory was defective. Neither could a direct answer be obtained as to the time when it was deemed advisable to arm the guards. The question of wages was taken up again, Mr. Frick stating that the rates at Homestead were higher than at any other mills, that the proposed reduction averaged 15 per cent. and yet the men would make still more money from month to month under the new terms than they made under the old. The examination of the Carnegie Chairman ended with the reading of a schedule of wages paid to tonnage men under the old scale.

Captain Rodgers, of the Little Bill, was the next witness. He told the story of the arrival of the Pinkertons, the trip of the barges up the river and the fight at the mill landing substantially as it has been related in the preceding pages of this volume.

Sheriff McCleary followed and was closely catechized as to his supposed official sponsorship for the Pinkertons. The Sheriff denied that he had promised to deputize the Pinkertons. Having been informed by Messrs. Knox & Reed, the Carnegie Company's attorneys, that the Pinkertons would be sent up and that a deputy would be needed to aid in preserving the peace, he had, he said, ordered Colonel Gray to go and that "if there was much opposition to their landing he should order the captain and the Pinkertons to come away.'' No amount of cross-examining could shake Mr. McCleary's assertion that the Pinkertons were not deputized and that Colonel Grey was not authorised to deputize them.

President Weihe, of the Amalgamated Association, explaineᶡ the sliding scale system, the propositions submitted by the Carnegie Company, and the workmen's reasons for rejecting those propositions. The reductions in wages resulting from the acceptance of the firm's terms would range, he said, from 10 to 30 per cent. As to improvements, the Association always made allowances for these, and no objection was offered if jobs were done away with. The change proposed in the scale-signing date would have set an example which other mills throughout the country would have been sure to follow.

Mr. Weihe was asked to state his views on arbitration. He declined to speak for the Association, but gave it as his individual opinion that arbitration, whether compulsory or by voluntary tribunals was an unsatisfactory resort, the issue being almost invariably against the workingman. The trouble in estimating wages resided in the fact that the firms could not be persuaded to tell the exact cost of production.

Hugh O'Donnell succeeded Mr. Weihe on the witness stand. He told of the organization of the advisory committee with himself as chairman and of the posting of guards outside the mill fence, who ''were told not to use force.''

''Were they ordered to use violence to keep men out?'' the witness was asked.

''No sir, they were not. Their purpose was to keep all out by peaceable methods.''

O'Donnell described the attempt of the Pinkertons to land and his own efforts to check the bloodshed which followed. "I am sure," he said "the crowd near the water had no guns."

"Who fired the first shot?" asked a committeeman.

"I cannot say."

"Do you know anything of the attempt to fire the barges with oil?"

"I decline to answer."

Resuming his story, O'Donnell recounted the incidents of the surrender and the terrible march to the rink. "The detectives," he said, "received most inhuman treatment, but our men did everything to protect them, as I can prove, and many received wounds on the trip to the town rink." Asked as to his wages, he replied that he earned $144 a month. His explanation of the antipathy of the laboring class to Pinkerton detectives was that, in the special case under consideration, the workmen looked upon the Pinkertons as "armed invaders and allies of capital," and also because "if the Pinkertons got possession they would aid the firm in bringing in non-union men."

Burgess McLuckie testified to being an employe of the Carnegie firm, earning from $60 to $65 a month. He volunteered the statement that "there is a gigantic conspiracy somewhere, aided and abetted by legislation, to deprive the workingmen of their rights under the constitution of this government—those of life, liberty and the pursuit of happiness," and illustrated this assertion by referring to the reduction of the tariff on billets, the identical article on which the compensation of the Homestead men was based. Carnegie and McKinley, in his opinion, were fellow conspirators in this case. He characterized the Pinkertons as "lazy thugs employed by unscrupulous capitalists."

Congressman Taylor interjected a remark as to the signs of prosperity in Homestead, and especially, the comfortable looking houses there. "Well," rejoined McLuckie, "let me ask you a question. Are those homes too good for workingmen to live in?" "Not half good enough," answered Mr. Taylor. "Thank you," said McLuckie. Everybody smiled at this little exchange of compliments.

William Roberts, a member of the advisory committee, gave a very clear statement of the causes of dissension at Homestead. The wage reductions, he held, affected not the men who were making exceptionally high wages but many who for eight weeks had not averaged $1 a day. For instance, one man who, under the old scale made $2.23 a day would make under the new one offered by the firm only $1.32, while the heater who made $4.31 suffered no reduction. Mr. Roberts advocated compulsory arbitration. In answer to a question regarding the comparative rates of wages in the Homestead and other mills, he said: "In the American iron works, Carnegie's principal competitor, a roller is paid 70 cents per ton while at Homestead he is paid only 22 or 23 cents. A plate-mill roller at Homestead is paid 14 cents per ton, while at Jones & Loughlin's he is paid 72 cents. The product is similar, it goes into the same market and is used for the same purpose."

Colonel James H. Gray, Sheriff McCleary's chief deputy, described the trip of the barges to Homestead, and corroborated the Sheriff's claims that the Pinkertons were not deputized and that orders had not been given to deputize them. He said positively that the Pinkertons did not fire a shot until they had to do so in self-defense. This concluded the second day's session of the committee.

When the committee re-convened on the morning of July 14, John A. Potter, general superintendent of the Homestead mills, was the first witness summoned. Mr. Potter furnished data as to the equipment and capacity of the mills, but expressed ignorancee as to the cost of producing a ton of steel. He assigned as the reason for reducing wages that the Carnegie firm was "ahead of competitors" and paying more than the owners of similar mills, and therefore thought it should have "some of the advantages." Mr. Potter had been on the Little Bill when the Pinkertons tried to land at Homestead, but had declined to take the responsibility of entering the mill yard by force.

The remainder of the morning was occupied principally with the hearing of Homestead workmen who testified as to the effect of Mr. Frick's propositions upon their respective earnings, and of watchmen and others who had been connected with the Pinkerton's expedition and who described their various experiences.

Mr. Frick was recalled and permitted to rebut some of the assertions made by the workingmen. To prove that his firm did not control the billet market he cited the fact that Jones & Laughlin's mill has a capacity of 1000 tons daily, while the output at Homestead is 800 tons daily. He again refused to give the labor cost of producing a ton of steel although Congressman Boatner twitted him with refusing to give the information "on which protective legislation is asked for."

"I do not think we asked for the legislation," observed Mr. Frick.

"You have been greatly misrepresented then," said Mr. Boatner grimly.

Mr. Frick estimated the value of the Homestead plant at from $5,000,000 to $6,000,000, and stated that the capitalization of the Carnegie Company was considerably in excess of $25,000,000.

Having heard all sides of the case, the committee closed its labors early in the afternoon and returned to Washington where congress awaited its report.

CHAPTER XI.

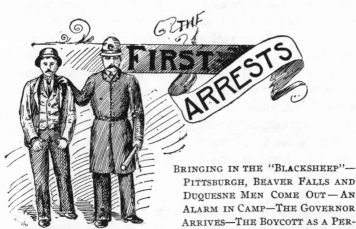

THE FIRST ARRESTS

BRINGING IN THE "BLACKSHEEP"—
PITTSBURGH, BEAVER FALLS AND
DUQUESNE MEN COME OUT—AN
ALARM IN CAMP—THE GOVERNOR
ARRIVES—THE BOYCOTT AS A PER-
SUADER—POLITICS TO THE RESCUE—MURDER CHARGED AND
WARRANTS ISSUED—McLUCKIE, O'DONNELL AND ROSS SURREN-
DER AND ARE RELEASED ON BAIL—GENERAL SNOWDEN'S DIS-
HEARTENING ANNOUNCEMENT.

THE locked-out men were not mistaken in their belief that the Carnegie Company would take advantage of the presence of the military to bring non-
union men into the mill. Troops were early detailed to
garrison the mill yard, and a line of sentries was posted
outside the fence, so that there could be no interference
by the workmen either from the railroad or the river.
The steamboat Tide was used as a special transport for
non-unionists, the first squads of whom came over from
Swissvale, on the Pennsylvania railroad, and were taken
across the river under cover of Colonel Hawkins' guns.
Agents of the firm were set to work in every large city

procuring recruits, and while it was found rather difficult to tempt men to risk the desperate chances of a
trip to Homestead to take the places of the conquerors
of the Pinkertons, a small number were secured each
day until, within a week after the first squad was brought
in, nearly one hundred men were quartered within the
mill enclosure. Hundreds of cots were provided for the
accommodation of the new hands, and large quantities
of food and other supplies were laid in. At the same
time, the firm advertised for proposals to build 100
houses on the City Farm plan of lots at Munhall station,
thus signifying its intention of establishing permanent
quarters for those who were to take the places of the old
employees.

On Friday, July 15, for the first time since the lock-
out began, smoke issued from the cupolas of the great
steel plant. The furnaces were lit at last, and the news
circulated rapidly throughout the town that the company
was suspected of having smuggled in enough non-unionists to renew operations. An excited mob rushed pell-
mell towards the mill yard, but was stopped short at the
picket lines, where the guards, with levelled bayonets,
barred progress.

As a matter of fact there were but few steelworkers
among the first hundred men brought in by the Tide.
Fifteen of them were carpenters, who were engaged on
a temporary lodging house between the machine pressing mill and the river, and a majority of the others were
waiters, cooks, clerks and bosses.

A final notice to the old employees was posted in
Homestead on July 16. It set forth that "individual"
applications for employment would be received by the

general superintendent until 6 P. M., Thursday, July 21 ; that it was the company's desire to retain those of its former workmen who had not taken part in the disturbances, and that the positions of those who failed to comply with this notice would be given to non-union men.

The locked-out men treated this manifesto with indifference, letting the prescribed period pass by without any sign of a desire to return to work on Mr. Frick's terms. Their sole reply was embodied in a circular issued July 22, wherein it was set forth that the workingmen of Homestead and the general public had a vested interest in the great industrial establishment built up by the labor of the one and indirectly sustained by tariff taxes paid by the other; that those interests would be asserted and defended in the courts and the halls of legislation and that the men rested their cause—"the cause of American liberty against anarchy on the one hand and despotism on the other, with the courts, the legislatures and the public conscience."

On this same day a large force of non-union men reported at the Carnegie offices in Pittsburgh and were shipped to Homestead on the Tide, starting from the Monongahela wharf amid the jeers of a crowd of onlookers. Similar trips were made every day thereafter, the safe arrival of the first batches of recruits having emboldened others. Once the ball was set rolling, the firm experienced little trouble in securing men. There is always an army of unemployed in the United States, and upon these as well as underpaid workers in various lines—clerks, struggling young professional men and others—who were tempted by the high wages said to be paid at Homestead the firm could and did draw freely. The Homestead leaders contended that it would be impossible to operate the mills without a force of expert steelworkers, but Mr. Frick seemed to care little about skill as long as he could secure men able and willing to learn the work entrusted to them. The mills, it appeared, were to be a school in which an entirely

BRINGING IN NON-UNIONISTS.

new set of artisans were to be instructed, regardless of the losses that must be sustained in the process.

In the meantime trouble was brewing in other concerns operated by the Carnegie Company. Mr. Frick had already signed the scale at the Pittsburgh and Beaver Falls mills, and expected to accomplish at these plants much of the work which was suspended at Homestead. The workmen at both places, however, sympathized with their brethren at Homestead and decided accordingly to break their contract with the firm and go out on strike until the trouble at Homestead should be fairly adjusted. The Pittsburgh men, employed at the Upper and Lower Union Mills in Lawrenceville, went out on July 15 and the Beaver Falls men on the following day. The mill at Duquesne was non-union, but there, too, the spirit of resistance manifested itself and on July 19, the men took preliminary steps toward entering the Amalgamated Association so as to be in proper shape to strike. On July 20 the Duquesne lodges were permanently organized and on the 23d a strike was declared.

Homestead was now, in a degree, under martial law, the power of the borough authorities being limited to the arrest of drunken and disorderly persons. Two companies of soldiers did guard duty on the streets and had orders to arrest any of Burgess McLuckie's special policemen found exceeding their duty.

Life in Camp Black was anything but a bed of roses. Colonel Hawkins' command spent two days and nights on the hills above Port Perry without tents and suffered much from the inclemency of the weather, broiling heat alternating with rain that drenched the men to the skin. A storm blew down most of the tents on the second day of the encampment.

The first alarm that brought the soldiers out occurred after midnight on July 15. Someone brought in word that the camp was to be attacked from the rear. Bugles were sounded, the drums beat to arms, and in a few minutes the Second and Third brigades were ready for action and threw out their skirmish lines, while the force of pickets was doubled. The alarm proved to be a false one ; nevertheless the Sixteenth regiment was kept under arms until daybreak.

It had been decided that the period of service at Homestead should take the place of the regular annual encampment of the National Guard, and Governor Pattison and his staff arrived accordingly on the 19th to conduct the annual inspection, to which a week's time was devoted. Some of the workmen supposed that the Governor might entertain the idea of mediating between the conflicting parties, but it was soon found that he harbored no such design. He visited the mills, inspected the scene of the battle with the Pinkertons and conversed informally with citizens of the town concerning the history of the trouble, but declined to interfere further, confining himself mainly to his official functions as Commander of the National Guard. Quarters were assigned to the Governor and his staff in three comfortable cottages belonging to the Carnegie Company, adjoining the Carnegie hotel on Eighth avenue, and opposite the main entrance to the steel works. General Snowden and his staff had been patronizing the hotel cuisine, previously sacred to the discriminating palates of the Carnegie officials. An odd incident temporarily deprived the General of this accommodation. One morning the head waiter, having formed the opinion that the troops were helping to take the bread out of the mouths of the workingmen, informed the proprietor that he could not be instrumental in conveying the staff of life to the mouths of "the enemy" and resigned on the spot. The head cook followed, and the under-waiters and cooks went out with their leaders. When the officers arrived for breakfast and found that there was nothing to eat, the air was made blue with profanity. The boycott was one which all the military force of the commonwealth was powerless to lift. After this, General Snowden had his meals prepared and served at headquarters by a colored cook drafted from one of the regiments. Young women who could be relied on not to indulge in a sympathetic strike were installed in the places of the cooks and waiters who had deserted from the hotel.

While the workmen were somewhat dismayed by the signs of activity within the mill enclosure, feeling, as they did, that the thin end of the non-union wedge had already been inserted, they stoutly refused to admit that the firm could find enough skilled steelworkers in the country to operate the mill or could successfully utilize green hands in the intricate work which it had taken old employees, in many cases, years to learn. This argument seemed invincible and was used on every hand as confirming the supposition that the firm was merely making a pretense of manning and operating the mill, so as to discourage the old hands and provoke a stampede back to work. Such devices as this, the men said, would be futile. The Homestead workers were firmly bound together and there would be no deserters from their ranks. Mr. Frick might be able to get non-union laborers, helpers, blacksmiths, mechanics, carpenters and painters, but all these had to depend on the skilled labor of the men who made the steel. Wtthout rollers, heaters, shearers, cutters and other trained workers, the mills could not start, and on these the Amalgamated Association had a solid hold and would maintain it.

"Our weapon," said Hugh O'Donnell, "will be the

boycott — the workingman's only effective weapon.
While Carnegie is seeking to starve us into submission,
we will endeavor to strike a blow at his every industry.
The strikes at Lawrenceville and Beaver Falls, and the
action of some of the carpenters' unions in refusing to
work in buildings where Carnegie's structural material
is used constitute the kind of assistance that we want.''

There was certainly abundant reason for anticipating
a general boycott of the Carnegie Company's product.
Labor unions in Pittsburgh, Chicago, Philadelphia and
elsewhere were holding meetings and pledging themselves to carry out the program outlined by O'Donnell
and it was even reported that the railroad brotherhoods
would interpose to prevent the transportation of freight
to and from the various Carnegie plants.

In any case there was no fear of actual suffering among
the locked-out men for a long time to come. Under the
rules of the Amalgamated Association, strike benefits
would be paid out of the treasury of the order and an
additional and comfortably large fund was created by
the contributions which flowed into Homestead daily
from every section of the country.

There was also a strong conviction among the men
that the Republican party leaders would come to the rescue. The political aspect of the wage dispute was explained in a previous chapter. This phase of the matter
was taken up with fierce avidity by the Democratic press
after the conflict of July 6, and the country rang with
denunciations of a protective policy which protected the
manufacturer only and left reduced wages and Pinkerton
lead to the workingman as his share of tariff benefits.
Genuine apprehension was felt among the Republican

politicians, and Republican newspaper organs, seeing
and dreading the disturbed condition of the labor world,
hardly dared respond to the sneers of the opposition.
The high tariff party had so long catered to the labor vote
that the problem of meeting labor's demands with regard
to Homestead was full of embarrassment, and it was
evident that President Harrison's prospects of re-election
were seriously threatened.

The leaders at Homestead, knowing the dependence
of the Carnegie Company on tariff legislation and believing that the fealty of Messrs. Carnegie and Frick to the
Republican party would be an all-powerful consideration
in a crisis wherein the presidency itself was at stake,
sent Hugh O'Donnell to New York to confer secretly
with General Clarkson and other ruling spirits in the
Republican national committee. O'Donnell left on this
mission on July 17. On the following day Mr. Frick
played another trump card, the forcing out of the military having been the first of a hand which the implacable
little chairman confidently asserted would turn out to be
all trumps.

Burgess John McLuckie was arrested on the charge of
murder.

And this was not all. The information, lodged before
Alderman McMasters, of Pittsburgh, in pursuance of
which the warrant for McLuckie's arrest was issued, included also the names of Hugh O'Donnell, Sylvester
Critchlow, Anthony Flaherty, Samuel Burkett, James
Flannigan and Hugh Ross. F. T. F. Lovejoy, secretary of the Carnegie Company, was the prosecutor and
he affirmed that the men named "did of their malice
aforethought feloniously and riotously with force and arms

and deadly weapons kill and murder one T. J. Connors then and there being in the peace of the Commonwealth of Pennsylvania." A second information charged the same persons with the murder of Silas Wain.

Three constables were sent to Homestead to make the arrests. They applied to General Snowden for assistance, which was promptly furnished, two companies of infantry being detailed to their support. At the same time the patrols were increased and two regiments were kept under arms so as to be ready for any contingency. No trouble was experienced, however. The accused had been forewarned and all, with the exception of O'Donnell and McLuckie, had locked up their houses and gone into hiding. The doughty burgess, strong in the consciousness of his innocence, went to Pittsburgh at an early hour, surrendered himself at the alderman's office and was committed to jail. Before the prison gates closed upon him, he informed the newspaper representatives that the Amalgamated men, in turn, would make informations against Carnegie, Frick and Potter. "We will make this man Frick come down on his knees so hard that the sound will be heard in the farthest corner of civilization" was honest John's last observation as he was led into durance.

Secretary Lovejoy also had something to say for the enlightenment of the public. "We have good cases against 1000 of these men," he said "and from now on from twelve to fifteen informations will be made every day. The laws of Pennsylvania are very broad on this subject. Persons who were on the premises at the time of the shooting are liable not only as accessories, but as principals."

McLuckie spent only one night in jail, being released

next morning on $10,000 bail after a brief hearing before Judge Magee in the county criminal court. He took the first train for Homestead and was received there with acclamations, the townspeople turning out *en masse* to receive him. A procession was formed in his honor, and to the strains of "Home, Sweet Home," performed with unusual energy by the crack brass band of the town, the hero of the hour was escorted to the rink, where he made a speech of thanks to the people.

Hugh O'Donnell no sooner heard that a warrant was out for his arrest than he suspended his operations in New York and returned to Homestead. Like McLuckie, he spared the constables the trouble of arresting him and, in company with Hugh Ross, proceeded to Pittsburgh with the intention of surrendering. The two men went directly into the criminal court and, without the aid of an attorney, presented themselves to Judge Magee. O'Donnell addressed the judge, explaining that he had not sought to evade the arrest and asking that the law take its course. The judge was non-plussed by the unprecedented behavior of the two workmen in thus walking calmly into what was, from their point of view, the "lion's den," but, after some questioning, advised them to surrender themselves at the office of Alderman Mc-Masters. This they did, and within an hour, they were behind prison bars. Two days later Peter Allen and Nathan Foy were arrested at their homes and lodged in jail.

An application for the admission of O'Donnell and his companions to bail was heard by Judge Magee on Saturday, July 23. Attorneys William J. Brennen and John F. Cox appeared for the defendants on behalf of the

Amalgamated Association, and District Attorney Clarence Burleigh and D. F. Patterson, Esq. represented the prosecution. The testimony of a number of Pinkerton detectives, newspaper reporters, deputy sheriffs and others was taken, showing conclusively O'Donnell's leadership and his presence at the battle in the mill yard. The defence argued that O'Donnell's part in the "riot" was that of a peacemaker. Judge Magee reserved his decision until Monday, when he finally admitted the four prisoners to bail in the sum of $10,000 each, the case having "within its possibility a conviction of murder in the second degree."

The succession of arrests had, of course, a depressing effect on the people of Homestead. A still more discouraging circumstance was General Snowden's announcement that the troops would be kept in Homestead until one side or the other should give in. As long as the troops remained the mill was so securely guarded that the question was not merely of providing against violence but of preventing the Amalgamated men from obtaining access to the non-unionists and bringing persuasion to bear upon them after the manner customary with labor organizations. General Snowden was denounced without stint for what the men construed as a desire on his part to play into the hands of the Carnegie Company. But the General did not seem to mind denunciations. The last attempt to subjugate him was made by the high constable of the borough on an occasion when a stray cow had paid the debt of nature within the lines of the encampment. The constable undertook to storm the enemy's works with a view to compelling the interment of the cow with the honors of war, but was seized and incarcerated over night in the guard house. With the fall of this functionary came the collapse of all that remained of civil authority in Homestead, and thereafter General Snowden's word was law.

The advisory committee was sorely perplexed over the disposition to be made of the guns taken from the Pinkertons. The Attorney General of the state was addressed on the subject but declined to give advice, and it was doubtful that the guns could lawfully be retained as the "spoils of war." Ultimately the individual holders of the weapons settled the matter in their own way by hiding the trophies where prying detectives would be unable to find them.

The death of George W. Rutter, at the Homeopathic hospital, Pittsburgh, on July 18 closed the list of fatalities on the side of the workingmen. Rutter remained in a delirium until the last, always imagining in his ravings that he was back on the bank of the Monongahela, fighting against the Pinkertons. He was buried at Verona, Pa., where his widow and children resided.

CHAPTER XII.

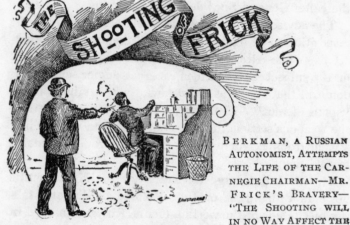

THE SHOOTING OF FRICK

BERKMAN, A RUSSIAN AUTONOMIST, ATTEMPTS THE LIFE OF THE CARNEGIE CHAIRMAN—MR. FRICK'S BRAVERY—"THE SHOOTING WILL IN NO WAY AFFECT THE HOMESTEAD STRIKE"—MILITIAMAN IAMS CHEERS THE ASSASSIN AND IS DRUMMED OUT OF CAMP—PUBLIC INDIGNATION OVER THE IAMS AFFAIR—SNOWDEN, HAWKINS, STREATOR AND NEFF INDICTED—WORKINGMEN PROSECUTE CARNEGIE OFFICIALS FOR MURDER.

"FRICK is shot!"

Such was the appalling announcement blazoned on bulletin boards, passed from mouth to mouth and hurried over the telegraph wires on the afternoon of Saturday, July 23, while O'Donnell and Ross were undergoing their preliminary hearing in the county court. The first question on every lip was, "Did a Homestead man do the shooting?" and great was the feeling of relief among the sympathizers of organized labor when it was learned that the would-be assassin, Alexander Berkman, was a Russian anarchist, and that his crime was prompt-

ed solely by the teachings of the infamous class of outlaws to which he belonged.

Berkman came to the United States in 1886, fresh
from the University of Odessa, where he had inbibed the
principals of the Autonomists—extreme Anarchists who
believe in redressing social wrongs by individual action.
He became a compositor in the office of Johann Most's
paper, *Die Freiheit*, wrote freely for Anarchistic publications and allied himself with the worst class of revolution-
ary plotters in the metropolis. The beginning of 1892
found him living with Emma Goldman, a Russian
woman of some note as a speech maker among the Anarchists, and spending much of his time in the beer halls
frequented by Anarchists and Nihilists. Berkman seemed
to be consumed with a desire to shine in the eyes of his
mistress and of the blatant, beer-sodden circle of which
she was the star, by giving a practical exemplification of
his fidelity to Autonomist doctrine.

"Who is the worst enemy of society in America?" he
asked himself, and when the Homestead trouble broke
out, he imagined that his question was answered.

Frick was the man—Frick, the oppressor of workmen,
the representative of the power of wealth and of might
antagonizing right. "Undoubtedly," thought Berkman,
"this man is society's arch-enemy and a fit mark for the
weapon of an Autonomist."

So the misguided wretch made up his mind to murder
the Carnegie chairman, and proceeded accordingly to
Pittsburgh, armed for assassination. In company with
Henry Bauer and Carl Knold, active anarchists of Allegheny City, Berkman inspected the *Chronicle-Telegraph*
building on Fifth Avenue, Pittsburgh, in which Mr.

Frick's office is located, and mapped out a program of attack. Representing himself as an employment agent, who desired to confer with the Carnegie chairman regarding the furnishing of non-union labor, he experienced little trouble in obtaining access to Mr. Frick's private room. He made several visits before the day of the shooting, and was suspected by no one. The neatly-attired, slight, young man who appeared so anxious to help the firm in its endeavors to procure workmen was one of the last men who would be supposed to harbor murderous designs.

At noon on the day set for the consummation of his plan, Berkman sent in his card to Mr. Frick, requesting an interview, but was referred to the clerk whose business it was to supervise the transportation of non-union men to Homestead. The clerk was out and Berkman was told to call again later. Shortly before two o'clock, Berkman returned and again asked to see Mr. Frick. He was informed that the Chairman was engaged. After waiting a few minutes in the hall outside the ante-room adjoining Mr. Frick's office, he came back once more, and finding nobody present but the office-boy, handed the lad his card and told him to take it in to the Chairman. The boy had hardly opened the door of Mr. Frick's office when Berkman rushed in, drew a revolver and opened fire. Mr. Frick, who was seated at his desk in conversation with Mr. Leishman, one of his partners, had his back turned to the intruder and offered an easy mark.

Berkman fired three shots in quick succession, the first two lodging in Mr. Frick's neck, while the third struck the ceiling. The assassin attempted to fire a fourth time, but the cartridge failed to explode. He snapped the trigger several times and finding that the revolver would not work, threw it on the ground, and, pulling out a stiletto, advanced upon Mr. Frick, who, wounded as he was, had risen to his feet to defend himself. Twice Berkman plunged the stiletto into Mr. Frick's side and he was about to strike a third time when the wounded man, summoning up all the strength left to him, seized his assailant's arm and grappled with him in a fierce struggle for life.

All this passed so rapidly that the clerks in the adjoining offices were unable to reach the scene of the encounter until the moment when Mr. Frick and Berkman clinched. When they entered, Berkman had the Chairman pressed against the large window looking out on Fifth avenue and was trying to release the hand that held the stiletto. Both men were covered with blood and a pool of blood was on the floor. On the street without, then thronged with Saturday afternoon promenaders, people stood transfixed with horror. Some shrieked helplessly. Some, with more presence of mind, ran to summon the police.

The clerks quickly released Mr. Frick from the grasp of his assailant and placed him on a lounge. Berkman dashed out of the office, with several clerks in pursuit, and was caught in the elevator, given in charge of the police and removed to the Central Station in a patrol wagon.

Dr. Litchfield, Mr. Frick's family physician, and a number of other medical men arrived promptly and took charge of the wounded man. Mr. Frick had not lost consciousness and was able to recognize and speak to the physicians. They wished to place him under the influence of chloroform while probing for the bullets, but he forbade this and submitted stoically to the operation, which lasted two hours. The extraordinary nerve of the man never left him. After the bullets had been extracted and his wounds bandaged, he conversed collectedly with visitors, signed several letters which had been written before the shooting and talked of being in condition to return to his office on Monday.

Meanwhile an excited multitude thronged the street outside the Carnegie offices and defied the efforts of the police to disperse it. At 6 o'clock an ambulance drove up, but it was not used. The news that Mr. Frick was to be removed to his private residence at Homewood, in the East End, had spread among the people and the desire to catch a glimpse of him made the mob unmanageable. Not until 7.45 o'clock was the removal accomplished. At that hour the crowd was drawn away by driving an ambulance to the rear of the Carnegie offices. The vehicle was driven quickly back again, and Mr. Frick was placed in it and carried off while the coast was clear.

Before being removed to his home, Mr. Frick sent this message to the reporters: "The shooting will in no way effect the Homestead strike."

Dangerous as the Carnegie Chairman's injuries were, his recovery was rapid, and two weeks after his encounter with Berkman he was able to return to his office and resume full charge of the firm's affairs to which, while on his sick bed, he had still continued to give a considerable measure of attention.

Berkman was taken to the county jail on Sunday night, there to await trial. He seemed indifferent to his fate and expressed regret that he had not succeeded in killing Frick. Bauer and Knold, his supposed accomplices, were locked up on the following day. A wagon load of Anarchist literature was seized at the house of Bauer, who acted as an agent for publications of this character.

The effect of the shooting on public opinion was strongly marked. The press of Pittsburgh was unanimous in expressing sympathy for Mr. Frick, and in so doing, voiced the general sentiment of the people. At Homestead much regret was expressed, and the workmen seemed to feel that, although Berkman did not represent them or their cause, directly or indirectly, his cowardly act was certain to prejudice their interests.

Undoubtedly the attempt to murder Mr. Frick served to hasten the defeat of the workingmen. The courage displayed by the Carnegie Chairman won him admiration in quarters where he had previously been condemned, and there were other circumstances which took the edge off the animosity generated by his harshness towards organized labor. During the crisis at Homestead, his young wife became a mother and, so powerfully did the events in which her husband was the central figure effect her that, for a time, she lay at the point of death. The child lived only a few days. Mr. Frick, it was said, in recognition of the fact that the New York *Sun* was the only newspaper in the country which took up the cudgels in his behalf, intended to name the little one Charles A. Dana Frick, after the editor of that journal. These incidents conspired to soften the popular heart somewhat, although Mr. Frick did not abate in the least his hostility towards the Amalgamated men and his determination to break the back of unionism in the Carnegie mills at any cost.

There was, however, one man in Allegheny county

who neither sympathized with Frick nor scrupled to express his regret that Berkman's weapons failed to do their work.

This man was W. L. Iams, a youth belonging to one of the best families in Greene County, who was serving in Company K, Tenth Regiment, under Colonel Hawkins.

Iams was stretched on the grass outside Lieutenant Colonel J. B. Streator's tent, chatting with a group of comrades, when the news of the attempt on Frick's life was brought in. Acting on the impulse of the moment, and doubtless without measuring the significance of his words, the young man jumped to his feet and shouted "Three cheers for the man who shot Frick." Colonel Streator heard the remark and, stepping out of his tent, asked who had uttered it. Receiving no response, he ordered the regiment drawn up in line in the company streets, and, after condemning the language used by Iams as treasonable, demanded from one company after another the name of the offender. When he came to Company K, Iams stepped forward from the ranks and said "I did it." The Colonel asked him why. "Because I do not like Frick" was the answer. Iams was ordered to apologize before the regiment but refused, and was thereupon sent to the guard-house and subjected, without the benefit of a trial by court-martial, to the most degrading punishment known under military law. He was first strung up by the thumbs with notice that he would be cut down as soon as he apologized. Although suffering exquisite torture, the young man remained firm and declined to retract his words. After hanging for a quarter of an hour, he lost consciousness and the regimental surgeon, Dr. Neff, ordered him to be cut down. Iams was then placed in the guard-house until his case was reported to Colonel Hawkins, at the headquarters of the provisional brigade. The report was returned with the approval of Colonel Hawkins and General Snowden and an order from the latter that the man be disgraced and drummed out of camp. Colonel Streator executed these directions to the letter. Iams' head and face were half shaved; his uniform was exchanged for an old pair of overalls and a shirt and dilapidated hat to match, and in this wretched condition he was led out of camp to the tune of the "Rogues' March." His sentence carried with it permanent exclusion from the National Guard and disenfranchisement.

Iams proceeded to Pittsburgh and, strange to say, became the lion of the hour. He announced his intention of prosecuting the officers concerned in his punishment and a score of attorneys volunteered their services as his counsel. Among these was Frank P. Iams, Esq., a cousin of the young man, who was engaged in practice at the Pittsburgh bar.

Within twenty-four hours the Iams case became a National *cause celebre*. It was discussed everywhere from Maine to California. Military authorities waxed warm over it. Legal authorities squabbled over it. Professional publicists were interviewed concerning it.

Editors made it the subject of tremendous publications. Pictures of Iams, hairless, mustacheless and defiant appeared in the illustrated weeklies. The Allegheny County Democrats, happening to have another convention on hand at this time, took the matter up in a political way, and as it happened that Colonel Streator was a

well-known and popular Democratic club man, "confusion worse confounded" followed the endeavors of the
workingmen in the convention to secure the passage of
resolutions excoriating the "brutal and inhuman" conduct of Iams' superior officers.

The preponderance of sentiment was everywhere
against the officers. In inflicting a punishment so severe
and unusual on a thoughtless youth, whose insubordin-
ate conduct might have been otherwise chastised with
equally good effect, and especially in denying him even
a drumhead court-martial, they were held guilty of ty-
rannically exceeding their authority.

Iams carried out his threat of prosecuting the officers
and indictments were subsequently found against General Snowden, Colonel Hawkins, Colonel Streator and
Surgeon Neff. The trial, however, resulted in the
acquittal of the defendants, the judge and jury being satisfied that whether the punishment inflicted on Iams
fitted the crime or not, military law permitted its inflic-
tion.

After two weeks' service, the military force at Homestead was reduced to three regiments of infantry, a
troop of cavalry and a battery, the retiring regiments
breaking camp on July 27 and 28. Those that remained
were booked for a term of service which was to end only
when the Carnegie mills were in undisturbed operation,
an order of things which was not to be finally established
until more than two months later.

Mr. Frick's illness did not stay the hand of Secretary
Lovejoy, who continued to lodge informations against
the participants in the affair of July 6. Pinkerton detectives and a few newspaper reporters who had

been placed on the Carnegie Company's pay-roll furnished the secretary with the necessary testimony. The
first of the workmen to be held without bail was Sylvester Critchlow, a daring fellow who had done active duty
as a sharpshooter in the mill-yard. Samuel Stewart, a
clerk in the mill, swore that he had seen Critchlow fire
at the men in the barges, and on this evidence the defendant was held liable for first degree murder and committed to jail pending his trial.

The workmen, for their part, proceeded to carry out
their threat of prosecuting the Carnegie officials. Hugh
Ross, himself under bail on the charge of murder, made
information before Alderman King, of the South Side,
Pittsburgh, charging that H. C. Frick, F. T. F. Lovejoy, Robert Pinkerton, William Pinkerton, J. A. Potter,
G. A. Corey, J. G. A. Leishman, H. M. Curry, C. W.
Bedell, Fred. Primer, W. H. Burt, Nevin McConnell,
James Dovey, John Cooper and Fred. W. Hinde "did
kill and murder John E. Morris, George W. Rutter,
Silas Wain and Joseph Sotak." The arrest of Chairman Frick was to be deferred until he should recover
from his wounds. As the Homestead men, for the most
part, had been arrested at such times and under such
circumstances as compelled them to spend a night in
jail, before securing a hearing in court on their application for admission to bail, Ross made special efforts to
have the Carnegie officials subjected to the same experience. This manœuvre, however, was defeated. Messrs.
Leishman, Lovejoy and Curry, hearing that warrants
were out for their arrest, went at once, in company with
a formidable array of counsel, to the criminal court
where Judge Ewing was sitting, and asked for admission

to bail. Judge Ewing said he could not hear the applications until the defendants had appeared before an alderman and either waived examination or been held for court; but with a degree of courtesy probably never before exhibited in a criminal court he dispatched a messenger for Alderman King, permitted the defendants to waive a hearing and then went on to consider the question of bail. This was speedily disposed of. The Judge declined to consider the representations made by the attorneys of the Amalgamated Association as to the entrance into the case of the elements of first degree murder. There was no equality, he held, between the Carnegie officials and the men in the conflict of July 6. The former were exercising their rights; the latter were rioters and trespassers, whom it was proper to oppose with arms. He, therefore, would admit the defendants to bail in the sum of $10,000.

Messrs. Dovey and McConnell, superintendents of departments in the Homestead mill, were arrested later and passed the night in jail. Superintendent Potter and G. A. Corey evaded the constables and presented themselves before Judge Ewing next morning. Alderman King was again brought into court and the four men were released on bail in the same manner as Messrs. Leishman, Lovejoy and Curry. The court ordered also that Mr. Frick give $10,000 bail and that it be taken at his home.

Judge Ewing was roundly denounced by the workingmen for the lengths to which he had gone to spare the Carnegie officials the humiliation which O'Donnell and his companions had been forced to endure. "Evidently," they said, "the judges are prejudiced against us and are

bent upon discriminating in favor of our rich and influential antagonists."

Another disquieting circumstance was the verdict arrived at by the coroner's jury in pursuance of the inquest
held on the men who were killed in the Homestead conflict. In each instance the killing was charged to an
"unlawful assembly," and the jury recommended that
"said unlawful assembly be certified to the September
sessions of the grand jury."

On August 2, Attorney Brennen presented to court a
petition signed by sixty-seven steel-workers of Pittsburgh
and Homestead, praying that a license be issued for the
establishment of a voluntary trade tribunal, in conform-
ity with an act passed in 1883, to arbitrate differences
in the steel trade. The acceptance of the terms of the
act must be mutual between employers and employed.
Mr. Brennen entertained hopes that the Carnegie firm,
seeing the willingness of the men to submit to arbitration, might yet consent to this mode of adjustment.
Secretary Lovejoy settled the matter definitely in the
negative by the brief statement that "The question of
recognizing the Amalgamated Association cannot be ar-
bitrated."

This was the last overture made to the firm on behalf
of the workmen. The latter, however, continued to
keep up their courage and maintained an almost unbrok-
en front, desertions being few and far between. Mass
meetings were held frequently and at these it was invariably agreed that the mill could not be operated with
non-union men, that sooner or later the firm must yield
to the pressure of circumstances and that, with the help
received from the treasury of the Amalgamated Associa-

tion and from other sources, the locked-out men could hold out, if necessary, for a year or more.

There were some who foresaw the collapse of these castles in the air, but, rather than place themselves under the suspicion of lukewarmness, they held their peace.

CHAPTER XIII.

Frick's Assailant Railroaded to the Penitentiary—The Iams
Trial,—Hanging by the Thumbs Approved by a Jury—The
Mills Filling Up—Sermons to Non-Unionists—Strikers Go
Through the Plant—The Relief Fund—Gompers Arrives
and Makes an Incendiary Speech—Pittsburgh and Ma-
honing Manufacturers Capitulate—William and Robert
Pinkerton on the Defensive.

ANARCHIST BERKMAN received but a short
shrift. He was placed on trial before Judge
McClung on September 19, appearing at the bar
without an attorney and without witnesses. His demeanor was cool and indifferent. District Attorney
Burleigh presented six indictments, charging the prisoner
with offenses ranging from felonious assault and battery
down to carrying concealed weapons.

Mr. Frick was placed on the stand and told the story
of the shooting, and the blood-stained garments worn by
the Carnegie chairman at the time of the attack were

put in evidence.   Corroborative testimony was furnished by Mr. Leishman and others.

The prosecution having closed its case, Berkman asked to be permitted to testify in his own behalf.   "I am not guilty," he said.   "I have a defense."   A German interpreter was assigned to assist him.   The Anarchist's defense consisted of an inflammatory address covering forty pages of closely written foolscap.   As rendered into English by the interpreter, sentence by sentence, it was almost unintelligible.   It proved, however, to be a review of the "blood-stained register of America," beginning with the "murder" of John Brown, cropping out again in the execution of the Chicago Anarchists who were concerned in the Haymarket massacre, and culminating in the descent of the Pinkertons upon Homestead.   The statement bristled with denunciations of capitalists as tyrants who oppress the workingmen, and the inference which it finally conveyed was that Berkman considered himself a martyr of the Chicago type whose exploits would serve to rivet the world's attention on the enormity of the Carnegie Company's crimes against labor.   Strangely enough, it seemed not to dawn upon the mind of this young fanatic that he and his fellow preachers of anarchy could not possibly be mistaken as representing the element that toils for a subsistence, and that a martyr to the cause of beer, blood and idleness must necessarily be an object of contempt in the estimation alike of the classes and the masses.

Judge McClung confined his charge to a few perfunctory remarks and the jury, without leaving the box, rendered a verdict of guilty on all six indictments.

Sentence was then imposed on each indictment, the penalties aggregating 22 years imprisonment, twenty-one in the penitentiary and one in the work-house.

The trial occupied just four hours, attesting that in this case at all events, justice ceased to travel with a leaden heel.

The Iams episode was not so easily disposed of. Prosecutions were entered against Colonels Hawkins and Streator and Surgeon Grim on the charge of aggravated assault and battery, and the defendants were held under bonds for trial at the September term of court. The trial began on October 27, before Judge W. D. Porter, and continued for ten days. The proceedings were watched with special interest by military men, owing to the issue involved between civil and military law and the prospective establishment of important precedents. Colonel J. R. Braddocks, of the Pittsburgh bar, State Senator Edward E. Robbins, of Greensburg, and J. M. Braden and Albert Sprowls, of Washington, Pa., appeared as counsel for the defendants ; and Frank P. Iams, a cousin of the disgraced militiaman, and John D. Watson, both of the Pittsburgh bar, conducted the prosecution.

The defense opened the proceedings by demanding that the indictment be quashed on the ground that the punishment of Iams was commensurate with the enormity of his offense against good order and military discipline, that it conformed to military law, and that jurisdiction in the case properly belonged to a military tribunal. After some intricate controversy, Judge Porter denied the plea and ordered the trial to go on.

Attorney Watson opened for the prosecution, giving a

graphic recital of the torture to which the prosecutor, Iams, had been subjected. Iams himself was placed on the stand and related his experiences, a fair conception of which may be formed from the following extract from his testimony:

"When I was first tied up I asked for a chew of tobacco. Soon I began to grow tired; my legs cramped; my head ached; my eyes felt as if they were being pushed from their sockets; the muscles in the back of my neck seemed as if they were being torn from the base of the skull. I suffered terrible agony. It seemed to me that I had been suspended in the air a week before being cut down. I saw Colonel Streator there. When I was cut down I was in a dazed condition; everything seemed blurred. The first thing I remember was when some one gave me some ammonia. I was lying on the ground; had a terrible headache. Some one gave me some whiskey. I remained in the guard tent all night."

Attorney Braden endeavored to show on cross-examination that Iams had prearranged to misbehave in order to secure his discharge; that he had swallowed tobacco in order to make him sick while under punishment, and that he had admitted to a friend that the punishment did not hurt him much, but the lawyer failed to shake the young man's testimony. Before leaving the stand, Iams stated that if the defendants were convicted it was his intention to bring a civil suit against them for damages.

Several members of Iams' company were called as witnesses and corroborated the details of the young man's story. John H. Gladden, an hospital nurse of the Tenth regiment, testified that he had seen Iams trussed up by the thumbs, but watched the proceedings only for ten minutes, as the sight sickened him. Private Kent swore that Colonel Streator, on hearing it rumored that Iams meant to shoot him on sight, said that he (Iams) "had better keep out of the way, or he would shoot him if he could hit at forty yards."

Senator Robbins, whose interest in the case was sharpened by the fact that he was quartermaster-general of the Tenth regiment, opened for the defense. He denied that the case had the elements of an assault, questioned the severity of Iams' punishment, and warned the jury that the conviction of the defendants must be followed by the destruction of discipline in the National Guard. Deputy Sheriff Gray was brought forward by the prosecution to tell the story of the lock-out at Homestead, the exhaustion of the Sheriff's powers and the fate of the Pinkertons, so as to make clear the gravity of the conditions with which the military had to cope. The defense interposed a statement to the effect that the Governor had exceeded his authority in ordering out the troops, but this was overruled by the court.

Colonel Streator's story did not materially conflict with that told by Iams. Colonel Hawkins testified that on the afternoon when Mr. Frick was attacked he received two communications by signal, one stating that Frick had been shot by a striker, the other that Frick was dead and that extraordinary precautions were necessary. He had thereupon ordered all commanders to be on the alert, to double their camp guards and to send out three extra patrols. While the camp was in this state Iams had proposed three cheers for the man who shot Frick. When Colonel Streator reported the affair, witness had said to him: "Colonel, you know your duty as a soldier." The situation was critical and prompt measures were needed.

Robert W. Herbert, a newspaper reporter, said that Iams had told him of his intention to shoot Streator, and that in speaking of General Snowden, the young man had said, "I will get even with that four-eyed ——— ——— ——— on the hill." One of the hospital nurses swore that Iams had made himself sick with tobacco, and another that Iams had been drinking and wanted to be confined in the guard-house. Surgeon Grimm illustrated for the court's edification the knot, known as a close-hitch, by which the rope was fastened on Iams' thumbs, and described it as not being a severe kind of knot. Veterans of the civil war bore witness that the punishment suffered by Iams was in accordance with the usages of war and that it was mild considering the gravity of the offense.

An amusing *lapsus linguae* marked the evidence of Colonel Norman M. Smith, of the Eighteenth regiment. Here was the colloquy:

ATTORNEY IAMS.—"You have hung men up by the thumbs in your regiment?"

COLONEL SMITH.—"I have never had occasion, but if I had, I would *cheerfully* do so—I mean, I would do so. I wish to strike out the word 'cheerfully.' That was a slip." Whereupon an expansive smile illumined every face in the court-room.

The closing speech for the defense, delivered by Senator Robbins, was a fine forensic effort, bearing in the main on the absence of malice and the necessity of extraordinary punishment when soldiers mutiny in the field. Attorney Iams, in closing for the prosecution, compared his relative to the Savior on the cross, and averred that the only reason why the youth was not permitted to die while suspended by the thumbs was because the defendants "wanted him alive next morning in order that they could shave his head and drum him out of camp." Judge Porter charged squarely in favor of the defense, telling the jury that, "If Colonel Streator, in punishing Iams, was actuated only by upright motives in an effort as an officer to maintain order, he should not be punished."

It took the jury twenty-one hours to arrive at a verdict. A few stood out for conviction on the charge of simple assault and battery, which had been ruled out by the court, and, to test the matter, an appeal was made to Judge Porter for instructions. The judge replied with a scathing rebuke. When the jurors next appeared they returned a verdict of acquittal, but directed that, in the aggravated assault and battery case, the costs be divided between Colonel Hawkins and Streator.

While there was much sympathy for Iams, this finding was commonly regarded as a just one, in view of the supreme necessity of maintaining discipline in the military service and the wide latitude permitted by military usage in punishing delinquencies in the field. It is safe to say, however, that the harsh penalties imposed upon Iams will never again be resorted to in the National Guard of Pennsylvania without reference to a court-martial.

While these events were in progress, the mills at Homestead were filling up rapidly with non-union men. The Tide kept up her daily trips, and the sight of brawny fellows with bundles, duly ticketed for "Fort Frick," became so common on the Monongahela wharf at Pittsburgh that people ceased to marvel at it and to curse and scoff at the blacksheep. By the first of August there were over 800 men at work, their board and lodging being provided within the mill enclosure. Regimental chaplains were secured to hold regular services on Sunday, with the assistance of a band which took the place of a choir. Chaplain Hays, of the Fifteenth regiment, preached the first sermon. His theme was "Saul of Tarsus," with which eminent biblical character he managed to connect Private Iams and the anarchists, denouncing both the latter as liberally as he praised the scriptural hero. After this sermon, the more illiterate of the non-unionists were firmly convinced that Saul of Tarsus was the leading non-unionist of his time besides being a regular martinet in military matters.

Superintendent Potter now claimed openly that the strike was broken, that about forty of the firm's old employees had quietly returned to work and that a majority of the rest were ready and anxious to return. The advisory board met these assertions with an emphatic denial, crediting Mr. Potter with making a "gigantic bluff," as Vice Chairman Thomas Crawford put it, for the purpose of discouraging the strikers.* Mr. Potter, however, invited the advisory board to send a committee to inspect the mill and verify his representations. The invitation was accepted and four skilled steelworkers went through the plant and narrowly inspected the work going on in every department. At a mass meeting of

---

*The term "strikers" is used here because, when the firm invited its employees to return to work, the lock-out ceased, and the union men were placed in the position of being on a strike.

the strikers, held on August 2, this committee reported
that, while it was true that a large number of men were
at work in the mill, little actual progress was being made,
and that the consequent loss to the firm was heavy
enough to justify the most sanguine expectations on the
side of the Amalgamated Association. The chief officers
of the Association were present when the report was
made, and delivered speeches full of enthusiasm and confidence. Every man at the meeting pledged himself to
stay out to the bitter end.

An attempt to "evangelize" the non-unionists was
made by the distribution of circulars appealing to their
manhood in the name of organized labor. These bills
were dropped into the mill yard from trains passing over
the Pemickey bridge and seemed to produce some effect,
inasmuch as several of the non-unionists left the mill
and accepted money from the Amalgamated Association
to take them to their homes. Unfortunately the ease
with which funds were obtained in this way led many of
the worst characters in the mill, after being dismissed for
laziness or misconduct, to make descents on the Association's treasury, backing up their demands with amazing
tales of the difficulties experienced in trying to operate
the mills with green hands, including accidents of the
most appalling description. Many of these fictions crept
into the newspapers and produced a sensation.

The relief fund established for the benefit of the strikers
was swelled daily by contributions from all parts of the
United States and Canada, ranging in amount from one
to twelve hundred dollars. Soliciting committees were
sent into the coal and coke regions and elsewhere and
met on every hand with a generous reception. An im-

mense sum was needed to meet the daily demands of the
army of the unemployed. The disbursing officers, however, husbanded their resources by refusing to give out
cash. To those in need of assistance orders on the grocery stores for provisions were issued. The amounts
given out in this way aggregated about $3,000 a day.

President Samuel Gompers, of the American Federation of Labor, with which the Amalgamated Association
is affiliated, arrived in Pittsburgh, accompanied by the
other executive officers of the Federation, on August 12
and settled down at once to the injection of new life into the Homestead campaign. On Saturday, the 14th,
he addressed 1500 men in the Homestead rink, throwing
a ferocious vigor into his remarks which verged on incendiarism. Of the assault on Mr. Frick he said:

"I have been asked for my opinion of the attack on the
life of Mr. Frick. I don't know why I should be asked
to go out of my way to give Berkman an additional
kick. I never heard of him until after he made his attack. The laws of Pennsylvania will take care of him.
I do know, however, that I have heard of thousands of
men being shot down by day and by night, each and
every one of whom was a better man than this despot,
Frick. Yet I have never been asked for my opinion of
any of these cases."

Mr. Gompers intimated that a boycott might be declared against the Carnegie Company, in spite of the
decisions of the Pennsylvania courts construing boycotting as conspiracy, and he added that he would not fear
to come personally within the borders of Pennsylvania
and declare it.

A highly encouraging event which took place at this
time was the signing of the scale by the Pittsburgh iron

manufacturers. The manufacturers' committee and the wage committee of the Amalgamated Association had been holding a succession of conferences, without approaching a settlement for a period of fully six weeks. Not until the second week in August did they arrive at an agreement. On the evening of the 11th the stubborn determination which characterized both sides was suddenly relaxed and the labor world was surprised with the announcement that the manufacturers had decided to sign the scale in consideration of a 10 per cent. reduction in the wages of finishers—the highest priced men employed in steel mills. They had originally demanded a reduction of puddlers' wages from $5.50 to $4.50 per ton. This the Association steadily resisted and with unquestionable justice. Even the *American Manufacturer*, the biased organ of the employers, was forced to admit editorially that the puddler, being a handicraftsman and in no wise affected by mechanical improvements, was not a proper subject for a wage reduction. Finding this demand hopelessly untenable, the manufacturers asked instead for a reduction in finishers' wages, and after fifteen useless conferences, suggested that the matter be referred for arbitration, as the Amalgamated committee had no power to act. The arbitration proposal was submitted to the lodges and overwhelmingly rejected, but the wage committee was authorized to act on a change in the finishers' scale. It was then decided to submit to the 10 per cent. reduction. The effect of this settlement was to give work at once to 40,000 idle men in the Pittsburgh district, and as the Mahoning Valley manufacturers and workmen quickly followed suit, the entire iron district of Western Pennsylvania and Eastern

Ohio was relieved from a situation pregnant with disaster to employers and workmen alike. The finishers were the only disgruntled ones, and so keenly did they resent what they professed to regard as unjust discrimination against their interests that a number of them seceded from the Amalgamated Association and formed a union of their own.

At Homestead the signing of the scale by the Manufacturers' Association was regarded as a capitulation to the power of organized labor which must force the Carnegie Company to abandon its individual fight. It was the belief that Mr. Frick had been chosen to bear the brunt of the general battle against the Amalgamated Association with the understanding that, if he won, all the mills in the Pittsburgh district would be made non-union; and the compromise agreed upon was accepted, therefore, as meaning that the other manufacturers had lost faith in Mr. Frick's ability to win, and that the Carnegie chairman himself could not rationally continue his fight, now that his brethren had fallen away from him. Subsequent events proved the baselessness of this supposition. It was merely one of many straws at which the Homestead men grasped eagerly in the face of the Carnegie firm's slow but sure fulfilment of its pledge to fill the mills with non-union workmen and rely solely thenceforward upon this class of labor.

The making of informations and counter-informations founded on the Pinkerton affair went on uninterruptedly. Fred. Primer was the first of the Pinkertons to be placed under arrest. He was held for court by Alderman King on the strength of testimony showing that the first shot on July 6 was fired from the barges. Primer, attended by the attorneys for the Carnegie firm, was hurried before Judge Ewing, who promptly released him on his own recognizance, stating very plainly at the same time that whatever trouble occurred at Homestead was of the workmen's own making and that no one else should be held responsible for the consequences. The court also held Edward Burke in $10,000 bail on the charge of murder preferred by Secretary Lovejoy. Burke had already acquired some notoriety by an altercation with Sheriff McCleary on the occasion of the Sheriff's last visit to Homestead before the arrival of the troops.

The reader has been informed of the inspiriting effect produced upon Sheriff McCleary by military protection. One of the first results thereof was the enlistment of a corps of deputies to take the place of the Homestead police, the latter officials being so thoroughly in sympathy with the strikers that they devoted their attention chiefly to the apprehension of non-union men who happened to stray out of the works. The sight of a non-unionist was always sufficient to incite an uproar and on several occasions riotous demonstrations were caused by the appearance on the streets of men who had the hardihood to leave the mill and walk abroad. The Sheriff kept adding to his force of deputies according as the military guard was reduced, until when the last of the troops left Homestead, there were enough civil officers employed to deal with any ordinary disorder.

The congressional investigation which was begun at Pittsburgh was resumed at Washington on July 22. Robert and William Pinkerton appeared to testify, and a committee of the Knights of Labor, consisting of Messrs. Hayes, Wright and Devlin, was also present and submitted to the investigating committee a series of questions to be put to the witnesses. The Pinkerton brothers presented a written statement, giving a history of their agency and an account of its methods. They upheld the character of their employees for trustworthiness and reliability, denied that it was customary for their men to carry arms or that the men ever wantonly or recklessly fired a shot or used weapons without being sworn in as deputy sheriffs or otherwise properly authorized, and alleged that the men sent to Homestead were to have been deputized and that Colonel Gray was understood to be authorized to deputize them.

When the sub-committee charged with the investigation came to sum up and prepare a report, it was found that the members were hopelessly divided, so that the work done, as far as it was likely to affect congressional action, might be considered as wasted. Some of the members, however, did not hesitate to give publicity to their individual views. Mr. Bynum held that if the Carnegie firm could legally bring in 300 Pinkerton guards, it would be equally justified in bringing in 10,000—that is to say, a full-sized army equipped to levy war. He spoke in very severe terms of Sheriff McCleary, describing him as a "poltroon," whose conduct during the riot was simply cowardly.

The House judiciary committee later received a supplementary statement from the Pinkerton brothers, replying to attacks made upon Pinkertonism by Senator Vest and Grand Master Workman Powderly of the K. of L. In this document many crimes were charged to members of secret labor organizations, and it was claimed that the organizations themselves, instead of showing sincere solicitude for law and order, by disciplining and controlling the guilty ones, were disposed to applaud outrages committed in their name and to elevate the criminals, when caught, to the dignity of martyrs. "Notwithstanding the protestations of the leaders at Homestead," said the Messrs. Pinkerton in conclusion, "no reasonable man can for a moment doubt that if the troops and deputy sheriffs were withdrawn, the non-union men now working in the mills would be murdered, and for no offense, no wrong, no injury to anyone."

PEMICKEY TRACK IN THE MILL YARD.

CHAPTER XIV.

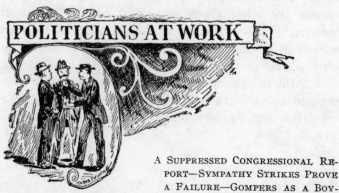

POLITICIANS AT WORK

A Suppressed Congressional Re-
port—Sympathy Strikes Prove
a Failure—Gompers as a Boy-
cott Wielder—The Slavs Weaken—Plans of the Republican
National Committee—Smooth Mr. Milholland Enlists Hugh
O'Donnell—Honest John McLuckie Refuses to be Muzzled—
The Milholland Scheme Falls Through—Outbreaks at
Homestead—The Search for Pinkerton Guns—Mr. Frick
Revisits the Mill.

F OR reasons which were never fully disclosed, the House
committee on Homestead, which entrusted to Representative Oates the preparation of a report to the general judiciary committee, rejected the report when completed and decided to let the whole matter drift over to
the next session of Congress. Mr. Oates found that the
differences between the Carnegie Company and its men
might have been adjusted, had Mr. Frick stated to the
conference committee the "bottom facts" prompting
the demand for a reduction of wages, but the officers of
the company invited trouble by failing to exercise "pa-
tience, indulgence and solicitude," and that Mr. Frick,

in particular, was "too stern, brusque and some-what autocratic." He condemned the employment of Pinkertons and argued that the company might have prevented bloodshed by relying solely on the constituted authorities for protection, although he conceded the in-efficiency of Sheriff McCleary. He condemned also as unlawful the action of the workmen in turning away the sheriff and in hanging in effigy Messrs. Frick and Potter, denied the right of the Amalgamated Asso-ciation to bar non-union men out of employment, and held that the men of Homestead had no legal right to resist the Pinkerton invasion and were answerable ac-cordingly to the Pennsylvania courts. In conclusion, Mr. Oates found that congress had no power to dispose of the questions involved. A satisfactory arbitration law could not be enacted and it was a debatable question whether or not congress could do anything to regulate or suppress Pinkertonism.

On August 3, Vice-President Morton appointed a committee of senators, composed of Messrs. Gallinger, Pfeffer, Hansbrough, Felton, Sanders, White and Hill to investigate the Pinkerton corporation. Action by this body was deferred until after the Presidential elec-tion, the chairman being a stalwart Republican and averse to the opening of proceedings which might fur-nish campaign material to the Democrats.

It was not long until the backbone of the sympathy strikes declared at the Carnegie mills at Lawrenceville, Duquesne and Beaver Falls showed signs of weakening. At Lawrenceville, the company took precautions similar to those taken at Homestead. An eight-foot board fence was built round the mill yard and no person was

admitted without a pass from the superintendent. The
strikers placed pickets on guard, but, despite their vigilance, several hundred non-union men were spirited in
and on August 1, the plate mill was started. One hundred and fifty uniformed policemen and the entire force
of city detectives were detailed, at the request of the
firm, to protect the mill property at this time. After
one day's service the majority of the officers were withdrawn, but enough were left on duty to guard all entrances and approaches to the mill. For the accommodation of the non-unionists, who dared not venture out,
cots were set up in the carpenter shop, a rough-and-
ready cuisine was improvised, and beer was brought in
from the neighboring breweries. The force of "scab"
employees increased rapidly, and in a short time, the
watchers without began to lose heart and relax their
vigilance. Nevertheless the Lawrenceville strike was
prolonged for a year, or twice as long as the strike at
Homestead, although the Lawrenceville men had signed
a contract with the Carnegie Company and had no
grievance of their own. When the strike was ultimately
declared off, few of the men who went out were employed again by the firm and many of them found themselves reduced to poverty.

The Duquesne strike was of short duration. The
men had been hastily organized and the new-born spirit
of unionism among them was not strong enough to
inspire and maintain mutual confidence. A report that
non-union men had been secured and that the mill
would be started on August 4 caused a stampede,
several hundred of the strikers discarding their allegiance to the Amalgamated Association and rushing pell-

mell to the mill when it opened up, fearing that their jobs were slipping away from them, perhaps forever.

Enraged at this defection, the strikers who held their ground, aided by a large body of men from Homestead, who had camped at Duquesne on the previous night, took possession of the mill gates and beat back those who were returning to work. Deputy sheriffs who were on the ground sent to General Wiley for assistance, which was promptly rendered, six companies of the Sixteenth Regiment being sent to the scene of disturbance on a work train. Eleven of the rioters were captured and taken to Pittsburgh, where they were held for a court trial. On the morning of August 8, the mill was again opened for work and the strikers, thoroughly disheartened, resumed their jobs in a body, every man, with the exception of those arrested for riot, getting his old place.

The strike at Beaver Falls, where 900 men are employed, with a weekly pay-roll of $12,000, lasted four months. It was free from disorder, the mill being shut down from the time the strike was declared. The financial loss to the town was so heavy and affected the business people so severely that it was deemed useless to stay out, and, when the firm re-opened the mill, the three Amalgamated lodges formally abandoned the strike and marched back to work in a body.

Sentiment at Homestead was kept warm by the unflagging efforts of the Amalgamated officials and of President Gompers, of the Federation of Labor. Mr. Gompers clung tenaciously to his idea of imposing a universal boycott upon Carnegie products, and the Homestead men accepted the suggestion with enthusiasm, believing that by this means the firm could be brought to its knees. Hugh O'Donnell was one of the most earnest advocates of the plan and stated through the press that it was bound to furnish a solution for the Homestead problem. As a preliminary step, the strikers issued a printed appeal to workingmen not to "work up the material shipped from the works of the Carnegie Steel Company during the present strike."

At a conference of the general officers of the Federation with Mr. Weihe on August 12, the boycott plan was considered and finally negatived, probably because of the well-known attitude of the Allegheny County courts towards persons concerned in this form of conspiracy. As Mr. Gompers and his colleagues had been holding up the boycott as a panacea, their backdown was regarded with much disfavor by the strikers, but a few red-hot speeches at a mass meeting on the following day, including the famous address by Mr. Gompers, an extract from which appears in the preceding chapter, put the rank and file in good humor again. There are times when oratory covers a multitude of sins.

Once out of range of the orator's power, however, the strikers had to meet and tacitly admit the force of some discouraging circumstances. Grumblings were heard even at the expense of Hugh O'Donnell and Burgess McLuckie. O'Donnell left Homestead mysteriously late in July and it was rumored that he had been detailed to confer with Republican leaders in the east with a view to bringing political pressure to bear on Messrs. Frick and Carnegie. The actual history of O'Donnell's mission is given here for the first time in print.

It has already been explained that C. L. Magee, of Pittsburgh, in addition to being interested as a Republican leader in the settlement of the Homestead troubles, was still more profoundly concerned in the affair by reason of his being Sheriff McCleary's bondsman. Mr. Magee was well aware that attempts to influence either Mr. Carnegie or Mr. Frick were a waste of energy. The next best step, in his opinion, was to influence the men of Homestead themselves, and, above all, to put a stop to the speech-making of Burgess McLuckie and others in opposition to the McKinley bill, to "free trade in labor" and other sins charged to the account of the Republican party just when the Republican party was least able to stand assaults. In pursuance of this purpose he communicated with John L. Milholland, of New York, chairman of the Republican committee on industrial affairs, advising him to arrive at an understanding with O'Donnell and McLuckie. Milholland, recognizing the critical nature of the situation, at once proceeded to Homestead, and induced O'Donnell to accompany him to New York. The young Homesteader left without confiding his plans to anybody. A reporter of the *New York World*, however, recognized Milholland, discovered what was on foot and informed the *World* by telegraph, whereupon the management of that journal detailed a special man to meet and shadow the travelers when they reached Philadelphia and also succeeded in placing a confidential agent in Milholland's office as stenographer, with instructions to watch developments in the Homestead affair.

The upshot of the conference in New York, to which

O'Donnell was a party, was that the young labor leader
pledged himself to use his influence to silence the anti-
tariff orators of Homestead, and particularly McLuckie,
and the Republican National Committee, in return,
guaranteed an early settlement of the wage trouble, to
the satisfaction of the workingmen.

On his return, O'Donnell told Hugh Dempsey, Master
Workman of D. A. 3, K. of L., of his agreement and enlisted Dempsey's aid in bringing McLuckie to terms.
Dempsey sought out the sturdy burgess, took him into
the parlor of a hotel and laid the Milholland scheme before him.

"It rests with you, John, to settle this whole trouble."
said the Master Workman.

"How so?" asked McLuckie.

"Well," said the other, "All you need do is to write
a few lines over your signature, stating that you have
been misquoted and to quit making Democratic speeches,
and the Republicans will give you anything you want
and settle the wage question, besides."

McLuckie's eyes blazed and his big fist came down on
the table with a bang. "So," he said, "you want me
not only to sacrifice my independence, but to write myself down a PUBLIC LIAR! If any other man made
such a proposal to me, Hugh, I would knock him
down."

"Don't be unreasonable, John," the Master Workman
argued. "Remember what is at stake. Remember
that it is in your hands to stop misery and bloodshed and
restore happiness to Homestead."

"Yes, at the price of my own character," rejoined the
big Burgess, hotly. "Say no more, Hugh. Come what

may, I shall never denounce myself to the American people as a liar and a hypocrite."

Here the conversation ended and the two men left the hotel. Just then Hugh O'Donnell came out of a hotel across the street, and seeing McLuckie and Dempsey hastened to join them.

"What do you think he has been asking me to do?" said McLuckie, with a contemptuous glance at Dempsey, and then he recounted the interview at the hotel.

O'Donnell laughed. "Why, John," he said, "it was I that asked Dempsey to talk to you. If you are as sensible a man as I take you to be, and are anxious to render real service to your friends here, you will do as the National Committee wants you to, and you'll never regret it."

McLuckie answered with bitterness that O'Donnell was mistaken in him, that his manhood was not for sale to the politicians, and that he would treat as an enemy any man who met him with proposals the acceptance of which would place him in a dubious light before the American people.

The endeavor to silence McLuckie and make him recant did not end here. The Burgess was warned by members of the Advisory Board that his anti-tariff talks were damaging the cause of the strikers; nevertheless he declined to put a bridle on his tongue and let slip no opportunity of speaking on the text, "Protection for the manufacturer and free trade in labor," with incidental references to the connection between high tariff, high fences and Pinkerton thugs.

Shortly after the meeting with O'Donnell and Dempsey, President Weihe assigned O'Donnell and McLuckie to speak at a labor meeting in Boston. Funds for the trip were supplied by the Boston people and O'Donnell was the purse bearer. When the men arrived in New York, O'Donnell urged McLuckie to go with him to Milholland's office, but without success. After the Boston meeting a reporter of the *Boston Herald* was detailed to accompany the men back to Homestead. Arriving in New York, O'Donnell again broached the subject of visiting Milholland, but McLuckie was obdurate. At this point, according to the Burgess' own story, O'Donnell left his two companions, promising to meet them at the depot in time to catch a morning train. McLuckie and the *Herald* man were on hand, but O'Donnell failed to keep his appointment. The day wore on without any sign of O'Donnell's coming. Finally McLuckie informed the *Herald* man that, as O'Donnell carried the purse, he was unable to pay his fare to Pittsburgh. The reporter advanced the necessary cash and they left New York without an inkling of the whereabouts of their missing companion.

It was afterwards ascertained that O'Donnell had hunted up Milholland to notify him of the impossibility of dealing with McLuckie and had probably forgotten his fellow-travelers in the excitement attending his "confab" with the great manipulator of industrial affairs for political purposes.

O'Donnell's course in these negotiations may be excused on the dual ground of inexperience in politics and a desire to benefit his townsmen by securing somehow a termination of the strike favorable to the wage-workers. He was dealing with sharp and not over-scrupulous practitioners, who dealt largely in promises and cared little about performance and less about any damage that might be sustained by O'Donnell himself, provided that their immediate aims were accomplished. The sole reward obtained by the young leader was seven months' confinement in the Allegheny County jail and abuse at the hands of rival leaders at Homestead. William Roberts was especially severe in his condemnation of both O'Donnell and McLuckie, crediting them with being partners in an unauthorized political move, which was sure to be barren of results. Mr. Roberts himself entered the employ of the Democratic National Committee as a stump speaker before the campaign was over, and remained an ardent low-tariff Democrat until the rejection of his application for a position in the Internal Revenue Collector's office at Pittsburgh convinced him of the error of his ways and led him to take the stump for protection.

Smarting under the criticisms to which he was subjected, Hugh O'Donnell went before the advisory board demanding that he be supported by a vote of confidence or else be permitted to resign. McLuckie seconded the request for a vote of confidence, and O'Donnell received his vindication.

The conduct of the Hungarian laborers caused the advisory board no little uneasiness. These unfortunates, always poorly paid, had, for the most part, no savings to fall back on and were quickly reduced to destitution. It was hard to expect them to starve for the sake of vindicating union principles, but at the same time it was looked upon as important to hold them in line with the other strikers, because a break, even among the lower class of workmen, would be very damaging to the union cause. The fear of a break among the Huns was a continual source of anxiety.

Mr. Frick, having recovered in a remarkably short time from the effects of his wounds, returned to his duties on August 5. A few days later, Messrs. Potter and Childs appeared on the streets of Homestead for the first time since July 6. They were on their way to attend a magistrate's hearing and had to pass through a crowd of several hundred men at the headquarters of the mechanics and laborers.. Both officials were cool and seemingly unconcerned. They were not molested in any way, the men merely gazing at them in silence as they passed.

Although the Gompers boycott turned out to be only a flash in the pan, the boycotting spirit found a foothold even among the children in Homestead. An amusing illustration of precocity in this regard was furnished in the little chapel at Munhall station on the Sunday after Mr. Gompers' arrival. Mrs. Agnew, the wife of a foreman at work in the Carnegie mill, and her daughter had charge of a Sunday school in this modest place of worship. With the echoes of Mr. Gompers' speech still ringing in their ears, a number of sober-faced boys assembled as usual for instructions, but, before the exercises had fairly commenced, every lad present arose and solemnly marched out. One of the urchins, when questioned, said that he didn't propose to be "teached by der wife an' daughter of no blacksheep." Happily, as soon as the F. of L. issued a no-boycott manifesto, Sunday school took up again at Munhall and went on without further mishap.

The life of the men at work in the mill was by no

means a pleasant one. They were closely confined, not daring to go out, for some time after the mill was first manned, unless on Saturdays, when those who cared to go to Pittsburgh were taken down on the Tide and allowed to remain away over Sunday. By the middle of August about 200 non-unionists were lodged in the company houses near the mill under protection of the military. The first of these that undertook to bring in his household goods, found that even military aid was insufficient. A crowd of strikers met the teamster

THE PEMICKEY BRIDGE.

who was hauling the goods at the ferry-boat and threatened him with severe handling if he again ventured to haul the property of a black-sheep through the streets of Homestead.

The first and only real outcropping of trouble between the workmen and the militia arose from conflicts between the crews of freight trains passing over the Pemicky bridge and a detail of soldiers stationed on the obnoxious Little Bill. The soldiers reported that trainmen or strikers concealed on the trains had fired upon them and they were instructed, if again assailed, to return the fire. On the evening of August 18, wild excitement was caused by the noise of a fusillade on the river front of the mill yard. If the statement of the militiamen on board the Little Bill is true, five revolver shots were fired at the boat from a freight train, the first shot coming from the engine and the others from the cars. The fire was returned from the boat and when the train reached the other side of the river, the batallion stationed on the hill above the B. & O. railroad, under the command of Captain Fred Windsor, also opened fire, the rattle of musket balls against the freight cars sounding like the patter of a hail storm. The men in the mill were panic-stricken, believing that the events of July 6 were about to be duplicated, and there was also a hubbub among the strikers, but the arrival of the provost marshal's guard quickly restored order. The conductor of the freight train stoutly affirmed that the shots which alarmed the soldiers on the Little Bill were merely torpedo explosions, and this was very probably the case, since it is in the last degree unlikely that a few men on a slowly moving freight would undertake to cope with a large number of soldiers on the boat and on shore. The soldiers were at all times consumed with anxiety to do some genuine fighting, and on this occasion the fire-eaters in the Fifteenth and Sixteenth regiments made no secret of their disappointment when they found that the incipient skirmish on the river was not to be followed by a "go" with the strikers.

Two days previous to this affair, the provost guard, under Major Crawford, had a brush with the townspeople which came within an ace of developing into a pitched battle. Frank Tracey, a non-union laborer, was arrested for larceny, and four of his brother blacksheep were taken with him to Alderman Oeffner's office by the arresting officer. Tracy was committed to jail amid the cheers of a crowd which had gathered in and around the magistrate's office. When the four non-unionists came out, the mob surged around them and some of the more violent suggested lynching or a ducking in the river as fit treatment for the "scabs." Clubs and stones were picked up, and the situation began to look serious when Major Crawford appeared at the head of a squad of men, with fixed bayonets and guns at half cock, and forced the crowd to disperse. Some of the citizens derided the soldiers as "pale-faced boys," and a stout young woman shook her fist under the line of military noses and threatened to extinguish the entire National Guard. Nevertheless, the non-unionists were enabled to return to the mill in safety and the last murmurings of the tumult were silenced by policemen and deputy sheriffs after Major Crawford left the scene.

Other outbreaks of similar character spurred to renewed vigilance the militia and the Sheriff's deputies, who had fallen into the habit of lounging and dozing in shady places, and within a few days after Major Crawford's collision with the mob, large numbers of non-union men succeeded in moving their goods from the ferry into the company houses without suffering molestation.

Pinkerton detectives began a systematic search for guns on August 28, but without result. The Winchesters taken from the guards on the barges had been smuggled into a safe place of concealment where even the Pinkertonian eye that "never sleeps" was unable to discover them.

On August 31, Mr. Frick visited the mill for the first time since the beginning of the wage trouble. He was accompanied by a detective, but needed no protection, as the strikers showed no disposition to grow wrathy over his presence. Mr. Frick made a complete inspection of the mill, pronounced the various departments to be in excellent working order and informed the reporters that the strike was a thing of the past.

CHAPTER XV.

D URING the month of August, the mill continued to
fill up rapidly with non-union recruits. Among
these there was an admixture of worthless characters, who went to Homestead only for the novelty of the
thing or for the purpose of securing a few square meals
and perhaps a little money from the Company without
imposing any special tax on their energies. Men of this
type rarely spent more than a day or two in the mill.
Once their curiosity or rapacity was satisfied they deserted, threw themselves into the arms of the strikers,
represented themselves as having been deluded by the

firm's agents and in the majority of cases secured pecuniary aid from the Amalgamated Association. The strikers invariably welcomed desertions and did not always trouble themselves to inquire minutely into the circumstances prompting the sudden change of heart on the part of the deserters. The stories told by the latter to the advisory board eclipsed Munchausen's wildest flights, winding up, as a rule, with the assurance that, owing to bad treatment and breaches of faith regarding the wages to be paid, almost the entire corps of non-union men was preparing to quit work.

The exodus of idlers and incapables did not, however, in any way impair the progress which Superintendent Potter and his new hands were making, despite the reports to the contrary circulated among the strikers. The force of employees increased rapidly and as the wages offered were considerably higher than the average earnings of clerks and young men just beginning a professional career, many representatives of those classes were attracted into the Carnegie Company's service. Among the persons of education and refinement thus enlisted were four once prominent brokers on the Pittsburgh oil exchange, Messrs. Linn L. Dilworth, C. D. Leslie, John McLaughlin and J. L. Agnew. Mr. Dilworth was set to work running an engine, Mr. Leslie became foreman of the cold saw department, and Mr. Agnew was placed in the armor-plate department. Mr. McLaughlin, who was at one time considered the "highest roller" on the Oil City and Pittsburgh floors, accommodated himself to the duties of a subordinate position at fair wages.

The completion of the last piece of armor-plate for the government cruiser Monterey, on September 3, made it plain enough that the works were being operated in earnest and that the expectation that the firm would be unable to execute its contracts with the government, as long as green hands were employed, was destined to be defeated. In any case, there was a special clause in the government contracts providing for an extension of time in the event of labor troubles, so that the firm had nothing to fear from that quarter. The answer of the strikers when confronted with the circumstances was that the material turned out was necessarily defective and must be rejected by the government. This claim, however, was not substantiated.

About this time sickness began to spread among the non-unionists. The Company physicians had their hands full and a large number of men had to be conveyed to the Pittsburgh hospitals. John McGeorge, a resident of Allegheny, was taken to his home and died there, and McGeorge's son, who had been working in the mill with his father, was also stricken down. The attending physician diagnosed the malady in these cases as typhoid fever and assigned as the cause the impurity of the water used for general consumption in the mill. At first the Company hushed up the rumors of the presence of what seemed to be an epidemic among the men, and it was not until many deaths had occurred that the matter was publicly ventilated. Of the mystery involved in this affair and the manner in which it was solved an account will be given in another chapter.

Weekly mass meetings, at which the men were assured that the company was only "making a bluff" and that, sooner or later the old hands would have to be reinstated, the Amalgamated Association recognized and wages kept up to a decent figure, kept life in the strikers' organization for an astonishingly long time. The loyalty of the workingmen to one another and their cheerful confidence in the power of unionist principles and unionist methods to overcome all obstacles were almost sublime. General officers of the Amalgamated Association took part in all these assemblages and distinguished themselves by inculcating a spirit of moderation and respect for the law. Other orators gave full rein to opinions surcharged with bitterness and resentment, and Mr. Frick, the Sheriff and the Common pleas judges came in for many an unmerciful scoring. John Oldshue, leader of the Slavs, figured in every meeting, interpreting for the benefit of his countrymen and delivering exhortations on his own account.

With the exception of an information for murder lodged against Edward Burke, who was already in jail on charges of riot and unlawful assemblage, Secretary Lovejoy's program of prosecutions remained untouched throughout the month of August. At the beginning of September, Mr. Lovejoy warmed up to his work again and caused warrants to be issued for the arrest of Hugh O'Donnell, Hugh Ross, Matthew Foy and William Foy for the murder of Detective John W. Klein. All the defendants were already under $10,000 bonds on the charge of killing T. J. Conners and Silas Wain, and the apparent design was to multiply the amount of bail until the resources of the union leaders were exhausted and confinement in jail could no longer be avoided. Matthew Foy was arrested at once. O'Donnell surrendered two weeks later, on his return from New York. Elmer E. Bales, Harry Bayne and Oscar

Colflesh were also arrested on charges of riot and conspiracy.

At the hearing on the conspiracy charge against Hugh O'Donnell, George W. Sarver, David Lynch, William T. Roberts and William McConegy, before Alderman McMasters, a sensation was created by the testimony of George S. Hotchkiss, an assistant superintendent in the employ of the Pinkerton agency. Hotchkiss swore that he had held several conferences with Jack Clifford, of the Homestead advisory board, and obtained from Clifford information incriminating O'Donnell and others. The nature of Clifford's revelations was not made known, objection to the admission of second-hand testimony being raised by attorney Brennen for the defense and sustained by the magistrate; but the report went out that Clifford had turned informer and caused consternation among the strikers. The members of the advisory board, however, defended their associate and explained that he had conferred with the Pinkerton man solely for the purpose of "pumping" him. Subsequent events bore out this assertion. The five men heard before 'Squire McMasters were held for a court trial.

Shortly after O'Donnell and his companions had been disposed of, Clifford was arrested on a second charge of murder, preferred by the industrious Lovejoy, and committed to jail. He was also held for conspiracy, but gave bail on this charge. Next day his application for bail on the murder charge was brought before Judge Ewing, as was also that of Matthew Foy. Foy, against whom there was practically no evidence, was released on $10,000 bail. The testimony against Clifford, however, was very damaging. Captain John Cooper, of the Pin-

kerton agency, swore that when the Pinkerton barges
approached the mill landing at Homestead, he saw Clifford among a crowd of strikers with a pistol in his hand,
and heard him shout, "You —— —— ——, don't come
ashore, or we'll kill all of you." Clifford, he said, was the
man who approached the barges with a white flag and arranged for the surrender. Samuel Stewart, a clerk in
the employ of the Carnegie Company, testified that he
saw Clifford attach a fuse to a piece of dynamite fixed in
an iron pipe and hurl this crude bomb at the barges,
and that he noticed a revolver sticking out of the defendant's pocket. On the strength of this testimony,
Clifford was committed for trial without bail. Judge
Ewing refused to hear evidence as to who fired the first
shot and said in his opinion : "The parties on the shore
had no duties to perform except to go away, or as good
citizens, to put down the crowd that this defendant,
Clifford, was with. There is no question—there *can* be
no question—of self-defense about it. I say that we
will not go into it, especially in this preliminary matter."

On September 21, the grand jury returned true bills
in all the Homestead cases presented to that body, 167
in number. The following is the list:

Murder of Silas Wain—James Close, Charles Martz,
George Diebold, —— Sanderson, Edward McVay, Peter
Allen, Sr., Jack Clifford, Matthew Foy, Hugh O'Don-
nell, John McLuckie, Sylvester Critchlow, Anthony Fla-
herty, Samuel Burkett, James Flannigan and Hugh
Ross.

Murder of T. J. Conners—James Close, Charles Martz,
George Diebold, —— Sanderson, Edward McVay, Peter
Allen, Sr., Jack Clifford, Matthew Foy, Hugh O'Don-

nell, John McLuckie, Sylvester Critchlow, Anthony Flaherty, Samuel Burkett, James Flannigan and Hugh Ross.

Murder of J. W. Kline—Jacob Stinner, Edward Burke, Jack Clifford, Hugh O'Donnell, Matthew Foy, William Foy and Hugh Ross.

Aggravated Riot—Hugh O'Donnell, G. W. Brown, Thos. H. Baynes, Isaac Byers, Harry Buck, Mark E. Baldwin, M. Cush, Frank Clark, Isaac Critchlow, Thos. J. Crawford, John Corcoran, John Dally, John Dierken, Jas. Dunn, John Edwards, Thos. Godfrey, W. H. Gaches, Jas. S. Hall, U. S. Grant Hess, —— Hennessey, Reid Kennedy, Thos. Kelly, Geo. W. Laughlin, H. H. Layman, Robt. G. Layman, Jack Lazear, Paddy McCool, David Maddigan, Owen Murphy, John McGovern, Wm. McLuckie, Punk, alias Pete McAllister, —— McLaughlin, William Oeffner, Dennis O'Donnell, John Alonzo Prim, Jack Prease, P. J. Rorke, Richard Scott, David H. Shanian, Newton Sharpe, John Sullivan, Oden Shoemaker, —— Taylor, George Holley or Wilkinson, Joseph Wayd, Peter Moran, Lewis Lewis, Patrick Fagan, W. H. Williams, Mike Naughton, Patrick Hayes "and certain other evil-disposed persons with force and arms, then and there, in manner and form aforesaid did make an aggravated riot, to the great terror and disturbance of all good citizens of the commonwealth, to the evil example of all others in like cases offending, contrary to the form of the act of the general assembly in such case made and provided, and againt the peace and dignity of the commonwealth of Pennsylvania."

Aggravated Riot—Peter Allen, Joseph Akers, Thos. Antes, Oliver P. Antes, Charles L. Atwood, E. G. Bail, Harry Bickerton, Wm. Bakely, Jack Bridges, Samuel Burkett, Ed. Burke, James Close, Jack Clifford, Thos. Connelly, Sylvester Critchlow, Robert Dalton, George Diebold, Fred. Gunston, Anthony Flaherty, James Flannigan, Matthew Foy, David Inchico, Evan Jones, E. C. McVay, John Murray, Peter Nan, Hugh Ross,

Benjamin Thomas, —— Sanderson, H. Troutman, W. Edward Williams, Oliver C. Coon, W. Mansfield.

Conspiracy—Hugh O'Donnell, Thos. N. Baynes, E. Bail, Isaac Byers, Wm. Bayard, G. W. Brown, Thos. J. Crawford, George Champeno, Isaac Critchlow, Miller Colgan, John Boyle, Jack Clifford, Dennis Cash, Oscar Colflesh, Wm. Conneghy, Mike Cummings, Wm. Combs, John Dierken, Pat Fagan, W. H. Gatches, Matthew Harris, Reed Kennedy, David Lynch, John Miller, O. S. Searight, John Murray, John McLuckie, Hugh Ross, Wm. T. Roberts, George Ryland, D. H. Hannon and George W. Sarver.

Having exhausted its catalogue of murder, riot and conspiracy charges, obtained true bills against 167 strikers, and buried the leading spirits among the Homesteaders beneath an avalanche of bail bonds, Mr. Frick now proceeded to play what he considered to be his trump card. The Supreme Court of Pennsylvania, of which at this time Hon. Edward Paxson, a close friend of C. L. Magee, was Chief Justice, came to Pittsburgh to hold its annual session. It was deemed possible that the Homestead affair might come before this body in some shape, after the lower courts disposed of it, but to nobody aside from the members of the Carnegie Company and their attorneys did it occur that the superior judiciary would, of its own motion, undertake to deal with the labor trouble at first hand.

This, however, was what Mr. Frick counted on as the culminating stroke which was to break the back of the Homestead strike. The step from the alderman's office to the supreme court room was one which probably no other individual or corporation in the state would have dreamt even of suggesting; but Mr. Frick managed to take it seemingly with as much ease as his secretary exhibited in getting a ward constable to lock up a few dozen of workingmen for riot or conspiracy.

The blow fell on the morning of September 30. The Chief Justice and his six associates met in the supreme court chamber of the county court house and held an hour's conference, at the expiration of which Judge Paxson sent for District Attorney Clarence Burleigh, and P. C. Knox, Esq., principal counsel for the Carnegie Company. When these two gentlemen arrived another hour was spent in consultation. Judge Paxson then sent for County Detective Harry Beltzhoover, whom he instructed to subscribe to an information made before him (Paxson) and to arrest the persons named therein. The information was worded as follows:

Commonwealth of Pennsylvania,

versus

David H. Shannon, John McLuckie, David Lynch, Thomas J. Crawford, Hugh O'Donnell, Harry Bayne, Elmer E. Ball, Isaac Byers, Henry Bayard, T. W. Brown, George Champene, Isaac Critchlow, Miller Colgan, John Coyle, Jack Clifford, Dennis M. Cush, William McConeghy, Michael Cummings, William Combs, John Durkes, Patrick Fagan, W. S. Gaches, Nathan Harris, Reid Kennedy, John Miller, O. O. Searight, John Murray, M. H. Thompson, Martin Murray, Hugh Ross, William T. Roberts, George Rylands and George W. Sarver.

Commonwealth of Pennsylvania, County of Allegheny.

Before me, the subscriber, Edward H. Paxson, chief justice of the supreme court of Pennsylvania and ex-officio justice of the court of oyer and terminer of Allegheny county, and a justice of the peace in and for the county of Allegheny, in the state of Pennsylvania, personally came Harry Beltzhoover, county detective, who upon oath administered according to law, deposeth and says that heretofore, to-wit, on or about the first day of July, A. D. 1892, the defendants above named, being inhabitants of and residents within the commonwealth of Pennsylvania and under protection of the laws of the commonwealth of Pennsylvania and owing allegiance and fidelity to the said commonwealth of Pennsylvania, not weighing the duty of their said allegiance, but wickedly devising and intending the peace and tranquility of the said commonwealth to disturb and stir, move and excite insurrection, rebellion and war against the said commonwealth of Pennsylvania, did at the borough of Homestead, and in the township of Mifflin, both within the county of Allegheny and state of Pennsylvania, and elsewhere within the state of Pennsylvania and beyond the borders of the state, unlawfully, falsely, maliciously and traitorously compass, imagine and intend to raise and levy war, insurrection and rebellion against the commonwealth of Pennsylvania, and in order to fulfil and bring into effect the said compassings, imaginations and intentions of them, the said defendants, afterward, to-wit, on the first day of July, A. D. 1892, and at divers other times at the borough of Homestead and in the township of Mifflin, with a great multitude of persons, numbering hundreds, armed and arrayed in a warlike manner, that is to say, with guns, revolvers, cannons, swords, knives, clubs and other warlike weapons, as well offensive as defensive, did then and there unlawfully, maliciously and traitorously join and assemble themselves together against the commonwealth of Pennsylvania, and then and there with force and arms did falsely and traitorously and in a hostile and warlike manner, array and dispose themselves against the said commonwealth of Pennsylvania and did ordain, prepare and levy war against the said commonwealth of Pennsylvania to the end that its constitution, laws and authority were defied, resisted and averted by the said defendants and their armed allies, contrary to the duty of allegiance and fidelity of the said defendants.

All of which the deponent states upon information received and believed by him, and he therefore prays that a warrant may issue, and the aforesaid defendants may be arrested and held to answer this charge of treason against the commonwealth of Pennsylvania.

The law under which the proceeding was brought is the Crimes act of 1860, under which the penalty for treason is fixed at a fine not exceeding $2,000 and imprisonment by separate and solitary confinement at labor, not exceeding twelve years.

It was announced that Judge Paxson would hear in person the application of any of the accused strikers for bail; that when the cases came before the grand jury he would instruct the jurymen as to what constitutes treason under the statutes of Pennsylvania, and that, if the cases should be brought to trial, he would sit on the bench in the court of oyer and terminer and try them himself. In short, Edward H. Paxson, Chief Justice of the Supreme Court of Pennsylvania, was master of the situation. The court of last resort had been by a Frickian turn of the wrist, converted into a court of preliminary resort, intermediate resort and all other known varieties of re-

ONE OF THE TRAITORS.

sort, and the strikers were led to understand accordingly that with Paxson armed to the teeth and ready to bring them to bay at all points, they might as well throw up the sponge at once and be done with it.

Detectives Farrell and Mills, assisted by a half dozen deputy sheriffs, were detailed to capture the defendants named in Beltzhoover's information. The task was not an easy one, for most of the reputed "traitors," realizing the difficulty of procuring bail, went into hiding and their friends took care to throw the officers off the track. Five of the men—Thomas Crawford, George Rylands, T. W. Brown, W. H. Baird and John Dierken —were caught on Friday, the day on which the warrant for their arrest was issued.

On Saturday, Attorneys Brennen and Cox went before Judge Paxson with a petition for the admission of the accused to bail. Messrs. Burleigh and Knox were called in, and, after a consultation, the Chief Justice made an order authorizing the release of any of the defendants on $10,000 bail at the discretion of any judge of the oyer and terminer court. Judges Kennedy and Porter heard the applications, but rejected the bondsmen offered except in the case of William Baird.

Despite the supposedly sacred character of the supreme bench, criticism of Judge Paxson's extraordinary action was freely indulged in by the members of the Pittsburgh bar and reproduced in the public press. Hardly a voice was raised in commendation of the Chief Justice's arbitrary interference, and the consensus of legal opinion, as mirrored in the newspapers, was to the effect that the disturbance at Homestead, being a purely local affair and directed against a private corporation, could not be construed as treason against the state.

The boldness with which this view of the case was stated by competent authorities gave much encouragement to the strikers, and at the regular weekly mass meeting, on Saturday, October 2, Vice-President Carney, of the Amalgamated Association, and other orators were emphatic in their claims that the treason charge was trumped up as a measure of intimidation and would fall to the ground if ever put to the test of a court trial. The strikers were, therefore, advised to stand their ground, and the Carnegie Company was warned that, when all the members of the advisory board were imprisoned, there would be other men to take their places, and that if all the men in Homestead were cast into jail the women would still be there to keep up the fight for the rights of organized labor. These sentiments were received with clamorous approval.

No little surprise was created by the publication of a statement from Major-General Snowden setting forth that he was originally responsible for the treason prosecution. During his sojourn at Homestead in command of the militia, General Snowden said, he had suggested to the Carnegie attorneys, Messrs. Knox and Reed, that the advisory committee was guilty of treason. The lawyers pooh-poohed the idea, but evidently thought better of it, for three weeks prior to the issuance of warrants by Judge Paxson, Mr. Knox met the General in Philadelphia and asked his help in the preparation of briefs. General Snowden responded that it would hardly be wise for him, while serving as commander of the state forces, to appear as counsel for the Carnegie Company. When the brief was prepared, however, it was sent to him to be passed upon and received his indorsement. General Snowden did not hesitate to say for publication that, in his opinion, death would be rather a mild penalty for members of the advisory committee.

Perhaps the most significant deliverance of the hour on the subject of the treason charge was that embodied in a letter written to the Pittsburgh *Commercial-Gazette* by the veteran jurist, Hon. Daniel Agnew, ex-chief justice of the Pennsylvania Supreme Court. Judge Agnew declared that the Homestead affair was riot and not treason. "It is easy," he said, "to distinguish treason from riot. It lies in the purpose or intent of the traitor to overthrow the government or subvert the law or destroy an institution of the state. Riot is a breach or violation of law, but *without a pnrpose against the state.*"

Those of the Homestead men charged with treason, who were not already held for murder, managed, for the most part, to find bail. Many continued in hiding. Burgess McLuckie, tired of running after bondsmen, had betaken himself to Youngstown, O., and, acting on the advice of Attorney W. T. Anderson, of that city, refused to return without a requisition. Honest John was lionized by the Youngstown people, delighted them with his speeches about high tariff and high fences and could have found a body guard any time to defy the Carnegie Company, the Supreme Court, the militia and all the other powers in Pennsylvania.

On the morning of Monday, October 10, the grand jury of Allegheny County assembled in the criminal court room, which was thronged with attorneys curious to watch the development of Judge Paxson's program. At 9.30 A. M., the Chief Justice entered accompanied by Judges Stowe, Kennedy, McClung and Porter, of the county courts, all of whom took seats on the bench while Judge Slagle sat with District Attorney Burleigh behind the clerk's desk.

The gravity of the occasion was felt by everyone and dead silence prevailed as Judge Kennedy opened the day's proceedings with a few words to the jurors stating that, in view of the unusual nature of the treason cases, Judge Paxson had "kindly consented" to instruct the jury.

The Chief Justice began his charge by explaining that his intervention was due to the supreme importance of furnishing an authoritative interpretation of the law in the Homestead cases and that he acted at the invitation of the county judges. He then entered upon a review of the conditions and events at Homestead. "The relation of employer and employee," he said, "is one of contract merely. Neither party has a right to coerce the other into the making of a contract to which the mind does not assent. The employer cannot compel his employee to work a day longer than he sees fit nor his contract calls for, nor for a wage that is unsatisfactory to him. It follows that the employee cannot compel his employer to give him work or to enter into a contract of hire, much less can he dictate the terms of employment. When the negotiations between the parties came to an end, the contract relations between them ceased. The men had no further demand upon the company, and they had no more interest or claim upon its property than has a domestic servant upon the household goods of his employer when he is discharged by the latter or when he voluntarily leaves his service, nor does it make any difference that a large number were discharged at one time; their aggregate rights rise no higher than their rights as individuals. The mutual right of the parties to contracts in regard to wages, and the character of the employment, whether by the piece or day, whether for ten hours or less, is as fixed and clear as any other right which we enjoy under the constitution and laws of this state. It is a right which belongs to every citizen, laborer or capitalist, and it is the plain duty of the state to protect them in the enjoyment of it."

The organization and plan of campaign of the Advisory Committee were reviewed at length, its chief object being stated as "to deprive the company of the use of its property and to prevent it from operating its works by the aid of men who were not members of the Amalgamated Association." Then followed a narrative of the Sheriff's preliminary manœuvres and of the Pinkerton expedition, as viewed from a strictly Paxsonian standpoint. After recounting the details of the battle at the mill landing, the surrender of the Pinkertons, and the occupation of Homestead by the military, the Chief Justice went on to say:

"We can have some sympathy with a mob driven to desperation by hunger as in the days of the French Revolution, but we have none for men receiving exceptionally high wages in resisting the law and resorting to violence and bloodshed in the assertion of imaginary rights, and entailing such a vast expense upon the tax-payers of the commonwealth. It was not a cry for bread to feed their famishing lips, resulting in a sudden outrage, with good provocation; it was a deliberate attempt by men without authority to control others in the enjoyment of their rights. * * * It is much to be feared that there is a diseased state of public opinion growing up with regard to disturbances of this nature, and an erroneous view of the law bearing upon these questions has found lodgment in the public mind. This is evidenced by the accounts of portions of the press, and it finds expression in the assurances of demagogues who pander to popular prejudices and in the schemes of artful politicians.''

Proceeding to the law in the case, the Chief Justice held that when the Carnegie Company employed watchmen to guard its works, "it mattered not to the rioters, nor to the public, who they were, nor whence they came. It was an act of unlawful violence to prevent their landing on the property of the company. That unlawful violence amounted at least to a riot upon the part of all concerned in it. If life was taken in pursuance of a purpose to resist the landing of the men by violence, the offense was murder, and perhaps treason.''

The legal definition of treason was then read and its supposed application to the Homestead conflict pointed out as follows:

"A mere mob, collected upon the impulse of the moment, without any definite object beyond the gratification of its sudden passions does not commit treason, although it destroys property and attacks human life.

But when a large number of men arm and organize themselves by divisions and companies, appoint officers and engage in a common purpose to defy the law, to resist its officers, and to deprive any portion of their fellow citizens of the rights to which they are entitled under the constitution and laws, it is a levying of war against the state, and the offense is treason ; much more so when the functions of the state government are usurped in a particular locality, the process of the commonwealth, and the lawful acts of its officers resisted and unlawful arrests made at the dictation of a body of men who have assumed the functions of a government in that locality ; and it is a state of war when a business plant has to be surrounded by the army of the state for weeks to protect it from unlawful violence at the hands of men formerly employed in it. Where a body of men have organized for a treasonable purpose, every step which any one of them takes in part execution of their common purpose is an overt act of treason in levying war. Every member of such asserted government, whether it be an advisory committee, or by whatever name it is called, who has participated in such usurpation, who has joined in a common purpose of resistance to the law and a denial of the rights of other citizens, has committed treason against the state. While the definition of this offense is the designing or accomplishment of the overturning of the government of the state, such intention need not extend to every portion of its territory. It is sufficient if it be an overturning of it in a particular locality, and such intent may be inferred from the acts committed. If they be such that the authority of the state is overturned in a particular locality, and a usurped authority substituted in its place, the parties committing it must be presumed to have intended to do what they have actually done. It is a maxim of criminal law that a man must be presumed to have intended that which is the natural and probable consequence of his acts. Thus, if a man assaults another with a deadly weapon, or aims a blow at a vital part, the law presumes that he intended to take life. Aliens domiciled within the state, and who enjoy its protection, owe temporary allegiance to it and are answerable for treason.''

In conclusion, Judge Paxson said: "We have reached the point in the history of the state when there are but two roads left us to pursue ; the one leads to order and good government, the other leads to anarchy. The great question which concerns the people of this country is the enforcement of the law and the preservation of order.''

While the events narrated in this chapter were in progress, while the workmen of Homestead were being taken to jail in batches and charge after charge heaped upon them, and while the Supreme Court of the state was engineering the last grand *coup* by which the revival of an obsolete offense was to be made instrumental in winding up the strike at Homestead, Mr. Andrew Carnegie was busily at work reaping encomiums for his philanthropy, which at this particular time found vent in the donation of a memorial library to the town of Ayr, in Scotland. The corner-stone of this edifice was laid by Mrs. Carnegie two days after the treason warrants were issued at Pittsburgh. An address of thanks was made by the mayor, to which Mr. Carnegie replied, part of his remarks being as follows: "I feel more strongly bound than ever to devote the remaining years of my life less to aims ending in self and more to the service of others, using my surplus wealth and spare time in the manner most likely to produce the greatest good to the masses of the people. From these masses comes the wealth which is entrusted to the owner only as administrator.'' A few groans and cries about Homestead were

all that reminded the audience which heard this gener-
ous-spirited speech that, at the very moment when Mr.
Carnegie was speaking, the wealth-givers in his own
employ were being hunted down as traitors, locked up
in jail and supplanted by cheaper workmen.

THE FERRY AT MUNHALL.

CHAPTER XVI.

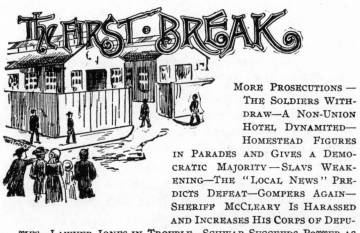

THE FIRST BREAK

MORE PROSECUTIONS — THE SOLDIERS WITH-DRAW—A NON-UNION HOTEL DYNAMITED—HOMESTEAD FIGURES IN PARADES AND GIVES A DEMOCRATIC MAJORITY—SLAVS WEAKENING—THE "LOCAL NEWS" PREDICTS DEFEAT—GOMPERS AGAIN—SHERIFF MCCLEARY IS HARASSED AND INCREASES HIS CORPS OF DEPUTIES—LAWYER JONES IN TROUBLE—SCHWAB SUCCEEDS POTTER AS SUPERINTENDENT—HOMESTEAD'S LAST RIOT—STRIKER ROBERTS HINTS AT DEFEAT—MECHANICS AND LABORERS GO BACK TO WORK.

A S an offset to the activity of Secretary Lovejoy, Burgess John McLuckie went before Alderman F. M. King on Wednesday, September 21, and lodged information for aggravated riot and conspiracy against H. C. Frick, George Lauder, Henry M. Curry, John G. A. Leishman, Otis Childs, F. T. F. Lovejoy, Lawrence C. Phipps, John A. Potter, G. A. Corey, J. F. Dovey, Nevin McConnell, William Pinkerton, Robert Pinkerton, John Cooper, C. W. Bedell, Fred Primer, W. H. Burt, Fred Heinde and others. In the information for conspiracy the defendants were charged with conspiring to "depress wages" and to incite riot by feloniously im-

porting a force of armed men. No arrests were made
on these informations. Blank bail bonds were signed
by the Mellon banking firm and filled in by the defendants.

Sheriff McCleary, while he no longer experienced
trouble in procuring a sufficient number of deputies at
$2.50 a day, to patrol every street in Homestead and en-
force order when necessary, found it a hard matter to in-
duce these emergency policemen to attend to their
duties. Non-union men coming out of the mill at noon
for dinner, were repeatedly assaulted, the intractable
element among the strikers caring little for the presence
of the sheriff's officers. Early in September, Mr. Mc-
Cleary quietly investigated the methods of his underlings, and ascertained that many of them were simply
taking a holiday at the county's expense. The force
was then reorganized, the loafers being summarily discharged. It was only now that the sheriff's pent-up
feelings found vent. He was utterly disgusted, he said,
and had come to the conclusion that, even if the salary
of the sheriff were increased to $15,000 a year, the man
who sought the office would be an idiot. The show of
authority which Mr. McCleary made had a visible effect
and when the deputies bestirred themselves order was
sufficiently restored, for the time being, to elicit from
Provost Marshal Mechling the opinion that, if the
sheriff kept on attending to business, the troops would
be withdrawn within two weeks.

Adjutant General Greenland was very severe on the
sheriff, whose incompetency, he said, was productive of
continual harassment to the troops. In General Greenland's opinion, it was in the sheriff's power, with twenty-

five deputies under his personal direction, to keep the peace at Homestead and enable the militia to withdraw.

The improvement in the work of the deputies had such a marked effect that, in the third week of September, the Fifteenth regiment was ordered home, and, on the last day of the month four companies of the Sixteenth regiment broke camp, leaving but four companies on the ground, one of which was posted on the hillside across the river from Homestead. Two weeks later, on October 13, the last of the militia received orders to leave, the first intimation of the good news being conveyed to the men when the band struck up "Home, Sweet Home" at the morning reveille. Tents were struck and baggage packed in short order, and at 10 A. M. the last vestige of the encampment was removed, and with a cheer that re-echoed among the hills the boys in blue marched to Munhall Station and were soon on the way to their homes in the oil country. The Homesteaders watched the departure without showing much feeling, although many of them, doubtless, experienced a consciousness of relief now that, after ninety-five days of military surveillance, the town was restored to the hands of the civil authorities. Henceforward the preservation of the peace was exclusively in the hands of the sheriff's deputies, thirty in number.

An outrage which caused considerable indignation about this time was the attempt made by unknown desperadoes to blow up the Mansion House, a hotel situated at the corner of Fifth avenue and Amity street, in the most populous quarter of Homestead. The establishment was conducted by Mrs. Marron, a widow who had been induced to come from Pittsburgh in order to provide boarding for employees of the Carnegie firm. She secured 40 boarders from among the clerks and non-union steelworkers employed in the mill. On the night of October 6, when the occupants of the hotel were sleeping, an explosive of some kind was thrown through a window of the dining-room on the ground floor. The missile exploded with great force, tore a hole through the floor and penetrated the cellar. Beyond the wrecking of an empty room, however, no damage was done. Mrs. Marron naturally laid the blame for the occurrence on the strikers, but they stoutly disclaimed responsibility and contended that the damage had been done by a natural gas explosion and not by a bomb thrown with intent to kill and destroy. Another theory which found favor among the men was that some wily foe to organized labor had done the mischief in order to discredit the cause of the strikers and hasten the end of the strike by altering the drift of public sympathy. Mr. Frick offered $1,000 for the arrest of the supposed dynamiter and $100 additional was offered by the advisory committee, but the reward was never earned.

The night of October 8 was made memorable by Homestead's share in the greatest Democratic parade held in Pittsburgh during the presidential campaign. Preparations for this event had been in progress for some time. In previous years Homestead had been a Republican stronghold, giving heavy majorities for high tariff candidates, but as has been signified in the preceding pages, political sentiment in the town had undergone a complete revulsion, and the men were determined to make this fact conspicuous in the Pittsburgh demonstration. Under the command of David Lynch and Charles

Guessner, 600 of the strikers marched in the parade, and were greeted with cheers all along the route. When the Homestead men arrived opposite the court house, they halted and gave three rousing cheers for Hugh O'Donnell and others of their associates who were confined in the county jail. Passing down Fifth Avenue, the Carnegie offices were reached. Here the marchers gave vent to their feelings in a chorus of groans.

Some of the transparencies carried in this notable procession spoke volumes for the influence of the Homestead trouble as a political factor. One bore a picture of a rooster and the inscription :

> "The cock will crow in '92
> Over Fort Frick and its Pinkerton crew."

On another appeared the query, "Who protects the 2,200 locked-out men in Lawrenceville?" and the response, "Ask McKinley," while on the reverse side was the defiant invitation:

> "Show us a man in a Pittsburgh mill
> Who had his wages raised by the McKinley bill."

The maker of this couplet may have been weak in the matter of rhythm, but the deadliness of his low tariff logic challenged and received admiration from the crowd.

Yet another legend worth noting was: "The Three (Dis) Graces—Protection for Carnegie, Persecution for his men and Pinkertons for support." At every glimpse of the mottoes quoted, the mob of on-lookers cheered lustily and it looked on that October night very much as though Pittsburgh, the headquarters of high tariff sentiment, had become suddenly inoculated with free-trade virus. There could be no mistaking the opinion of the crowd as to Mr. Frick and the Pinkertons. Evidently the friends of these worthies had accepted discretion as being the better part of valor and remained at home.

The eclat with which the Homesteaders performed their part of the political display in Pittsburgh encouraged them to repeat the demonstration still more energetically in their own town. October 23 was fixed as the date on which the cession of Homestead to the Democracy was to be celebrated. On that evening the town was profusely decorated, Chinese lanterns, bunting, starry flags and red fire contributing to the picturesqueness of the scene. The parade, held in honor of Cleveland and Stevenson, was headed by the best known Republicans in the district, including such notables as Thomas J. Crawford, W. T. Roberts, Captain O. C. Coon and William Gaches. Prominent among the emblems carried was a live sheep painted black, beside which stood a man arrayed as a negro wench. On the float occupied by this group was the motto, ''This is Protection.'' As the float moved along the street, men, women and children strained their lungs with the cry of ''Carnegie's Blacksheep!'' The success of the Homestead demonstration was the ''last straw,'' and Republican missionaries visited the benighted town no more.

The Hungarians continued to grow more and more restless as they saw the number of men in the mill increase and the chances of their getting back their jobs diminish correspondingly. All these foreigners belonged to the laboring class and it was especially hard for them to stand the strain of a long period of idleness. Arnold Frank, a representative of the race who continued in the

employ of the Carnegie Company, devoted himself to
quiet missionary work among his compatriots and took
frequent occasion to inform the newspapers that a break
in the ranks of the Slavs might be looked for at any
time.   Mr. Frank claimed to be the recipient of daily
applications for jobs from Hungarian strikers and that
these men were sick and tired of hardships endured for
the benefit of an organization which did not even admit
them to membership.   Slav leaders, who were loyal to
the Amalgamated Association, rebutted Mr. Frank's
statements, alleging that their fellow-countrymen received their full share of strike benefits and were just
as steadfast as any other class among the strikers.

Another cause of disquietude was a sudden change of
base on the part of the Homestead *Local News*, which
was originally the mouth-piece of the advisory board.
In its issue of October 15, the *News* editorially reviewed
the situation, setting forth that there were now over 2000
workmen in the mill, 200 of these being former Homestead employees, that recruits were daily being received
and preparations being made to accommodate a large additional number of non-unionists; and that business
men and intelligent members of the Amalgamated Association privately admitted that the battle was lost.   In
conclusion the article held these two conclusions to be
indisputable: "First—The Carnegie Company is gradually succeeding.   Second—The great Homestead strike
is gradually dying out."   The treachery of the *News*, as
the men regarded it, provoked unbounded indignation
among the strikers.   Nevertheless the truth of the statement made by the paper was privately conceded by many
Homestead people, and especially by the store-keepers,

whose capacity for doing business on trust was being taxed to an extent threatening some of them with bankruptcy. The sympathies of these people were entirely with the Amalgamated Association; but, on the other hand, the prospect of heavy loss to themselves, in case the strike should be a failure, stared them in the face, and the apparent success of the Carnegie Company in manning its works boded ill for the prospect of their recouping themselves.

One assertion made by the *News*, viz.: that 200 former Homestead employees had returned to work, was stigmatized as an absolute falsehood by the union leaders, who insisted that not one union man had forsaken his allegiance.

Two days later, a quartet of unionists, including a heater, a mechanic, an engineer and a laborer, applied for and obtained work. This was the first break in the ranks of the strikers that was openly made and admitted at Amalgamated headquarters.

A visit from Gompers at this time was a positive godsend. The pugnacious chief of the Federation arrived in state on October 21 and was met by a brass band and almost the entire population of the town. A procession was formed and the welcome visitor was escorted to the rink to the inspiring strains of "See, the Conquering Hero Comes." All representatives of the press, with the exception of the correspondent of the Pittsburgh *Leader*, were excluded from the meeting which followed, the preference given the *Leader* being due to the reputation exclusively enjoyed by that journal for giving fair treatment to organized labor. Thomas Crawford presided over the assemblage. Mr. Gompers made a vigorous speech, in the course of which he said :

"On a former occasion I explained the purpose underlying this contest, but a new feature has since developed. The militia has been withdrawn and the civil authority prevails. But we see the judges on the bench trying to distort the laws against the people of Homestead and against justice. Judge Paxson, holding the most honored position on the bench of this state, recently, in charging the grand jury regarding the men of Homestead, impressed upon their minds that these men were guilty of treason. When that charge was published in the press of the country it not only shocked the laboring men, their wives and children, but even the lawyers who could not or would not depend on his action.

"I am not a lawyer, but I don't think it necessary to be one to know what constitutes treason and what patriotism. Shall patriotism be measured by the yard-stick of the Carnegie firm or be weighed as their pig iron? Is it because these men in those latter days like those in Boston harbor, declared they had some rights and dared maintain them that they shall be declared traitors? The men who lost their blood and limbs on the field of battle to maintain and preserve this country and knock off the shackles of millions of slaves can not be construed as traitors, Judge Paxson's charge notwithstanding. Now some of your men are in prison, others out on bail, but you are now out three and one-half months on strike with your ranks practically unbroken. I would not ask you to stand out one moment longer than your rights demanded, but are there not some acts of the Carnegie firm that show you that you are working in a winning cause? Because you are here in Homestead you don't know the great victory you have won. In all great lockouts there are certain inconveniences to suffer and these must be endured, but if you were to end the struggle to-day you have won a victory. There are employers fair and unfair, and when they think of offering a reduction of wages to their employees in the future the fight you have waged will have some effect in the carrying out of this resolve. Don't you think your stand will have its effect on the workmen of this country? Not only here, but throughout the civilized globe, this fight will have its effect. The fraternity of the wage-workers of the civilized world is at hand. Be true to yourselves, one to the other, open and above board; and above all confer with those who are leading you and have your interest at stake and act with them jointly. No matter whether they may appear the enemies of our constitution or our country's institutions, it matters little. We propose to defend our country, its flag with its stars and stripes, in the face of those who would tear it down, for it represents our sovereign rights. We want to maintain the rights of the people and their manhood and we can only do this by organization—ready to stand by one another, ready to defend our constitution, the people of this country, the wageworkers and especially those of Homestead."

President Sheehan and Vice-President Carney, of the Amalgamated Association and others followed with brief addresses, declaring the fight to be practically won by the strikers and exhorting them to stand firm to the end. The men were much encouraged by these exhortations and comforted themselves with the reflection that when so many competent authorities predicted victory, the expectation of defeat must be merely the chimera of a diseased imagination.

Towards the end of October assaults on non-unionists became very frequent. Men were waylaid and beaten while going to and from work, and the non-union boarding houses were bombarded with bricks and stones. The attacking parties were seldom arrested, the deputies being rather disposed to keep under cover than to do aggressive detective work. A detail of coal and iron police was brought in to assist in quelling the disorders, but without improving the state of affairs to any perceptible extent, as many as six non-unionists being attacked with slung-shots and other weapons in a single evening, despite the vigilance of deputies and policemen combined.

At length Sheriff McCleary, perceiving that a dangerous crisis was threatened, added 50 deputies to his force and thus succeeded in checking the tendency to lawlessness. Ninety-one of the non-union workmen were also sworn in as deputies.

The sheriff attributed the spread of insubordination mainly to the influence of Hon. D. R. Jones, an attorney who had at one time been president of the Miners' Union and who had served two terms in the legislature. Mr. Jones was called in to defend James Holleran, who had resisted arrest for disordorly conduct and been aided by a number of strikers at whose hands the deputy sheriffs received rough usage. At the hearing, which was held before 'Squire Oeffner, Mr. Jones said that "the person under arrest and all others not only exercised a right but performed a sacred duty in resisting unless the officer had a warrant for the arrest." The defendant was held in $500 bail for court, but his friends construed Attorney Jones' remarks as exonerating Holleran and all others who undertook to resist a deputy venturing to make an arrest without a warrant. In this way, the sheriff contended, the disorderly element was

incited to misconduct and Mr. Jones should be held responsible. Application was made before Judge McClung
by the sheriff's attorney asking that Mr. Jones be summoned to explain his action in court. An order was
made accordingly and Mr. Jones in response set up the
defense that his utterances had been misrepresented and
misunderstood and that he had not aimed at kindling
disaffection and lawlessness. This explanation was accepted and the matter dismissed.

The prevalence of disorder caused a meeting of protest to be held by the leading professional and business
men of Homestead, and resolutions were adopted calling
upon the sheriff, in case the trouble continued and he
should be unable to suppress it, to apply to the Governor
for aid. The members of the advisory board also condemned the disposition to defy the law and used their
best efforts to put a stop to the misdeeds of the rougher
element.

William Gaches, treasurer of the strikers' organization, was kept busy, day in and day out, receiving and disbursing funds for the relief of the strikers, although as
time wore on, the golden stream of contributions began
to dwindle unpleasantly. A goodly lift was given to
the relief fund by the celebration of "Homestead Day"
in Chicago, on October 29, when each of the 90,000
union workmen in that city was expected to contribute
a day's wages. The receipts from this source were estimated by the newspapers at $40,000. Even that sum,
however, was only a stop-gap. A mint of money was
needed to support the 4,000 idle men at Homestead,
and, however generous the subscriptions from abroad, it
was impossible that the enormous expense of maintain-

ing this army of unemployed persons could be kept up much longer.

Mr. Frick was a steady visitor to the works and made arrangements for elaborate improvements. He rather surprised the strikers by removing John A. Potter from the superintendency and substituting Charles M. Schwab, who had been serving as manager of the Braddock mill. As Mr. Schwab was known to be a genial and amiable gentleman, and Mr. Potter was the reverse of popular, the strikers formed the conclusion that the removal of the latter was intended to placate them, and perhaps to serve as a means of hastening desertions from the Amalgamated ranks. Mr. Potter lost nothing by the change, inasmuch as he was appointed chief mechanical engineer of the Carnegie Company, a transfer which was equivalent to a promotion.

The first week of November was marked by a feeling of unusual uneasiness among the Amalgamated men. Dissatisfaction was rife among the mechanics and desertions from their ranks began to multiply rapidly. Superintendent Schwab labored industriously among the old hands, holding out extraordinary inducements to tempt back to work those whose superior skill rendered their services almost indispensable.

The Federation officials sought to buoy the men up and revive the determined spirit which had been exhibited in the early stages of the conflict. Mr. Gompers taxed his powers of oratory to the utmost. William Weihe, Chris. Evans, David Lynch and others made stirring appeals; but all without avail. Disaffection had found a lodgment and it was too late now to prevent the stampede which every one felt was soon to come.

Such was the condition of things when election day, November 8, was ushered in. The grand effort by which Homestead was to discard Republicanism as a rebuke to advocates of one-sided protection was to be the last combined effort of any kind that the workingmen of the devoted town were to make. Hugh O'Donnell, then confined in the county jail, was the only Homesteader of prominence that refused to go over to the Democracy. Hugh was, of course, debarred from voting, but he made up for this deprivation by sending out for publication a letter in which he said: "All the enemies of the locked-out men at Homestead are Democrats from Governor Pattison down, including General Snowden, Chief Justice Paxson, the New York *Sun* and other Democratic papers."

The election returns gave Homestead to the Democrats by an average majority of 137. David Lynch, who was a candidate for the legislature, received the highest vote, his majority being 300. The strikers were jubilant over the result and held high carnival on the day after election.

On Sunday, November 14, Homestead saw its last riotous demonstration. The affair arose out of an altercation between two colored non-unionists and a striker. The striker knocked down one of the negroes and was joined in an instant by a crowd of men, women and children, eager to lend a hand. The negroes drew revolvers and fled, firing into the crowd as they ran. At City Farm Lane, six more negroes joined the fugitives, and the whole party ran to their boarding-house and barred themselves in. An angry mob surrounded the house, tore down the fence and was about to burn the place, when a posse of deputies and borough officers arrived and placed the negroes under arrest. While the prisoners were on their way to the lock-up they were assailed with stones and clubs, and it was only by drawing revolvers and threatening to fire that the deputies succeeded in protecting themselves and the poor wretches in their custody. The striker who was concerned in the beginning of the outbreak and one of his companions were also placed under arrest. These men, as well as most of the negroes, were pretty severely wounded.

The usual Saturday afternoon meeting on November 13 was marked by symptoms indicating only too plainly that the end was near at hand. William T. Roberts, fresh from a campaigning tour in the East, made an address substantially conceding that the cause of unionism at Homestead was on its last legs. He spoke of the desertion of the finishers from the ranks of the Amalgamated Association as an assault on the integrity of organized labor inspired by the Carnegie people for the purpose of defeating the Homestead men and added, "In view of the confidence you have placed in me, I don't propose to come here and tell you that everything is rosy when it is not. If you think with this combined opposition in your own ranks you can fight it out to the end, I am with you." The men, being asked what they wished to do, shouted with one voice, "Fight it out to the end!" There were few among them, however, that did not comprehend the intent of Mr. Robert's words. The first doubt of ability to go on with the strike had been openly expressed by one of their own leaders and listened to without protest. This was the beginning of the end.

Another circumstance showing that a crisis was at hand was the convocation of the advisory boards of Homestead, Lawrenceville and Beaver Falls at the Pittsburgh headquarters of the Amalgamated Association, to consider the question whether or not the strikes at those places should be declared off. It could not be ignored that enthusiasm was flagging, and the flow of contributions falling off to a degree that was positively perilous. The committeemen, nevertheless, could not nerve themselves to face the consequences of ordering a discontinuance. Had they done so the failure of the strikes would undoubtedly have been charged up to their account by the majority of their fellow-workmen, and they would be in the position of making a thankless sacrifice.

The reader has already been informed of the manner in which the Lawrenceville and Beaver Falls strikes came to an end. At Homestead, the mechanics and laborers were the first to weaken. These men, to the number of about 2000, met on the morning of Thursday, November 18, and appointed a committee to wait upon the Amalgamated men and submit the proposition that the strike be declared off and the mechanics and laborers be released from further obligations. The Amalgamated men met in the evening, with President Weihe in the chair.

The proposition of the mechanics and laborers was rejected by a vote of 106 to 75.

A ballot was then taken on the advisability of continuing the strike and resulted in an affirmative decision by a vote of 224 to 129.

A committee was appointed to notify the mechanics and laborers that they could act as they liked, but

that the Amalgamated Association would not be responsible for their actions.

Next morning the mechanics and laborers re-convened,
received the report of the committee of the Amalgamated Association, and agreed unanimously to return to
work, but under no circumstances to accept tonnage
jobs, as by so doing they would trespass on the rights of
the Amalgamated men.

The meeting adjourned quickly, and the men proceeded at once to the mill and put in their applications
for reinstatement. More than half of the mechanics
were turned away, as the number of vacancies was limited, but the laborers were all put to work or assured of
employment in a few days. So great was the rush of
returning prodigals that two clerks were required to
make out passes for the applicants. Chairman Frick was
on hand to supervise the re-employment of the old men
and enjoyed, in his undemonstrative way, the successful
culmination of his plans to break up unionism in
Homestead.

CHAPTER XVII.

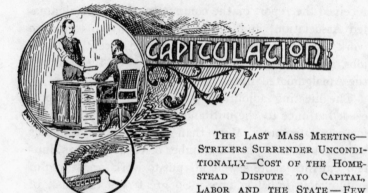

CAPITULATION

THE LAST MASS MEETING—
STRIKERS SURRENDER UNCONDI-
TIONALLY—COST OF THE HOME-
STEAD DISPUTE TO CAPITAL,
LABOR AND THE STATE — FEW
OLD HANDS GET WORK AND
POVERTY STALKS ABROAD—NOBLE SERVICE OF RELIEF COMMIT-
TEES—THE COMING OF SANTA CLAUS—CONGRESSIONAL INVESTI-
GATIONS WIND UP WITHOUT ACCOMPLISHING ANYTHING—A BATCH
OF USELESS REPORTS—THE KEARNS ANTI-PINKERTON BILL BE-
COMES A LAW IN PENNSYLVANIA.

THE secession of the mechanics and laborers was all
that was wanting to complete the discouragement
of the tonnage men. The usual mass meeting was
held in the rink on Saturday, November 20, but the
leaders, perceiving that a crisis was imminent, decided
to exclude all who were not members of the lodges and
only about 500 strikers took part in the secret deliberations which followed. Addresses were made by Vice
Presidents Lynch and Carney, of the Amalgamated
Association. Thomas Crawford, Chairman of the
Advisory Board, was not present, and the information
was conveyed to the meeting that he had resigned in or-

der to take a position in a mill at Uniontown, **Pa.**, and
that Richard Hotchkiss, Secretary of the board, had
been appointed to fill the vacancy. The discussion
turned mainly on the necessity, now self-evident, **of**
abandoning the strike and declaring the Homestead **mill**
open to union men. It was manifestly the sense of the
meeting that this step should be taken, but the men re-
coiled from it, and, after a debate lasting four hours, action was deferred until the following day.

It was a mournful little band that assembled in the
rink on Sunday morning. In that memorable meeting-
place which had again and again resounded with trium-
phant oratory and with the plaudits of sanguine multi-
tudes, less than 300 dispirited men now came together
to register the confirmation of their defeat. There were
some who argued passionately against capitulation. To
yield, they said, would be to hasten the disintegration
of the Amalgamated Association. Better go naked and
starve than sacrifice the principles on the vindication of
which the men of Homestead had staked everything.
But this reasoning was of no avail. A standing vote
was taken on the question of declaring the mill open and
the proposition was carried by 101 to 91.

There was no outburst when the result was declared.
The men sat and stared at one another for a few seconds,
and then dropped out of the hall in twos and threes,
some of them giving vent to their feelings in bitter denunciations of the action of the majority.

The news caused little excitement through the town.
It was no more than had been expected, and, for the
most part, the people were glad of it, for it had long
been understood that the continuance of the unequal

struggle with the Carnegie Company meant an increased burden of debt and poverty.

It was among the outside sympathizers that the keenest regret was felt over the failure of the strike. Messrs. Powderly, Devlin, Wright and other high officers of the K. of L. deplored the collapse, and here and there K. of L. men took occasion to lay the blame on the shoulders of Samuel Gompers and his associates in the management of the Federation.

Hugh O'Donnell gave his opinion of the ending of the strike in the appended letter to the Pittsburgh *Leader:*

"EDITOR LEADER:—In reply to your request for an expression of opinion concerning the action of the men at Homestead in declaring the strike off, I can say but little at the present time. Owing to the fact that certain of my acts in that most memorable struggle are *sub judice*, I am not in a position to criticize the acts of my late associates. Great battles are rarely, if ever, fought as planned. The world has never witnessed before so much suffering and sacrifice for a cause. The action of the three thousand laborers and mechanics who came out with our men on pure principle alone is unexampled in the history of labor struggles.

"But to the men in the Lawrenceville and Beaver Falls mills too much praise cannot be given. Their loyalty and steadfastness to the principles for which they were contending should never be forgotten. Out of consideration for them I regret that the Homestead struggle should have terminated in the manner in which it did.   HUGH O'DONNELL.

"Allegheny county jail, November 21."

Secretary Lovejoy contented himself with assuring the newspapers that the surrender would have no effect on the cases of the strikers under arrest, as far as the Carnegie firm was concerned.

On Monday the Advisory board disbanded and the dissolution of the workingmen's once great and powerful organization was complete.

The battle for the preservation of the integrity of this body had been fought at a fearful cost. The outlay on the side of the Carnegie Company has never been made known, but it cannot have fallen short of $250,000. The workmen, in the course of twenty weeks of idleness, lost $850,000 in wages, and the expense to the state of maintaining the militia at Homestead was about $500,000. In round numbers then, the total cost of the strike to all parties involved, allowing for the pay of deputy sheriffs, the expense of court trials and the relief funds, may be set down at *two million dollars*, an enormous sum to be paid for the gratification of Mr. Frick's desire to get rid of unions and unionism. Inasmuch, however, as but a small portion of this amount came out of the coffers of the Carnegie Company, Mr. Frick had no reason to feel dissatisfied. His victory was in reality, a cheap one. Had he not precipitated a bloody conflict by shipping Pinkertons to Homestead and in this way secured the support of the entire military force of Pennsylvania, there is no telling how long the strike might have been continued and how heavy the loss that might have been inflicted on the firm by the stoppage of operations.

The last restraint having been removed, hundreds of men who had been active among the strikers now thronged the mill office and besieged the officials with applications for positions. Superintendent Schwab began receiving the applicants at 9 o'clock on Monday morning. At that hour about 500 men were in line.

The men were admitted in groups of five and those who
were not black-listed as dangerous rioters received per-
mits authorizing them to file their applications with the
superintendents of the various departments. The line
of waiting ones kept constantly growing and it was not
until 4 o'clock that Mr. Schwab and his assistants were
enabled to wind up·their labors. Unfortunately the
number of vacancies was so small that but few of the
old employees could be accommodated by the super-

DISCUSSING THE SURRENDER.

intendents, and fully 2,500 men were left to keep the
wolf from the door as best they could, without the
assurance of early employment. The prospect confronting these unfortunates was disheartening in the extreme.
Most of them were already embarrassed in consequence
of their long idleness. Rent and taxes were unpaid,
the endurance of grocers and butchers was exhausted,
and with winter at hand and no money in sight to pur-

chase the necessaries of life, what was to become of these destitute workingmen and their families?

The Amalgamated Association came at once to the relief of its own members, a large number of whom were on the blacklist, by voting the payment of $6 a week to each as long as he should be out of employment. The ordinary financial resources of the lodges would not have justified this step, but contributions continued to come in and the special necessity for relief now exhibited was recognized by union workingmen everywhere.

The events of the next two weeks after the strike was declared off showed but little brightening of the outlook. By actual count there were 2,715 men on the pay rolls of the mill on the day when the mechanics and laborers went back to work. Two weeks later there were 3,121 men employed in the works, from which showing it will be seen that out of 2,200 men who had applied for reinstatement only 406 obtained employment. Almost all of these were laborers.

At the call of Burgess Hollingshead, successor to Honest John McLuckie, a meeting of citizens was held to consider plans for the relief of the many cases of absolute destitution reported in the town. Dr. Purman presided and J. H. Rose acted as secretary. David Lynch explained to those present that the Amalgamated men would take care of themselves, but that the suffering among those for whom the Association could not undertake to provide was intense and demanded prompt measures for its alleviation. A committee consisting of David Lynch, William Gaches and Harry Bayne was appointed to investigate the immediate needs of the people, and a fund was started on the spot by the subscrip-

tion of $200 among the citizens in attendance.   After a
few days' work the sub-committee reported to the general committee, and on the strength of the information
presented the following appeal was adopted:

"There are 218 families in Homestead and vicinity
in a state of destitution.   This fact has been ascertained
by a competent committee, consisting of three persons,
appointed at a citizens' meeting held on Friday evening,
December 2, 1892.   The undersigned committee was
appointed as a result of the above investigation to issue
this appeal to the country, asking public aid in caring
for these destitute families.   The strike is over, but less
than 800 of the 3,800 former workmen of the Carnegie
Steel Company have as yet secured employment in the
mill, and only a limited number elsewhere.   It is highly
improbable that this vast body of unemployed men
will be able to secure work for many weeks to come.
This means prolonged and increasing distress.   The
people of Homestead, although liberal in their contributions, are unable to provide for the demands of such
general want.   This call is an urgent one, and the public must assist us."

The general relief committee perfected its organization
by electing Burgess Hollingshead president, William
Gaches, treasurer, and George Hadfield, secretary.   Mr.
Hollingshead was authorized to receive money contributions and turn them over to the treasurer, and to Mr.
Hadfield was assigned the duty of receiving donations of
food, fuel and clothing.

One of the first subscriptions received was the sum of
$25 from the employees of Kaufman Brothers of Phila-
delphia, transmitted by the city editor of the Philadelphia
Record.   Others poured in rapidly, the business people
of Pittsburgh being especially liberal in their response

to the demands upon them. The Building Trades council appointed a committee to take charge of the Pittsburgh donations, with Vice President Michael Sharran
at the head. Mr. Sharran, assisted by Mr. D. S. Mitchell,
labored with untiring activity and these two men were
instrumental in securing thousands of dollars worth of
supplies.

Among the most liberal contributors was Mrs. J. M.
Gusky, head of the great clothing firm of J. M. Gusky
& Company, a lady noted for her charities and always
foremost to respond in emergencies such as that occur-
ing at Homestead.

Kaufmann Brothers and Eisner & Philipps gave an
immense quantity of clothing. W. M. Laird contributed a sufficient quantity of shoes for all claimants, and
the large grocery and commission firms forwarded provisions of all kinds.

The Pittsburgh *Press* raised a fund of $2,500 in addi-
tion to supplies of clothing and other necessaries, and
the *Dispatch* collected over $700, to which was added
$300 from the charitable people of Washington, D. C.

As Christmas drew near, public sympathy was more
and more keenly aroused in behalf of the Homestead
sufferers. A few days before that holiday of holidays,
the children in the Homestead public schools were instructed to write letters to Santa Claus, asking for whatever they most desired. Nearly all the letters contained
requests for shoes and other necessaries. Many of them
were published in the newspapers and spoke volumes
for the unhappy condition of the poorer class of strikers
and their families.

Santa Claus was not missing, however, when the

eventful morning came, nor were the other essentials of a merry Christmas conspicuous by their absence. One thousand turkeys came from the kind hearted working-men of McKeesport and 300 from Mrs. Gusky, and the heart of every child was gladdened by the gift of a picture book and a box of candy from Kaufmann Bros. of Pittsburgh.

The Homestead relief committee kept up its good work until the end of March, by which time the necessities of the people ceased to be pressing. A report was then published showing receipts amounting to $5,587.28, of which $4,926.79 had been expended in relieving distressed families. A committee of three was appointed to use the unexpended balance in relief work, and the general committee then dissolved, having excellently discharged its mission.

Reference has already been made to the appointment of a committee of United States senators to investigate the Homestead affair and the postponement of action by Senator Gallinger, the Republican chairman of that committee, until after the presidential election. Within two weeks after election day, Senators Gallinger and Pfeffer began the inquiry at Chicago, where a hearing was given to Pinkerton agents and authorities on police methods, the latter submitting opinions on the best means of coping with labor disturbances. Chief of Police McClaughrey advocated the removal of the police force in great cities from the field of politics and placing municipal departments under a civil service system, and Marshal Hitchcock suggested the enactment of a law providing a severe penalty for refusing to serve on a *posse comitatus.* On November 23, Messrs. Gallinger and Pfeffer arrived in Pittsburgh. The other members of the committee, Messrs. Hansbrough, of North Dakota ; Felton, of California; Sanders, of Montana; White, of Lousiana, and Hill, of New York, did not find it convenient to attend. The testimony taken was mainly a repetition of that given before the House Committee. Captain Rodgers repeated his tale of the adventures of the Little Bill; Superintendent Potter told of the innocence of the purpose entertained in the bringing in of the Pinkertonian Three Hundred ; William Weihe explained how easily the trouble could have been adjusted if the Carnegie firm had desired an amicable settlement and condemned the facilities afforded for the importation of cheap labor in violation of the contract labor law ; David Lynch and William G. Roberts testified to the peaceable disposition of the Homestead men prior to the Pinkerton invasion and their respect for the property rights of their employers; A. C. Robertson, a politician who had formerly been a glass blower, condemned arbitration, whether voluntary or compulsory, as a failure, and ex-Judge Thomas Mellon declared the employment of armed guards during strikes to be necessary because there is "too much politics" to permit of the proper enforcement of the law.

After a visit to the Homestead mill, the committee proceeded directly to New York where the testimony of Robert A. Pinkerton and Captain Heinde was heard. The Pinkerton chief described the men sent to Homestead as model citizens. It had been agreed, he said, that the guards should be sworn in as deputy sheriffs. There had been no firing from the barges until after the captain was shot, and then only in sheer self-defense.

Witness claimed that his agency had lost $15,000 by the Homestead affair, owing to the seizure of 225 rifles and other property, and the cost of caring for men hurt in the battle. He thought it doubtful that Mr. Carnegie would reimburse the agency. Being asked if he thought that the violence committed at Homestead was due to the strikers or to the rabble attracted there, he said: "I think it was committed by the strikers, their leaders and the advisory committee itself." Captain Heinde's evidence was merely a recital of the events of July 6. With his examination the investigation was concluded.

The report of the committee, presented to the senate on February 11, 1893, denounced the employment of Pinkertons as "an utterly vicious system, responsible for much of the ill-feeling and bad blood displayed by the working classes," and suggested that if Mr. Frick had carried out the humane policy enunciated by Mr. Carnegie in his famous article in the *Forum*, the Homestead strike might have been avoided. At the same time, it declared that there was "no excuse for the scenes of disorder and terrorism for which the strikers were themselves responsible," and that "laboring men should learn the lesson that they cannot better their condition by violating the law or resisting lawful authority." The committee doubted the power of Congress to mend matters by legislation, and advised arbitration as the only middle ground on which employer and employe could meet without depreciating the rights of either.

About this time the House committee on investigation of the Homestead strike awoke from its lethargy and Messrs. Ray and Broderick, the Republican members, handed in a minority report, condemning the employ-

ment of armed guards, but advising that legislation on
this question be left to the several states. In the judgment of the minority of the committee the "present
system of federal taxation" had nothing to do with the
Homestead strike, which was in reality a struggle for
supremacy between organized capital and organized
labor.

The majority report was presented shortly afterwards.
It held that Mr. Frick should have united with the
sheriff of Allegheny county, without regard to the ineffic-
iency of that officer, in an appeal to the governor, instead of undertaking to crush the strikers on his own
account; criticized the Amalgamated Association as a
body the members of which were encouraged to become
intemperate zealots, denied the right of the Homestead
men to oppose the landing of the Pinkertons, and ended
by suggesting that it be left to the several states to enact
laws regulating Pinkertonism.

Individual minority reports were presented as follows:

By Mr. Broderick, advocating the passage of a compulsory arbitration law by the states.

By Mr. Buchanan, of New Jersey, declaring the investigation to have acted as a boomerang against the
Democrats in that it showed a high protective tariff to
be productive of high wages.

By Mr. Boatner, claiming that, under the clause of
the constitution which authorizes the inter-state com-
merce law, inter-state carriers can be prevented from
hiring Pinkertons.

By Mr. Stockdale, of Mississippi, claiming that' the
Pinkertons were trespassers; and

By Messrs. Bynum and Layton confessing their inability to find a remedy for conflicts between capital and labor.

All the reports cited having been duly read and filed away by the two branches of Congress, the Homestead question was thereupon dropped by general consent and, its political utility having vanished, was heard of no more in the national legislature.

The Pennsylvania legislature, which assembled in January, 1893, was obliged to meet the Pinkerton question squarely. All the members of the lower branch of that body—the House of Representatives—and one-half of the members of the senate came fresh from the people, having been chosen in the November elections, and a large proportion of them stood pledged to their constituents to aid in the passage of an anti-Pinkerton bill. Many measures of this character were introduced, but that upon which support was centered, by common consent, was a bill introduced by Representative John Kearns, of Pittsburgh, a gentleman in close touch with organized labor. The Kearns bill was entitled "An Act relative to the appointing of special deputies, marshals, detectives or policemen by sheriffs, mayors or other persons authorized by law to make such appointments, and by individuals, associations or corporations incorporated under the laws of this State or any other State of the United States, and making it a misdemeanor for persons to exercise the functions of an officer without authority."

The bill underwent some vicissitudes, which delayed its passage until May, although introduced early in January and advanced on the House calendar through Mr. Kearns' energetic efforts. At one stage in its progress, a proviso was added requiring that any person appointed or deputized to perform the duties of special deputy, marshal, policeman or detective should be "of known good moral character and temperate habits" and should give bond in a considerable sum for the faithful performance of his duties. This provision was attacked because of its being presumably aimed at the low class of detectives employed by the Law and Order society of Pittsburgh, which was just then making war on Sunday newspapers and lobbying against a bill for the protection of journals publishing Sunday editions, and for this reason it was eliminated. The word "detectives" was stricken out of the title and, as it was feared that the bill might interfere with the appointment of regular policemen in municipalities, a special proviso to prevent such a result was added in the senate.

As finally enacted into a law, signed by the governor, and placed upon the statute books, the measure reads as follows:

SECTION 1. Be it enacted by the Senate and House of Representatives of the Commonwealth of Pennsylvania in General Assembly met, and it is hereby enacted by the authority of the same, That no sheriff of a county, mayor of a city, or other person authorized by law to appoint special deputies, marshals or policemen in this Commonwealth to preserve the public peace and prevent or quell public disturbances, and no individuals, association, company or corporation incorporated under the laws of this State or of any other State of the United States and doing business in this State, shall hereafter appoint or employ as such special deputy, marshal or policeman any person who shall not be a citizen of this Commonwealth.

SECTION 2. That any person who shall in this

Commonwealth without due authority pretend or hold himself out to any one as a deputy sheriff, marshal, policeman, constable or peace officer, shall be deemed guilty of misdemeanor.

SECTION 3. Any person or persons, company or association, or any person in the employ of such company or association violating any of the provisions of this act shall be guilty of a misdemeanor and upon conviction shall be sentenced to pay a fine not exceeding five hundred dollars, or undergo an imprisonment not exceeding one year, or both or either at the discretion of the court.

Provided, That if any company or association be convicted under this act it shall be sentenced to pay a fine not exceeding five thousand dollars.

Provided further, That the provisions of this act shall not be construed as applying to policemen, constables or specials appointed by municipalities for municipal purposes.

As long as the Kearns act stands—and it is safe to say that it is not likely ever to be repealed—the Pinkerton Detective Agency is effectually barred out of Pennsylvania.

CHAPTER XVIII.

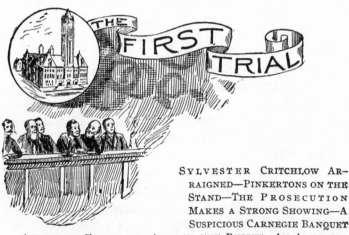

SYLVESTER CRITCHLOW AR-
RAIGNED—PINKERTONS ON THE
STAND—THE PROSECUTION
MAKES A STRONG SHOWING—A
SUSPICIOUS CARNEGIE BANQUET
—ATTORNEYS ERWIN AND ARGO TO THE RESCUE—AN ALIBI FOR
THE DEFENSE—JOHN S. ROBB ATTACKS MR. ERWIN—THE "NORTH-
WESTERN WHIRLWIND'S" MAGNIFICENT ORATION—HE CAPTURES
THE COURT AND CONFOUNDS THE PROSECUTION—"NOT GUILTY"
—THE BACKBONE OF THE MURDER CHARGES BROKEN.

SYLVESTER CRITCHLOW was the first of the
Homestead men to be placed on trial in the Allegheny County Criminal Court, the charge against
him being the murder of T. J. Connors.

On the morning of November 18, 1892, Critchlow
was arraigned before Judges Kennedy and McClung.
A great crowd assembled in the court room, curious to
observe the opening scenes in the memorable legal
battle which was to ensue, but to the great disappointment of the throng, the judges ordered the room to be

cleared of all except members of the bar, witnesses, jurors and reporters.

The prisoner was perfectly cool and self possessed. His wife and mother sat near him, watching with womanly solicitude every step in the proceedings, the issue of which meant so much to both.

The array of legal talent on both sides was formidable. The prosecution was in the hands of District Attorney Burleigh, assisted by Messrs. D. F. Patterson, John S. Robb, E. Y. Breck, P. C. Knox and Assistant District Attorney Harry Goehring. Counsel for the defense were: Messrs. W. W. Erwin and G. W. Argo, of St. Paul, Minn.; E. A. Montooth, Thomas M. Marshall, William J. Brennen and William Reardon, of Pittsburgh, and John F. Cox, of Homestead.

Immediately upon the opening of court, Critchlow was ordered to stand up, and having heard the charge read, pleaded not guilty in a clear, firm tone of voice. Attorney Brennen asked to have the indictment quashed on the ground of an irregularity in the drawing of the grand jury panel. The motion was overruled, and the selection of jurors began, this process being conducted by Mr. Burleigh for the prosecution and Mr. Marshall for the defense. Within a few hours, the following "good men and true" were selected: Peter Roth, John Herron, James Marshall, Amos Mashey, Chris Wiggand, C. S. Eaton, Chris A. Sende, James M. Wright, D. J. Herlehy, W. A. Freyvogel, Burns Wadsworth and Louis Jackman.

The District Attorney, in his opening speech, after having given the conventional explanation as to degrees of murder, asked the jury to avoid the impression that the case on trial was one of treason or was to be considered in connection with Homestead. "We are," he said, "simply trying Sylvester Critchlow for the murder of T. J. Connors, who was killed in the barges at Homestead on July 6. The barges were there lawfully and for a peaceable purpose. . . . We will show that Sylvester Critchlow was behind the barricade with a rifle, shooting down to the barges within easy range of Connors, and firing in a direction in which he would likely hit Connors."

"You must also remember, gentlemen, that the Commonwealth of Pennsylvania is the prosecutor and Sylvester Critchlow is the defendant. There is no private prosecutor here. The case will be prosecuted by public officials and no one else will be allowed to interfere. Other counsel may appear in the case, but they will be in subordination to the district attorney."

Dr. McKennan, Superintendent W. A. Cowan, of the West Penn hospital and Rev. Father Leonard Lynch were the first witnesses examined. They testified to the death of Connors and the nature of his wound.

Captain John W. Cooper, of the Pinkerton agency, followed with the familiar story of the river expedition and the battle at the landing. He also swore positively to the position of Connors at the time when he was shot and the hour at which he fell.

Captain Cooper was subjected to a searching cross-examination by Mr. Brennen, but went through the ordeal without permitting himself to become confused. Mr. Brennen sought to show (1) that the witness was not of good moral character and (2) that Connors was accidentally shot by one of his own comrades.

At one point the cross-examination ran as follows:

MR. BRENNEN.—Were you not a "Hey Rube" for a circus for nine years?

MR. BURLEIGH.—What in the name of common sense is a "Hey Rube?"

JUDGE KENNEDY.—Yes, Mr. Brennen, we would like to know what you mean by a "Hey Rube."

MR. BRENNEN.—I mean a circus fighter. The witness knows what I mean.

WITNESS.—I was detailed by the Pinkerton agency to accompany the Barnum circus in the capacity of a detective. I was with the circus for nine years.

W. H. Burt, also a Pinkerton detective, recounted the incidents of the fight at the landing and described the shooting of Connors as follows: "I knew T. J. Connors. He was on the boat. I saw him between 11 and 12 o'clock that day. That was before he was shot. He was near the bow of the boat. Three or four minutes later I saw two men picking him up. He had fallen about twenty-five feet from the bow of the boat. He was placed on a table and a medical student from Chicago, who had hired as a guard, bandaged the wound on Connors' arm."

Detectives P. J. Connors and Joseph Malley gave evidence of similar tenor to that of the two preceding witnesses, and Captain Rodgers and Deputy Sheriff Gray repeated their well-worn story of the Little Bill.

This stage of the proceedings was reached on the afternoon of Saturday, November 19, at the customary hour of adjournment. The court decided to hold a night session, and accordingly at 7 P. M. the examination of witnesses was resumed.

J. M. Dickson, H. H. Hervey and J. H. Slocum, clerks in the employ of the Carnegie firm, swore that on the morning of July 6 they saw Critchlow with a gun in his hand going towards the mill gate. Each of them positively identified the prisoner.

Charles Reese, a newspaper artist, being sworn, said that he saw Critchlow, with a gun in his hands, occupying an exposed position in the mill yard, near the pump house. Somebody had said to witness, "There is Critchlow. He is a regular dare devil." Mr. Brennen elicited from the witness the fact that he had attended a gathering of newspaper reporters called together by Capt. E. Y. Breck, attorney for the Carnegie firm, at the time when the Critchlow case was before the grand jury. This affair had created no little scandal when it occurred, some of the newspapers openly stating that Captain Breck had invited those whom he intended to use as witnesses to a banquet for the purpose of "coaching" them. Mr. Reese, however, denied that there had been a banquet or that he had received any formal invitation from Captain Breck. Nevertheless, the evidence was regarded as establishing a reasonable presumption of the use of unfair methods by the prosecution.

Isaac J. Jury, a constable residing in Homestead, swore that he saw Critchlow in the mill yard and advised him to get out, but that his warning was not heeded.

The most damaging testimony of all was given by Samuel Stewart, a clerk in the Homestead mill. He said :

"I know Sylvester Critchlow ; saw him near the Company office between 8 and 9 o'clock on the morning of

July 6; next saw him back of the barricades, near the pump house on the river bank; he was kneeling back of the barricade, a gun in his hands; the gun projected through the barricade between the second and third beams; the barricade was built of steel 'I' beams; his gun was pointed toward the barges; the bows of the barges were nearest to the barricades; you could see into the boats from where Critchlow was kneeling; the door of the outer barge was open; I saw Critchlow fire once in the direction of the barge; saw him aim carefully and pull the trigger; I remained there about 20 minutes; Critchlow was there when I arrived, and was still there when I left; I cannot tell the kind of gun Critchlow had, except that it was a single barrel."

On cross-examination witness stated that he also saw Anthony Flaherty, Joseph A. Hall and James Flannagan shoot from behind the barricade. He stuck firmly to his story in the face of Mr. Brennen's questioning. Stewart's examination ended the Saturday night session.

When the trial was resumed on Monday morning, Detective Malley was again placed on the stand and swore to having seen Critchlow on the river bank with a gun in his hands and to have heard him called by name. Photographs of the burning barges, the barricades and the mill yard, taken by order of the Carnegie Company on July 6, were put in evidence, and here the commonwealth rested.

Attorney George W. Argo made the opening speech for the defense. He explained that he and his colleague, Mr. Irwin, had been sent by the laboring element of the Northwest to assist in the defense of the Homestead men. "As far as I am concerned," he said, "I was not selected on account of any extraordinary ability, but because for years I have been in touch with labor. At one time I was a barge builder near this city. My parents resided in Washington County.''

In setting forth the reasons for demanding an acquittal, Mr. Argo enlarged upon the enlistment of armed men to invade Homestead ''within two days of the anniversary of the signing of the Declaration of Independence'' and, after describing the expedition of the Pinkertons went on to say:

''These men were not laboring men. It was an invasion of armed men employed by a man named Frick; it was an assault upon this grand old commonwealth; it was an assault upon the state in which the Declaration of Independence was signed; this armed body of men who invaded this state and trampled upon the soil made sacred by the feet of Washington; these men were not under the command of any regular officer of this county; they were men who could not be sworn in as deputies or special officers. Under the evidence in this case these men made an attack upon the people of Homestead; there is not any evidence that Frick owned one dollar's worth of property in Homestead. These men sneaked in on a dark, foggy night; they were met, not by strikers, for there is no evidence that there was a strike, but by the good people of the town, who, when the armed foe attempted to land told the latter not to come ashore; begged of them not to interfere with their rights, begged of them not to attempt to land. Not a particle of evidence has been given that these foreign emissaries had any right there. The men, the peaceable citizens, attempted to defend their rights. A young man named Foy went down to the gang-plank to plead with the men not to come ashore. He was met by a lot of armed men. Becoming alarmed he turned to go back, when he slipped and fell across the plank. As he fell he was shot in the back by some one on the barges. That was the beginning of the terrible battle. It will appear in evidence in this case that the first shots were fired from the barges and not by the people on shore. We will show you that preparations had been made for this trouble one month before it occurred. We will show that a stockade or high fence had been built around the works, a fence like that built in the west to repel Indian attacks. This fence was full of portholes, and resembled the outer wall of a fort. There is no evidence that the people who were on the banks on the morning of the invasion were strikers. They were peaceable citizens of Homestead. Every man in that crowd had a right to defend himself with arms; the law gives to every man the right to defend himself, to defend his family; to defend his neighbors and his friends; this right is given every man by a power higher than the law of man. The people were attacked by an armed foe and they had the right to use weapons in self-defense. The evidence shows that the men on the barges were in command of officers whose names are known, who have testified in this case, yet your honorable district attorney has made no effort to bring these men to justice. Thus he becomes a defender of these armed invaders of your county."

Mr. Argo further outlined the plan of defense as showing that the Critchlow who was seen behind the barricades was another Critchlow and that the prisoner was not present when Connors met his death.

W. M. Erwin followed with a spirited address in which he said that the prosecution rested entirely on the theory that there had been a riot, which he character-ized as a "doubly damned fiction." "Is there," he asked, "another such hard-hearted, villianous man within the limits of the land as this man Frick, whom we find hob-nobbing with the leaders of the Republic. This man Frick, whose name will be more notorious than that of the man who fired the Ephesian dome, dia not apply to your courts or your legislature, but violated the agreement with his men, and assumed, like a tyrant, to act as arbiter; this most brutal tyrant of all tyrants tried to force his men to bow to his will by an armed force of invaders. Thus have these scoundrels defied the laws of the commonwealth. Carnegie bent the eternal laws of God and the poorer imitations by man. We will show that the defendants only tried to straighten these laws. If there is no Judas Iscariot among you, gentlemen of the jury, you will plant the flag of independence on your hills.''

Captain O. C. Coon, of Homestead, was the first witness called by the defense. He testified that he was at the mill landing when the Pinkerton barges arrived, and described the opening of the battle as follows:

"When the plank was thrown out my attention was called to a man on the barge; he had a gun in his hand; there was a boy on the shore; he was tantalizing the man; the latter raised his gun to shoot the boy; I said to him: 'For God's sake don't shoot that boy, for he is only a boy.' I asked him if he was a deputy sheriff, he said no; I asked him if he was a guardsman, he said no; I then said 'you are a Pinkerton'; he replied that he was, and, holding up his gun, said his party was going to enter the mill in fifteen minutes; the boy on shore continued to call the man on the barge; the latter raised his gun and aimed at the boy, but someone pushed his gun down; when he raised it again he had it drawn on me; about that time a boy came running down to where we were, slipped and fell across the gang plank; a minute later there was a shot from the barge, and I heard afterward that the boy on the plank was shot in the side; the first shot fired after the landing was fired by either the second or third man on the plank; I do not know who he was; I went there to try and preserve order ; I never saw Critchlow to know him until I saw him in court to-day."

Charles Mansfield, of Homestead, effectually offset the evidence of Charles Reese. He swore that he had been in the mill yard and conversed with Reese. Asked as to the nature of the conversation, he said :

"I was in a cupola with Mr. Reese. I saw a man named Critchlow go into the pump-house. I said to Reese, 'There goes Critchlow into the place where Morris was killed. He will be killed sure. You had better get a good sketch of him.' "

MR. BRENNEN—"Was the man you pointed out to Reese the defendant ? "

"No, sir."

"Who was the man ?"

"I do not wish to state."

"Was his name Critchlow ?"

"It was."

Numerous witnesses were then introduced to prove an alibi for the defendant. Samuel Rothrauff, J. Miller Colgan and J. J. Baird testified that they saw Critchlow in Braddock before 10 A. M. on July 6. Mrs. Bridget Coyle said that she saw him at 3 P. M. a mile distant from the mill on his way home. "There's no lie about it," exclaimed Mrs. Coyle, in answer to Attorney Patterson's questions, "but you're trying to make me tell a lie, and I wouldn't do it for all the money Carnegie has." Three witnesses corroborated Mrs. Coyle's statement and a half-dozen others accounted for Critchlow's movements in the evening.

The taking of all this testimony occupied the court throughout a second night session.

On Tuesday, the fourth day of the trial, the defendant testified in his own behalf, denying that he had been on the Carnegie Company's grounds at any time on the day of the battle. A light suit of clothes which he claimed to have worn on that day was exhibited as an offset to the evidence of witnesses for the prosecution who coincided in the statement that the Critchlow whom they had seen wore dark clothing.

Critchlow's wife was sworn and said that at 4 P. M. on July 6, at which hour, it was alleged, defendant had been behind the barricades, he was at home sleeping.

This closed the case for the defense.

Only one witness was called by the commonwealth in rebuttal, and his evidence was valueless.

Mr. Marshall, for the defense, submitted a number of points, among which was the contention that, when it is certain that one or more persons committed a crime, but it is uncertain which, all must be acquitted.

Mr. D. F. Patterson responded for the prosecution, taking special exception to the plea against individual liability.

Four hours were allowed to each side for the closing arguments.

Mr. Robb, for the commonwealth, arraigned the defense in scathing language for seeking to belittle the laws of the commonwealth in the eyes of the jury. "There is, gentlemen," he said "some mysterious power that comes from the blue sky above the clouds that leads us away from the law; we have been told this by an attorney from the other side. Has it come to this, as we are told, that there is not law enough in Allegheny county or Pennsylvania for a plain cause? We have been told, but thank God those who made the statement are not citizens of our state, that we are all, from the man who sits on the supreme bench to the district attorney, corrupt. We have been told that in their cause there has been a mysterious, swimming atmosphere, something that would develop in this cause. But when you hear his honor you will know how plain is your duty and how plain is the law.''

And again:

"The Carnegie company may have done wrong; we all do wrong, but is that any reason why our laws and our great flag, which was referred to so eloquently by the gentleman on the other side in his opening address should be trampled underfoot by rioters? My forefathers were not so high as the forefathers of the gentleman who addressed you yesterday; mine were only privates; his were away-up officers. But if I were not a better citizen of Allegheny county than to advise a jury to disregard its solemn oath I should hope that I should be stricken dead.''

Mr. Erwin, who, since the delivery of his fiery speech of Monday, had come to be known among the members of the bar as the "Northwestern Whirlwind," followed Mr. Robb. There was dead silence in the court-room when he began. Surely he would respond in kind to Mr. Robb's virulent attack on him! But no. The Westerner was too shrewd to let himself be drawn off into the mere by-ways of argument, and with but a passing contemptuous allusion to Mr. Robb's onslaught, he proceeded calmly and impressively with the discussion of the main issue. As one of the newspapers put it, ''The strategy of the prosecution to lead into a by-path had failed, and he stuck to the high road and tramped defiantly along the highest part of it.''

After a few preparatory remarks, including his brief reference to Mr. Robb's speech, which he characterized as a "gauzy affair,'' Mr. Erwin plunged into his subject as follows:

"Unhappily for you, and I think for the county, the propelling causes that led to the riots at Homestead are not shown in evidence. Under your oaths you cannot merely presume on them. I think that is unfortunate for the country, the state and the city. After the news of the battle flashed over the wires calm minds awaited the result of the investigation. That it has not been touched is a matter of sincere regret. You are now put in an iron vest by your oaths, and you can presume nothing except such presumptions as are legal and presumable. We of the defense are in no way responsible for this. A man has the right to rebut only the testimony addressed against him, and that is so strong that if you committed the murder you would not have a chance to prove I did it. And thus we are bound hand and foot, and our mouths are open to receive what the prosecution presents.''

Mr. Erwin defined indictments as mere accusations, and said that the law's presumption of innocence was as a shield on which the prosecution must pile evidence until the weight is so heavy that it breaks the prisoner down. The speaker referred to the important part that intuition plays in law cases, and said in that respect women often possessed it more acutely because they were nearer like the angels. Going further, he adverted to the exclusion of any evidence that there was a strike at Homestead or that Mr. Frick had hired an armed body there. The constitution, he said, still gives the people right to bear arms in their defense.

"The cloven foot of the power that invoked this invasion of Pennsylvania has been hidden from you," continued he. "I know not whether accidentally, but it has been concealed. You know, though, that it was Frick, the blackest name there ever was; you know that Frick, whoever he may be, put on board the Little Bill arms and men for this invasion of Pennsylvania.

And, therefore, you are bound to presume that if the proceeding had a just excuse it should be shown, and the absence of it is favorable to the prisoner. What was there that even justified Frick in arming men like that? You do not know. I cannot but presume that it is so black he dare not show it in this open forum before the republic. The great question with you, gentlemen, is, under the evidence we have before us, was this battle at Homestead a riot or an authorized invasion? That's the first question. If you answer it was an invasion that's the end of it. It requires no proclamation of the governor to resist an invasion. I do not see how under the evidence you can see anything else than an invasion. I would like to have shown you what an irresponsible constabulary the Pinkertons are, but that is denied us."

Mr. Erwin sarcastically said that Mr. Robb in his endeavor to carry them by storm became the personification of a rioter, and forgot to tell them that if Mr. Frick had not sent the Pinkertons to Homestead there would never have been a battle. There may have seemed a reason to Frick, but the state had not shown anything of that. People for self-aggrandizement may often do things that, if shown in court, might convict them of what they charge against others, and that is murder.

"If you find there is no excuse for that invasion the people of Homestead should have pursued and shot the Pinkertons even at God's altar, and further still have gone across the line that separates the dead from life and shot them while they lay on the bosom of the prince of hell," shouted Erwin in a particularly passionate outburst that seemed to appal the court. "If there was no invasion, you must ask yourselves was the riot such as to make the people on the shore responsible for that tumult. Who were on those boats? Three hundred men from the slums of Philadelphia and Chicago, armed with 150 Winchesters, and revolvers and maces. And they were under captains and had waived their right to think for themselves; had sworn to obey their captain when he told them to kill the people at Homestead. This shows you the abandonment of individuality and concentration of power under one executive head; and that is the primary principle that constitutes war. Were the people on the mill shore who had fired on the Pinkertons down the river? Not one of them. Is there any evidence that the people on shore were responsible for that firing down on the shore? Not a particle. Perhaps the prosecution did not go into it for fear they might show that Frick was guilty of murder. The evidence has not been put to you to show that the people on shore were there to repel any but 'scabs.' If you cannot determine these points you should acquit the defendant."

Mr. Erwin then went into an analysis of the testimony of the Pinkerton witnesses for the prosecution; and defined detectives as men who could not make a living at any honorable pursuit, and preferred to hunt men instead of serving the Almighty by working by the sweat of their brows. He said it was hardly possible the jury could like a human hyena. Had the Pinkertons been honorable men the district attorney would have shown the jury evidence of such and thus helped to strengthen their statements. The speaker justified burning oil and dynamite and anything else that could be thought of if used against the Pinkertons. There was no intent in the gathering of the crowd on shore; and, therefore, the individual up for justice could not be held guilty for what happened. Erwin held that if Critchlow was on the scene of battle he had a perfect right to be there. It was a point of law older than Rome, copied by Cicero, that when arms are used all political laws are set at naught. The resistance of the Homestead people was a "majestic" performance. Were not three hundred rifles cowed by eight behind the barricade?

Stewart, "that magnificent volunteer witness," was a preposterous liar and a "squirt" who was eyeing the fighters.

Here the orator asked his colleagues how long he had to speak and was told to go on without regard to time. Taking up a synopsis of the testimony he proceeded to analyze the statements of witnesses for the commonwealth with telling effect. His sarcastic commentaries set the court-room in a roar, even the tipstaves being so amused that they forgot to cry order until Judge Kennedy aroused them.

The witnesses for the defense, Mr. Erwin said, were all reputable citizens of Homestead. He thought it impossible to construct a better alibi than had been proven for Critchlow. No machinations of testimony could make such an excellent alibi as the one presented. In view of it all, he could not look for any decision other than in favor of acquittal, even though the district attorney had so artfully presented the testimony as almost to compel the jury to decide for the commonwealth against their consciences.

In conclusion the speaker pictured the misery that would be inflicted on Critchlow's family, if the bread winner were snatched away.

"That is the greatest speech ever delivered in this court house," remarked the veteran, Thomas M. Marshall, when Mr. Erwin had finished. "I want to retire from the bar now, for I have been snuffed out."

On Wednesday morning Mr. Marshall spoke. He laid much stress on the surreptitious entry of the Pinkertons and the assumption that somebody had authority to give these private hirelings orders to shoot. "The order from Captain Cooper and Captain Heinde to shoot entitled them to be shot," said the speaker vehemently. "When there is war," he continued, "the man that arrives first on the battlefield has the right to shoot first. But why did the Pinkertons come down upon Homestead like thieves in the night? Who is it that likes darkness? Why did not Mr. Frick say he was bringing these men here to protect his property and not to intimidate people? Why did they steal into Homestead with guns that shot sixteen times?"

Mr. Marshall attacked the evidence for the prosecution,

and especially the identification of Critchlow by the Pinkertons, who could only have seen the man once or twice, if they had seen him at all, and were, therefore, not qualified to swear to his identity. He held that the district attorney had no right to throw the weight of his talents and influence against the defendant. That officer's client was the commonwealth, and yet Mr. Robb spoke of "our clients" as if Frick and the commonwealth were identical. "I don't believe," said Mr. Marshall ironically, "that H. Clay Frick had anything to do with this prosecution, oh, no! I don't believe that anybody connected with the Carnegie Company had anything to do with the attempt to take away the lives of these Homestead men. And this man Lovejoy who made these informations, he had nothing to do with the Carnegie interests; oh, no! Love—joy! L–o–v–e–j–o–y! I don't say his name should be Loveblood; but I do say that there are several people in the Carnegie Company who should have their names changed."

In concluding his address, Mr. Marshall said: "The real capitalist is the workingman, the producer, who has nothing but his paltry $3 a day, while the lordlings, the so-called manufacturers, walk abroad as social gods and revel in the luxury made by the sweat of the workingman's brow."

District Attorney Burleigh, in his speech closing the case for the commonwealth, volunteered the statement that he was in the pay of no man but was there solely to plead for justice in the name of the commonwealth. He taxed the defense with relying mainly on artifice and meretricious oratory; scouted the idea that the Pinkertons were "invaders," and declared that Mr. Erwin's defense of the right "to shoot down on the very bosom of the prince of hell," three hundred men "caged like rats in those barges," was anarchy—red, rampant anarchy!

Mr. Burleigh contended that the Carnegie Company in massing and attempting to land the Pinkertons with the permission of the Sheriff, acted within its legal rights. The landing had been attempted at night because it was desired to avoid a breach of the peace.

The closing portion of the address was given up to an endeavor to discredit the testimony adduced to establish an alibi for the defendant.

Judge Kennedy occupied only forty minutes in charging the jury. He held that a man mixing with a riotous crowd and not helping to quell the disturbance was as guilty as the active participants. The Carnegie Company had a lawful right to protect its property, even with Pinkerton detectives, no matter whence the guards came, and the people on the shore had no right to shoot down the men on the barges.

After one hour's deliberation the jury returned a verdict of "Not Guilty," to the surprise of the court and the delight of Critchlow's weeping wife, who remained near him to the last.

The news of the acquittal spread rapidly, and at Homestead an enthusiastic crowd watched every train from Pittsburgh in the hope of meeting Critchlow with an appropriate demonstration. The people were disappointed, however, for the lion of the occasion was doomed to remain a caged lion, being remanded to jail on additional charges—two of murder, two of riot and one of conspiracy.

At the same time the public made up its mind from the turn which affairs had taken in the Critchlow case that a conviction could not be secured against any of the Homestead men. The officials of the Amalgamated Association were jubilant and gave vent to their satisfaction by waiting in a body upon Attorney Erwin at the Monongahela House and formally congratulating him on the success which he had achieved President Garland acting as spokesman.

On the Carnegie Company's side there was a corresponding feeling of disappointment and three months were allowed to elapse before the trial of the Homestead cases proper—that is to say, those based on the battle with the Pinkertons—was resumed.

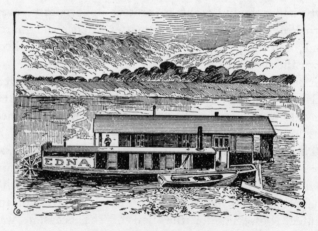

THE WORKMEN'S DISPATCH BOAT.

CHAPTER XIX.

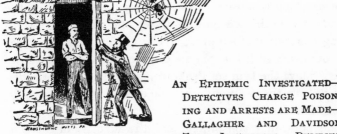

WEAVING NEW TOILS.

THE prevalence of disease among the non-union men
in the Carnegie mill, and the alarming increase of
mortality in the months of September and October
were touched upon in an earlier chapter. It was not
until December that the first intimation of the existence
of a criminal cause for the species of epidemic which
struck down man after man and baffled expert physicians and chemists reached the public. The Carnegie
Company had concealed the truth as far as possible, endeavoring from the first to counteract the statements
sent abroad by the Amalgamated Association to the effect
that bad food, bad water, and bad sanitary arrangements

were killing off the "blacksheep" like cattle stricken with a murrain.

The malady was a virulent form of diarrhœa or cholera morbus, for which the medical men employed to treat the sufferers were unable to account. All sorts of remedial measures were tried by the firm. Only the purest food was used. Notices were posted warning the men not to drink from the water plugs ordinarily serving as a source of supply, and chemically pure water was provided. Still the plague did not abate. Suspecting foul play, the firm set Pinkerton detectives to work, distributing them among the cooks and waiters as assistants, and in this way evidence was secured of a wholesale poisoning conspiracy, and the identity of the conspirators was believed to be established by confessions obtained from two accesories.

On December 5, J. H. Ford, a Pinkerton detective, made information before Alderman McMasters against Robert J. Beatty, a cook in the mill, on a charge of felonious assault and battery, in administering poison to the non-union men at Homestead. It was learned that Beatty was about to start for Cincinnati on the steamboat Nellie Hudson and an officer boarded the boat to apprehend him, but was not permitted to make the arrest. Beatty was subsequently arrested in Louisville and brought back to Pittsburgh on requisition papers issued by Governor Pattison.

The confession on which the Carnegie Company based its charge against Beatty was made by Patrick Gallagher, a cook in restaurant No. 1 in the Homestead mill. Its publication, which followed immediately on the arrest of Beatty, caused a tremendous sensation, inasmuch as it named as the arch-conspirator, the designer and executive head of the plot, no less a personage than Hugh F. Dempsey, master workman of D. A. 3, K. of L.

Gallagher deposed that late in August, he was approached by Beatty with a proposition to put in the tea and coffee made by him for the Carnegie Company's men, something which would render the men sick and unfit for work ; that Beatty took him, in company with J. M. Davidson, to see Hugh F. Dempsey, who was to furnish the preparation to be used ; that about the 7th or 8th of September affiant received from Dempsey a bottle containing a yellow powder, which, Dempsey said, contained three doses, each being sufficient for a pot of tea or coffee containing thirty gallons; that affiant used the powder with the result of making workmen sick and unable to work ; that additional powders were given him by Dempsey and Beatty and administered by him to the workmen, and that affiant received for his services $3 from Beatty and $25 from Dempsey, with the assurance of $23.85 more from the latter.

Despite the plausibility and coherency of the charges and the *prima facie* evidence in support of them, the Amalgamated men unanimously set down this new move of the company as a scheme devised in order to prejudice their cause. It was urged, in particular, that the relations between the Association and the K. of L. were not such as to render it probable that Dempsey would jeopardize his liberty and perhaps his life by engaging in a villainous plot in the interest of the former. Dempsey himself stoutly denied the charges, and his denial was supported by Beatty.

At the hearing before Alderman McMasters, Beatty

was defended by William J. Brennen, Esq. Captain Breck appeared for the prosecution. J. M. Davidson was the first witness examined. A summary of his testimony is appended:

"I am 50 years of age, reside in the Seventeenth ward, Pittsburgh, and have been a river cook nearly all my life. I have known Beatty two or three years. In the latter part of August, Patrick Gallagher and I met Beatty on Wood street, and Beatty recognized me as "Jimmy" Davidson. I have known Gallagher for fifteen years. It was understood that we were all to go to Homestead as cooks and that we were to take something with us to put in the food given the non-union men in order to make them sick and unfit for work. When we met Beatty he took us to the office of the K. of L., on Third Avenue. There we met Hugh Dempsey, who, I understand, is master workman for this district. I am not a member of the K. of L. While we were in the office, Gallagher and Dempsey did most of the talking. Beatty suggested that it would be well for us to dose the men at Homestead with croton oil. He said croton oil could be used safely; that we could carry bottles of it in our pockets and when we were at work in the cook-houses we could put it on our fingers and rub it on the inside of the soup bowls and coffee cups. I objected to the use of croton oil on the ground that it was a deadly drug, and I did not want to run the risk of killing any one. Dempsey said he could furnish us with powders that would do the work effectively and safely; that the powders had been used on non-union men in Chicago, and that by their use a strike had been broken in four days. He said that while it would make the men sick, it was not dangerous. Dempsey said that if we would go to Homestead and administer these powders he would guarantee us $50 each and our expenses. We did not get any powders from Dempsey that day. Gallagher, Beatty and myself

then left Dempsey's office. We took a walk about
town discussing our plans and the contract we had
undertaken. Beatty told us that if we did the work
well there would be a gold watch and chain in it for
each of us in addition to the money we were to receive.
I did not go to Homestead until September 30. Gallagher, who had been there for some time, left the day
before I arrived. Two days later he returned and
worked about the restaurant in the mill. Before Gallagher went to Homestead the first time we called on
Mr. Dempsey. He gave us a small jar of some kind of
powder. He said there was enough of the stuff in the
jar for three powders, each one sufficient to 'fix' thirty
gallons of tea or coffee. I suppose there was nine or
ten teaspoonsful of the stuff in the bottle. Dempsey
told Gallagher to divide it into three equal parts. This
Gallagher took with him to Homestead. The day before
I went to Homestead Beatty gave me some powders to
deliver to Gallagher. This was in Dempsey's office, or
K. of L. hall. I met Gallagher on the street and gave
him the package. He opened it and told me there were
nine powders in the package. The bottle containing
some of the stuff was given to Gallagher by Dempsey in
my presence. This was in K. of L. hall and Beatty was
present. Gallagher was to use his own discretion
whether he put it in the tea or coffee. I next saw
Beatty about September 30.

"Some time in September Gallagher came back,
and Beatty and I went to the K. of L. hall. Dempsey
asked him how the powders worked. He said successfully, and wanted more and Dempsey said he would
get more. After I came back I again met Beatty.
We talked about the success the powders had, and
Beatty seemed pleased. I had quit work on October 15.
About December 1, I met Beatty at Cavanaugh's saloon.
Gallagher was with us and we then went to Gallagher's
room, where we discussed the powders, and I asked
Beatty what was in the powders. He said rhubarb and
snuff and other things. He didn't say who furnished

them. While we were talking he mentioned Lynch, Crawford and Dr. Purman. Gallagher presented his bill of expenses to Dempsey and he asked me where mine was, and I made it out and gave it to Dempsey. Dempsey said the money was exhausted and we would have to wait. Beatty said the powders didn't seem to be a success. Gallagher told Dempsey that the powders had been used in cook house No. 1. I saw Beatty again two weeks later on Wood street. We talked over Gallagher's success in administering the powders. Met him again a week later; that was after I had quit work in Homestead."

On cross-examination witness said that Beatty gave him $2 and Dempsey $12. Mr. Brennen was unable to shake his testimony.

Pinkerton Detective Ford deposed to having overheard a conversation carried on by Beatty, Gallagher and Davidson concerning the powders used at Homestead. Witness hired adjoining rooms for Gallagher and himself, and induced Gallagher to entertain the other two men in his quarters, he (Ford) furnishing liquor for the party. He kept a man stationed in the room next Gallagher's and received daily reports of what took place. On confronting Davidson with proof of his guilt, Davidson made a full confession.

Louis Wolfe, of Anapolis, Md., said that ne had served as steward of restaurants Nos 1, 4 and 5 in the Carnegie mill. Witness hired Gallagher as cook and had seen Beatty in the mill. On September 7, witness' wife came on from Anapolis and he invited thirty or forty friends to supper in honor of her arrival. Many of the guests were taken ill and Mrs. Wolfe suffered terribly from cramps and vomited a great deal. Her weight was soon reduced from 120 to 66 pounds. Witness himself fell ill and lost 38 pounds.

J. O. Nesbitt swore that he had attended the supper given by Wolfe, fell ill immediately afterwards, was in bed five weeks and had not yet fully recovered.

W. E. Bullock, pay roll clerk in the Carnegie office at Homestead, had also been at the supper, sickened, lost sixteen pounds in eight days and was still ailing.

Mr. Brennen made a long argument for his client, alleging that the two informers were "miserable, contemptible rascals who had put up a job on an innocent man in order to shield themselves." The magistrate, however, believing a good *prima facie* case to have been made out, held Beatty for court in $5,000 bail.

As if to accentuate the force of the poisoning charge several more deaths from sickness contracted in the mill now occurred, the symptoms being identical in all cases.

District Attorney Burleigh proceeded without loss of time against Dempsey and Davidson, the information against the men being lodged by County Detective Beltzhoover. Dempsey surrendered himself and was released on $2,500 bail. Gallagher, against whom an information had been made by William E. Griffith, one of the workmen who had been poisoned, was arrested and sent to jail in default of $5,000 bail. Davidson was also arrested, but was released on $3,000 bail.

Hugh F. Dempsey was the first of the accused men to stand trial, being arraigned before Judge Stowe on January 12, 1893. The indictment against him contained four counts, 2 charging felonious assault and battery with intent to murder, and two felonious assault and battery with intent to "make sick." The defendant was represented by Messrs. Marshall, Montooth, Brennen and L. K. Porter. District Attorney Burleigh, Captain Breck and John S. Robb appeared for the Commonwealth. The jury selected was composed as follows: Harry T. Anderson, L. P. Boyer, Michael Brown, David Duff, Charles H. Kretzer and William G. Murray, all farmers; Daniel Bohannon, painter; Louis Blumenschein, gardener; . David C. Brickell, gent; Alex. D. Guy, merchant; Edward Letzkus, clerk, and John H. Wilson, manufacturer.

Captain Breck, in his opening speech, admitted that no man could be convicted of crime on the evidence of an accomplice, but promised to furnish ample testimony corroborative of the confessions made by Gallagher and Davidson. He laid special stress on the reports of the physicians who had treated the men supposed to have been poisoned at Homestead.

A numerous array of witnesses was brought forward by the prosecution. Attorney L. K. Porter conducted most of the cross-examinations for the defense.

Dr. Weible, surgeon for the Carnegie Company, submitted a tabulated report of the cases treated by him in the mill.

Louis Wolfe repeated the testimony which he gave at the Beatty hearing.

George W. Amy, Henry P. Thompson and Louis H. Craig, all of Chicora, Butler County, deposed to having worked in the Homestead mill and being stricken with disease, from which none of them had fully recovered. Dr. J. L. Campbell, of Chicora, had treated these men and described their symptoms, which, he said, he hau ascribed to mineral poisoning. He was certain that antimony had been given.

Stephen Loveless, of Butler, William H. Johnston, a watchman in the mill; Benjamin Weaver, a steelworker residing at Homestead, and Wilmot Herr, a watchman, deposed to having been attacked by the prevailing malady.

Dr. McGeary, of Homestead, had treated William H. Johnston and was convinced that his patient suffered from arsenical poisoning. In his opinion, impure water, spoiled meat or climatic conditions could not have caused the sickness which occurred in the mill.

Charles H. Smith, an engineer in the Carnegie works, said that he had fallen ill twice and lost 55 pounds. Three doctors were unable to restore his health fully.

William E. Griffith, the man named in the indictment as the victim of the poisoning plot, said that he had been serving in restaurant No. 6 as head waiter. On September 11 or 12, after eating supper in the restaurant, he was seized with diarrhoea and vomiting and was then laid up for a week. On October 6, after drinking some coffee, witness took sick again. This time he was prostrated for eight weeks. Dr. A. P. Vogleman, of Homestead, had treated Griffith and thought that the patient might have been made ill by drinking bad water.

Dr. McGeary (recalled) and Dr. E. W. Dean testified to the conditions attending the case of J. W. Van Winkle, who had died at the Homeopathic Hospital. They thought it safe to pronounce his death due to arsenical poisoning.

Numerous other witnesses gave testimony similar to

the foregoing, nearly a week being occupied in listening to the stories of those who had been poisoned and to the diagnoses learnedly set forth by medical men.

On the fifth day of the trial, Gallagher, the informer, was placed on the witness stand and repeated the narrative embodied in his previously published confession, with some new embellishments. In describing his first interview with Dempsey, Gallagher said:

"When we entered Dempsey's office a lady who was present retired; the door was then locked; we sat down; Beatty said to Dempsey: 'These are the two men;' we talked about the weather for a few minutes after which Dempsey said to me and Mr. Davidson: 'I suppose you know what we want?' We said we knew a little about it. Dempsey then said: 'Well, we want to get the men in the Homestead mill on the trot.' Beatty then spoke about using croton oil. Davidson and I said we wouldn't use it. Dempsey then spoke about breaking a street car strike in Chicago—the State street strike. He said powders had been used; that if we would use these powders in the Homestead mill it would make the men sick and that we could break the strike in about ten days."

Gallagher also swore that Beatty's trip to Cincinnati was for the purpose of getting two more cooks to finish the poisoning job. Dempsey had subsequently shown him a dispatch from Cincinnati, which read, "Two good agents on the road." When witness went to work in the mill the second time two cooks came from Cincinnati. They were Tony Gilfoil and William Coleman. Witness took them to a hotel and paid their bills; but was warned by Dempsey not to let the new comers know of his (Dempsey's) connection with the plot.

Gallagher further deposed that, after leaving the mill

finally, he had, in the presence of Davidson, presented a bill to Dempsey, which the latter O. K'd. He had also signed a receipt for $25, which Dempsey gave him in the dispatcher's office of the Citizens' Traction Line. The bill marked "O. K." was identified and offered in evidence.

Attorney Marshall subjected Gallagher to a trying cross-examination but without impairing his testimony.

J. M. Davidson repeated in court the evidence given by him at the Beatty hearing.

George W. Crail, dispatcher of the Citizens' Traction Line, corroborated Gallagher's statement as to the receipt of $25 from Dempsey. Dempsey, the witness claimed, came into his office and said: "Crail, if a man comes in here and asks if I left anything for him, give him this money."

The death of L. B. Hebron from sickness contracted in the mill was attested by the mother and brother of the deceased, and Captain A. E. Hunt, of the Pittsburgh Testing Laboratory, then stated the result of an analysis of sick bed accumulations furnished him by Mrs. Hebron. The analysis showed the presence of croton oil and arsenic.

J. D. Flynn, manager of the Western Union Telegraph Company in Pittsburg, produced a copy of a telegram sent to Dempsey from Cincinnati, on September 26. It read: "Send me $20 ; in a pinch ; two good agents on the road.—BEATTY." It was shown by a messenger boy that the telegram was delivered to a man in Dempsey's office, who signed for it.

Thomas M. Marshall, Esq., made the opening speech for the defense, the principal points set forth in which were, (1) That the sickness in the Homestead mill was merely incident to an epidemic from which soldiers and others outside the mill were suffering, and (2) That the men sent into the mill by Dempsey and paid for their services were detailed by Dempsey as scouts.

Dr. George T. McCord, being sworn, stated that the conditions of life among the non-union men in the Homestead mill were very favorable to the development of diarrhœa, dysentery and kindred complaints. He had treated one man who was taken sick with diarrhœa in the mill and cured him.

Dr. John Purman, of Homestead, told of the filthy condition of City Farm lane, and said he had under treatment numerous cases of diarrhœa and dysentery not incurred in the mill.

Nine members of Battery B, Eighteenth regiment, N. G. P., swore that they were afflicted with precisely the same complaint that attacked the non-union workmen.

Other witnesses testified as to the impurity of the water supply in the mill and the invariable prevalence of diarrhœa and kindred diseases among the millworkers during the hot season.

E. W. Robertson, who occupied the cell next to Gallagher's in the county jail, said that Gallagher had told him that Dempsey was an innocent man.

Hugh F. Dempsey, being sworn in his own defense, stated that he had employed Gallagher and Davidson, on Beatty's recommendation, to get work in the Homestead mill and report to him how things were running. Nothing had ever been said about putting poison in food, and witness knew nothing of a poison plot. The $25 paid by him to Gallagher was a loan.

On cross-examination, Dempsey stated that it was through the Knights of Labor in New York, who were striving to procure a settlement of the Homestead trouble, that he became interested in the affair. He gave a synopsis of one of Davidson's reports to him on the number of men employed and the output, and said that Gallagher made reports of like tenor.

While Dempsey was giving his testimony, resolutions affirming implicit faith in his honesty and innocence of wrong-doing were being adopted by District Assembly No. 3, and on the evening of the same day he was re-elected to the position of master workman by acclamation. This strong expression of confidence on the part of his fellow workmen might, it was thought, have some influence for good on the determination of Dempsey's case.

With the exception of Prof. George Hay, a chemist, who swore that Captain Hunt could not possibly have discovered traces of croton oil in nine drops of oleaginous liquid, all the remaining witnesses for the defense were called to prove Dempsey's good character.

Attorney L. K. Porter made the opening argument for the defense. He charged the prosecution with unfairness in having a chemical examination made without permitting the attendance of an expert on the part of the defense and dilated upon the reasons for presuming that an epidemic of stomach troubles would naturally occur in an establishment where 2,678 men were lodged and fed in close quarters and practically without outdoor exercise. The doctors disagreed and most of them had never treated poison cases. How could a man be convicted on such testimony? The men who claimed to have been poisoned had, for the most part, admitted that they had suffered from diarrhœa and vomiting before and why should it be surmised that the attacks which beset them in the mill arose from other than natural causes? The majority of the non-union men came from distant points and were liable to be affected by change of climate.

Gallagher, Mr. Porter said, being a self-confessed accomplice, was unworthy of credit. He was a spy, procured by Pinkerton Detective Ford, and the fact that he was left at large for five weeks after his confession indicated in what a questionable relation he stood to the prime movers in the prosecution of Dempsey. Dempsey, the speaker said, was the honored choice of 600,000 men for the chieftanship of the K. of L. in the Pittsburgh district. He was a frank and generous man, to whose kind heart no one ever appealed in vain. Was it humanly probable that this man would have bribed Gallagher to poison men? Would he, if such had been his purpose, have conferred with Gallagher and have given him money in broad daylight? The issue was between Gallagher, the hired informer, and Dempsey, the honorable citizen, whom it was proposed to take away from his wife and home on the testimony of strangers without title to belief.

Attorney Marshall followed his colleague with a telling analysis of the evidence for the commonwealth. He read from the report of the mill physician, Dr. Weible, figures showing that there was actually more sickness in the mill, in proportion to the number of men employed, before Gallagher went there than at any time afterwards. He also showed by Gallagher's testimony that on the day of the Wolfe family's supper, the coffee

which Gallagher claimed to have dosed was all used up
at dinner time and, as there was none left over, where,
Mr. Marshall asked, did the poison come from by which
the Wolfes' claimed to have been sickened.   After com-
menting on the improbability of Dempsey's employing
strangers to aid him in a poisoning plot, Mr. Marshall
said in conclusion: "We ask you to put the stamp of your
disapproval on these corruptionists and send Hugh
Dempsey home to those who love him, a free man, with
a character as spotless as it was before these two worthless, degraded creatures tried to ruin it."

Mr. Robb closed for the prosecution.   His strongest
point consisted in ridiculing the idea that if Dempsey
wanted reports on the operations of the mill he would
have sent cooks instead of steelworkers to secure them.

Judge Stowe charged the jury in a perfectly dispas-
sionate and unbiased manner.   This was on the morning of Friday, January 20, the seventh day of the trial.
The jury remained out less than three hours and brought
in a verdict of "Guilty as indicted."   A demand for a
new trial was promptly made and, pending the hearing
of the application, Dempsey was liberated on $2,500
bail.

On January 24, Robert W. Beatty was placed on trial,
charged with "felonious assault in administering, or
employing persons to administer, poison" to the non-
union men in the Carnegie steel plant.   The same
counsel appeared on both sides that figured in the
Dempsey case, with the exception of District Attorney
Burleigh, whose place was taken by his assistant, Harry
Goehring.   William M. Erwin, the "Western Cyclone"
also appeared in court and joined the attorneys for the
defense.

Captain Breck opened the case for the commonwealth by reading the testimony brought out on his side in the Dempsey case. There were 67,000 words of this matter and, before the reading was concluded, most of the Captain's auditors sank into a gentle slumber. The array of medical men and.diarrhœa victims previously examined was then marshaled into court and re-examined and cross-examined for the benefit of the jury which was supposed not to be cognizant of the evidence submitted when Dempsey was on trial. Not until Charles McKinnie was put on the stand was an element of interest infused into the proceedings. McKinnie said that he was a riverman, knew Beatty well, and had been approached by the prisoner with a proposition to go to Homestead and dose the men with croton oil. He had refused to have anything to do with such contemptible work. The witness testified in a straightforward manner and made a visible impression on the jury.

Gallagher and Davidson repeated their former testimony with some variations, Davidson in his efforts to shield himself managing to contradict Gallagher in many points.

Charles C. Comstock swore that he had met Beatty in the mill and been advised by the latter to get out or the powders would fix him.

Many other witnesses were called to bear testimony 'to having seen Beatty in the mill at various times.

Attorney Brennen opened the case for the defense and at one point in his address amazed his auditory by stating his ability to prove, with reference to the supper at Wolfe's house, that "*the tea that was drank at this banquet was all consumed at the dinner the day before.*"

Mr. Brennen's slip of the tongue was much enjoyed. Undismayed by the effect of his inadvertent Hibernicism, the doughty little attorney proceeded to set forth the strong points of the case for the defendant, laying special emphasis on the declaration that there was nothing suspicious in the employment of cooks as detectives, inasmuch as the cookhouses were the most convenient headquarters for the kind of espionage which Dempsey had instituted.

Many witnesses were called to testify to the occurrence among the soldiers of a similar epidemic to that which beset the non-union steelworkers, and to prove the bad character of Gallagher and Davidson. Borough officials from Homestead swore that City Farm lane, which is close to the Carnegie works, was in a filthy, disease-breeding condition and physicians corroborated this evidence and showed that much sickness resulted from this cause.

Hugh F. Dempsey was summoned to the stand and told his story in about the same terms as were used by him when he testified on his own trial. He explained that nobody had authorized or requested him to send spies to Homestead. He had acted simply "in the interest of labor organizations."

Professor Hay again rebutted Captain Hunt's claim of having detected traces of croton oil in material furnished him by the mother of L. B. Hebron, and Dr. C. C. Wiley, surgeon of the Eighteenth regiment, stated that the conditions at Homestead conduced strongly to the spread of diarrhœa, cholera morbus and kindred complaints.

Robert J. Beatty, being sworn in his own defense,

said that he had worked in the water house and pump house at the Carnegie mills for nearly a year prior to the lock-out. He was a member of Boxmakers' Lodge No. 52, K. of L. Witness denied all parts of the testimony of Gallagher and Davidson which tended to incriminate him. His telegram concerning "two good agents on the road," referred, he said, to two men supplied by a labor organization in Cincinnati, of whom he knew no more than this. He had received for expenses $33 from Dempsey and some money from David Lynch, Thomas Crawford and other Homestead men.

The closing speeches on both sides and the judge's charge, being substantially identical with those delivered in the Dempsey case, need not be outlined here.

The jury evidently had its mind made up before withdrawing. After only nine minutes' consideration, a verdict of "guilty as indicted" was agreed upon.

A strong fight was made to secure a new trial for Dempsey, but without success, and on February 21, the convicted men were called up for sentence. Dempsey and Beatty were each sentenced to seven years' imprisonment in the penitentiary, and Gallagher and Davidson, who had pleaded guilty, were sentenced respectively to five and three years' imprisonment.

Dempsey's attorneys took an appeal to the supreme court, which was negatived, and later applied for a pardon for their client on the strength of a recantation made by Gallagher, but subsequently repudiated by him. Gallagher made affidavit that the story told by him in court was false and that he had been suborned to commit perjury by detectives and others in the service of the Carnegie Company. Hardly was the ink on the affidavit dry, however, until this paragon of mendacity made a third "confession," reaffirming his original testimony. The pardon board denied the application **on** Dempsey's behalf, and the ex-master workman was **thus** deprived of his last hope and doomed to serve his full term in prison.

OFFICES IN THE MILL YARD.

CHAPTER XX.

The Denouement.

CLIFFORD TRIED FOR HIS LIFE—
ALIBI TESTIMONY—ATTORNEYS
ERWIN AND ANDERSON WIN NEW
LAURELS—"NOT GUILTY"—HUGH
O'DONNELL AT THE BAR—THE HOMESTEAD LEADER AS A
REPORTER AND PEACEMAKER—WEAK TESTIMONY FOR THE PROSE-
CUTION—MAJOR MONTOOTH RIDICULES THE DISTRICT ATTORNEY'S
SUBSTITUTE—O'DONNELL ACQUITTED—THE CARNEGIE LAWYERS
ABANDON THE FIELD—BERKMAN'S ACCOMPLICES DISPOSED OF.

ON February 2, 1893, Jack Clifford was put on trial
before Judge Stowe, on an indictment charging
him, jointly with Hugh Ross, Hugh O'Donnell,
Burgess McLuckie and others, with the murder of Detective T. J. Connors. The counsel on both sides were the
same that appeared in the Critchlow case, with the
exception that W. S. Anderson, an eminent criminal
lawyer of Youngstown, Ohio, was added to the side of
the defense. The jury selected was as follows: John
Erichson, J. L. Hammitt, Andrew Hepp, Jr., W. G.
Bigham, Henry Lloyd, H. A. Price, John Stauffer, D.
C. Mayer, Andrew Donnelly, T. C. Rafferty, John M.
Hamilton and Patrick Kearney.

Early in the proceedings, Judge Stowe served notice

on the defense that he would not permit any line of
argument or cross-examination tending to justify the
killing of the Pinkertons. No matter who the invaders
were or what their purpose, the court held, the killing
was not justified. Mr. Erwin engaged in a tilt with the
court over this ruling, citing the mode of procedure in
the Critchlow case as precedent, but was summarily
silenced.

The testimony offered by the prosecution differed little
from that given against Critchlow. Pinkerton detectives
identified Clifford and swore to having seen him in the
forefront of the crowd that gathered to prevent the landing of the Pinkerton forces in the mill yard. Clifford
was armed with a pistol, they said, and was active in
building barricades and later in arranging the surrender.
It was he that waved the white flag from the river bank
and, in company with O'Donnell and others, guaranteed
protection to the Pinkertons, if they would lay down
their arms and come on shore. He had also aided in
caring for the wounded and getting them off the barges.

George L. Johnson, a mill-worker, testified to having
seen Clifford carry what appeared to him to be a powder
canister in the direction of the brass cannon which was
mounted in the gas house. Witness admitted that he
had been employed by the Carnegie Company and had
gone out on strike, but returned to work at his old job
on July 5. He took no part in the fight with the Pinkertons, but was merely a spectator. This colloquy
followed:

MR. BRENNEN.—"You made no effort to stop it?"

"No, sir."

"You were there considerable time and did not attempt
to spike the cannon?

"No, sir ; I did not."

An objection to such cross-examination was raised by the prosecution and sustained by the court.

MR. ERWIN.—"Your honor, I think if this witness did not withdraw from the scene of the disturbance he too was a rioter and an accomplice, and as such his evidence would have to be corroborated?"

THE COURT.—"No, it would have been unhealthy for him to have interfered and the objection is over-ruled."

Robert Pollock swore that he saw Clifford at the pump house throwing bottles filled with ignited oil at the barges, and also at the fire engine pumping oil through hose while other men were throwing lighted waste in the stream of oil flowing towards the barges.

C. S. Capehart, a clerk, had seen Clifford throwing dynamite, and William J. Henderson had seen him distributing stick dynamite to men who walked to the bank and threw the missiles at the barges.

As in the Critchlow trial, the defense set up for Clifford rested entirely on alibi testimony, his counsel undertaking to show that he was asleep and knew nothing of the fight until after Connors was shot, and that his part in the trouble of July 6 was confined to an attempt to save the Pinkertons at the risk of his own life.

Captain O. C. Coon, Charles Mansfield, of the *Homestead Local News*, Andrew Soulier and others, stated that they had witnessed the opening of the conflict between the Pinkertons and the workmen and that Clifford was not among the combatants.

Mrs. Annie Malloy, a widow residing in Mifflin township about two miles from the scene of the disturbance, swore that Clifford slept at her house on the night before July 6, and that she did not waken him until about 11.15 A. M. on that day. Her statements were corroborated by her daughters Maggie and Dora, the former of whom was said to be Clifford's sweetheart. Additional evidence sustaining the alibi was given by Mrs. Riley, with whom Clifford boarded, Constable Charles Stewart, President Garland, of the Amalgamated Association and P. H. McEvey, Vice-President of the Association.

Determined efforts were made by Attorney Erwin to show by witnesses that the crowd which gathered on the river bank to meet the Pinkertons was there for a peaceable purpose and that the Pinkertons were the actual rioters, but the prosecution objected to testimony of this character and its objections were sustained.

The closing speeches for the defense, delivered by Messrs. Erwin and Anderson, were masterpieces of forensic eloquence, and they were heard by a gathering such as has rarely assembled in a Pennsylvania court room. Legal practitioners, young and old, were there to watch the climax in this struggle of legal giants. Labor leaders sat side by side with capitalists. The classes and the masses were alike represented, and observed with equally keen interest the closing scene of the drama which, for all they knew, was to end in a tragedy. The prisoner himself was perhaps the coolest person in the throng. His nerve remained unshaken to the last.

After Mr. Robb had made his address for the prosecution, in the course of which he characterized the battle at Homestead as "the most fanatical piece of barbarity ever witnessed," Mr. Erwin spoke. He said, in part:

"At this time a grave responsibility rests upon me, for it now becomes my duty to address your conscience. It is a serious duty, your honor, (turning to the bench) to judge your fellow men's conscience. I am a stranger among you, but I do not fear your crowd, your array of lawyers or your judge, but I do fear my God. I am an officer of the court. I must obey it. I will obey it. I will walk in the line which it sets. We are here to try a citizen of Pennsylvania, born here, for taking the life of a man who, twenty-four hours after landing on your soil, was carried wounded from the boat with his smoking rifle in his hands. Your citizens ask me to ask you if you will believe these men who shot down McCoy and others of your citizens, or those self-confessed red-handed murderers. I stand here, and by the spirits of your dead citizens shot from your mills, I appeal to you for justice. I stand before a jury of Pennsylvania kings; there are no kings in Pennsylvania but the jury. There is no just adjudication but the jury box. It was the discovery of ages—to find some body wherein the conscience should be free.

*   *   *   *   *   *   *   *

"Now the duty of the commonwealth is plain in this case. It must convince your minds and your consciences that the defendant is guilty. Who says this Pennsylvania boy killed Connors? Nobody. They want to say and want you to say a great riot was in progress. I deny it. A riot is some act done by several persons unlawful in its character. I deny that there was any riot on the shore that day; the state does not prove that the defendant had a gun in his hand that day. They do try to prove by one witness that he had a revolver in his hand. The doctor testified that the wound that killed Connors was a rifle bullet. Then how can they accuse the defendant of the crime? They first (the state) must prove to you that there was a riot

there that day and that Clifford was there, participating
in that riotous proceeding, either aiding or abetting.
They offer us Pinkertons—Pinkertons to a Pennsylvania jury, gentlemen—who came into this state with
guns, who are murderers of your citizens, making their
children orphans. One of the attorneys for the prosecution, in his fervid manner, stigmatized that gathering of
Homestead people as anarchy. I say that invasion of
the Pinkertons was the highest evidence of anarchy.
You saw these little Carnegie clerks come here and testify that they had gone behind these barricades spy-
ing around, while bullets, as they say, were flying
fast and furious. That is simply absurd. It would have
been the highest act of bravery. It might be so, but
it is not reasonable and I would stigmatize it as a lie. It
is a tenet of the law that it is better that ninety-nine
guilty persons should escape than that one innocent
man should suffer. Will you believe the sheriff who
would try to pull the wool over your eyes and
endeavor to launch this defendant into eternity? Will
you believe the testimony of the defendant or this
red-handed Pinkerton? No, this is not a question
between labor and capital, and it amused me to have
the learned counsel on the other side assert it. It is
claimed by the prosecution that Clifford was at the
landing firing at these men when they landed; that there
was a cessation for four hours after. I deny this, for
witness after witness for the prosecution went upon the
stand and swore to the contrary. What is the purpose
of this move by the prosecution? It is simply a trick;
a pure trick of the law to show that there was a
cessation of firing which would permit the people of
Homestead to withdraw. There was no cessation, but
these Pinks poured out a continuous fire upon these
defenseless people on the hillside from port-holes cut
in the barges. Self-defense is a cardinal principle
not depending upon the law of the state, but upon
God. It does not depend upon man. Oh! how

weak is that attempt of man to try to prove wrong that which God has implanted in every man. That old doctrine that a man must retreat from a man with a sword or a stone in order to preserve the peace, has been swept away by the introduction of the Winchester rifle. Can you show me a man who can retreat from a fire of 300 rifles? Just so long as you can show me that there is no possibility for them to escape from that deadly fire, just so long do I contend they had a right to return that fire. There is another point of the prosecution to prove as an evidence of riot the fact that these people were on the Carnegie property and were using vile language. I deny that this can be shown as riot."

ATTORNEY BURLEIGH—We don't attempt to show it.

MR. ERWIN—I don't know what you don't attempt to show.

Attorney Erwin then read the law in definition of riot.

Continuing he said: "There is no proof here that they were assembled as rioters ; not the least scintilla of such a gathering. But on the other side I will show a riotous gathering."

MR. BURLEIGH—We object. Your honor has already ruled against such proceedings.

COURT—Yes.

MR. ERWIN—I know your honor has, and I therefore offer an exception that you will not permit me to speak of it. I will not speak of it. As I understand, Justice is represented blindfolded, with a scale in her hand equally weighing in both pans and with a sword in her hand. It is a sad thing that one of her exponents should——

COURT—Stop that. I won't allow any such line of argument.

MR. ERWIN—I am limited by the court and can't discuss the material necessary to be introduced in this case, but I will say that, through the objections of the district attorney, we have been denied a fair trial for our client.

Attorney Anderson followed Mr. Erwin. After outlining the case in a few graphic words, he said :

"Mr. Robb has attempted to tell you while he depicted that horrible act of the people on the bank that there was another side to that story. He forgot to tell you that a man from a foreign state raised and leveled his rifle and in spite of earnest pleadings shot a young man down. He forgot to tell you that not a shot was fired from the river bank until that young man lay weltering in his life blood. I will try to show you that the trouble did not come from the men on the shore, but from the men in the barges sent there. I want to see, and so do you, what the commonwealth of Pennsylvania wants to prove. It does not claim, because there is no evidence to prove it, that Jack Clifford fired that shot that killed Connors. Because Clifford was there they want to hold him responsible for an act committed by another party. Before they do it they must prove that he was acting and assisting those men to acts of violence. It matters not what was done after 12 o'clock. It matters not if he threw that dynamite or the can of powder. Because before that you must be convinced that Jack Clifford was there when Connors was shot. You might wonder at that ; that it is not a crime to throw burning oil or dynamite, but the prosecution specifies a particular charge against Jack Clifford. They claim that he was on the bank of the river in the forenoon when Connors was killed. How have they proved it. Let us look at the forenoon. They prove it by three detectives and three persons residing around Homestead—but six witnesses ; purely identification. Three of these men saw Clifford before that morning. It is well for the jury to consider these men and the prisoner. Men gathered from the slums of the cities of New York, Chicago and Philadelphia; men without employment, men without character, men who can be impeached by their testimony. Suppose a difficulty arose in Chicago and a person came here to employ a body of men to go there and suppress it, what sort of men would go there? Would a lawyer have the cinch? Oh, no. Would the banker leave his duties? Oh, no. Would the business man? Oh, no. But the idlers—the scrub of your city—would be the ones who would go. Then I say to you is this not sufficient to show the character of these people who invaded your state and are attempting to swear away the life of Jack Clifford? Upon whose testimony is this crime to be fixed upon Clifford? By three Pinkertons who, in the excitement of that battle and having never seen him before, swear that they saw him there. How do they prove it? By, as they say, a pink shirt on Clifford. Think of it, looking out in a crowd of 500 people and picking out a man with his coat buttoned up, could they be so collected in their thoughts as to distinguish him by a small portion of a pink shirt visible? I say they never did identify him there. But they did not fix this point of identification until brave Jack Clifford, in spite of the hail of bullets, went down and saved these men's lives. It was then, if at all, this pink shirt identification was fixed in their minds. These brave, true, honest men of your community with as keen perceptions as these Pinkertons, were in that boat, and yet they come on the stand and swear they did not see Clifford there. Captain Coon, who knew Clifford for years and was standing at the gangway watching what was going on, swears that Jack Clifford was not there. Then again, there is the old man Gray, a watchman at that mill, with an eye as keen as any Pinkerton's, who swears that Jack Clifford was not there that morning. Then, I say, is it just in this commonwealth where a man is on trial for his liberty and his life, that the testi-

mony of reputable witnesses of your state is of no more
weight than that of the Pinkertons? I know not what effect
the testimony of these employees may have upon you ; but
I do know that the employer has held the lash over his
employees and forced them to testify in their interest.
I do not know whether it has been done in this case.''

Here the speaker discussed at length the testimony
offered to establish an alibi for the prisoner and begged
the jury to weigh carefully in the balance the statements
of the opposing witnesses bearing on the subject.

In conclusion he said:

''The life and liberty of Jack Clifford are as dear to
him as yours are to you. There may be some one who
looks to him with an interest. There may be a gray-
haired mother depending upon him, and there is no love
like a mother's. That mother is waiting for your verdict. It is better that ninety-nine guilty escape than
one innocent shall suffer. I ask at your hands justice
for Jack Clifford. I ask it upon the oath you have
sworn faithfully to fulfill and I ask it in the tears of his
mother. Gentlemen, I leave Jack Clifford in your
hands.''

Judge Stowe's charge was a plain statement of the law
in the case, without the least tincture of bias one way or
the other.

The jury occupied less than two hours in deliberation
and brought in a verdict of acquittal. Clifford was then
remanded to jail to await trial on the other indictments
found against him.

The import of the verdict was unmistakable. It meant
that, for the second time, the people of Allegheny
County, speaking through their representatives in the
jury box, refused to be governed by the letter of the law

in the matter of punishing the men of Homestead as rioters and murderers, and that the continuance of the prosecutions would be a waste of time, energy and money. Such was the construction generally put upon it, and most probably the Carnegie Company and its counsel formed the same judgment. Nevertheless, the district attorney announced that every one of the Homestead cases would be brought to trial and as an earnest of sincerity, Hugh O'Donnell was brought forward to face a jury of his peers on February 13, the fifth day after Clifford's safe deliverance.

The young leader looked pale and thin as a result of his imprisonment, but his eye was as clear and his voice as firm as on the day when he marshaled the fighting men at the barricades, and there was no sign of flinching in his demeanor as he stood up to enter his plea of "not guilty."

The attorneys engaged in the case were the same that served in the preceding trials, excepting that Major E. A. Montooth and Mr. John F. Cox relieved the counsel who had previously taken the most active part for the defense. The following jurors were selected: Fred Vogel, William Richardson, Charles Beuchler, John Sproul, M. J. Byrne, Henry Brooker, A. C. Flood, Henry Eisenhauer, John McGann, John Geisler, Peter Stragen and William Dramble.

The case for the prosecution differed little from that advanced against Clifford and Critchlow. Pinkerton detectives, sheriff's deputies, mill clerks and reporters repeated the old, old story of the events of July 6, while Mr. D. F. Patterson, who conducted the direct examination as a substitute for the district attorney, elicited from each statements showing O'Donnell's ostensible participation in the battle.

The line of cross-examination pursued by the defense showed that the intention was to prove that O'Donnell was present at the battle as a newspaper correspondent, and that, when he interfered actively, it was in the capacity of a peacemaker. Several newspaper men testified that the defendant was known as a correspondent of the Tri-State News Bureau and of various daily papers, and that, in a spirit of professional fraternity, he had taken care of the reporters during the fight and secured for them a convenient headquarters of observation in the cupola of the mill. Only one out of a dozen reporters examined specifically incriminated O'Donnell, and the evidence of that one was vitiated by the knowledge that he had sold out to the Carnegie Company at the beginning of the Homestead trouble and had acted throughout as a spy.

The prosecution could not have made a weaker showing, all things considered, and the work of the other side was, therefore, comparatively easy.

Captain O. C. Coon, who accompanied O'Donnell to the river bank on the morning of July 6, was the star witness for the defense. O'Donnell, he said, went to the scene of the trouble for the express purpose of preventing bloodshed, and used every effort to check the combatants even to the extent of pushing angry men back from the water's edge after the firing had started. The witness had also seen O'Donnell, on the day after the surrender, rescue from the hands of a mob of strikers a poor wretch who was supposed to be a straggler from the Pinkerton forces.

Dr. John Purman testified in the same strain. He swore that O'Donnell came to his office with three wounded men on the morning of July 6. A crowd gathered on the street without, and O'Donnell exhorted them to go peaceably to their homes and avoid going to the mill-yard. Later in the day, witness met O'Donnell on the street. A crowd surrounded the young leader, cursing him, and some one said, "You are a ——— of a leader, staying away from the mill." O'Donnell answered, "There are no leaders; everyone acts for himself. If you want to do me a favor you will stop this and go to your homes."

Numerous other witnesses gave testimony corroborative of the assumption that the defendant had taken no part in the riot other than as a law-abiding citizen anxious to preserve the peace. O'Donnell's wife was placed on the stand, but her evidence was unimportant.

After the attorneys for the defense had practically won their case, it was decided to let O'Donnell testify in his own behalf. There was some doubt about the prudence of this move, and that it was not without foundation was shown by the difficulty which O'Donnell experienced in escaping damaging admissions.

In his direct examination by Mr. Brennen, O'Donnell told a straightforward and impressive story. He told of his residence of seven or eight years in Homestead, his newspaper correspondence and other personal matters, and then went on to describe, in graphic terms, his doings on the day of the riot. On that eventful morning, he said he had gone to the river bank, arriving just when the gang-plank was being run out from the barges. He begged the Pinkertons not to land and not to shoot, reminding them of the presence of women and children and the certainty of wholesale loss of life if violence should be resorted to. After the first skirmish, he had gone to the Postal Telegraph offices and notified the Mercy and South Side Hospitals to send ambulances. If he had had only a few minutes more time to gain the bow of the barges before the fighting began, not a shot would have been fired. In no manner had he aided or abetted the trouble which occurred that day, nor did he at any time encourage the use of violence in preventing the introduction of non-union men into the Homestead mill.

Mr. Patterson, in his cross-examination, tried to extract from O'Donnell the admission that the workmen maintained an armed military organization, but was unsuccessful. He managed, however to force the defendant to name some of the men who were among the combatants on the river bank.

Attorney Robb closed for the prosecution, in an address which was mainly devoted to picturing the trouble at Homestead as a revolution conducted by a band of assassins, thirsting for Pinkerton blood. He referred to Hugh O'Donnell as having been summoned by a whistle signal to "marshal his standing army and begin a battle to the death."

Major Montooth closed for the defense. He contended that the substitution of Mr. Patterson, the attorney hired by the Carnegie Company, in the place of the public prosecutor was sufficient reason why Hugh O'Donnell should be acquitted. Mr. Robb interrupted to ask the court if this was good law. Judge Stowe answered in the negative. Nevertheless, the shaft had been too well aimed to miss its mark because of this interference, and the point made by Major Montooth was undoubtedly appreciated by the jury.

Judge Stowe charged the jury briefly and to the same effect as in the Clifford case. The jurors stayed out from 7 o'clock in the evening until 9:30 o'clock on the next morning. When they filed into court there was nothing in their faces to indicate whether they brought good or bad news for the defendant. O'Donnell was quite cool and collected, nodding pleasantly to his wife and niece when he was brought in from the jail, and betraying no sign of emotion except a slight heaving of the chest at the moment when the foreman of the jury drew the sealed verdict from his pocket. "We find the prisoner not guilty," were the words that rang out upon the death-like stillness of the court-room—welcome words to almost everybody present. A murmur of approval was heard, but was hushed when the court officials rapped for order. The jury was dismissed without comment. Then O'Donnell, with tears of joy coursing down his cheeks, turned to his faithful wife and embraced her tenderly, while friends thronged around to proffer their congratulations. O'Donnell was recommitted to jail, pending a hearing on the remaining charges against him, but was shortly afterward released on bail. His was the last of the Homestead cases brought to trial. Realizing that it was impossible to obtain the conviction of any of the Homestead men, the attorneys for the Carnegie Company made overtures to their opponents which resulted in the dropping of all prosecutions on both sides. Ex-Burgess McLuckie protested vigorously against abandoning the case against H. C. Frick, in which he himself was the principal prosecutor, but his protest was overruled and, aside from the trials of Dempsey and Beatty, Homestead was heard of no more in the criminal court.

The anarchists, Carl Knold and Henry Bauer, whose arrest in connection with Berkman's attempt on the life of Mr. Frick was mentioned in an earlier chapter, were brought to trial a few days before Hugh O'Donnell on indictments charging them with conspiracy and with being accessories to Berkman's crime. It was shown that Berkman was harbored by Knold at the residence of Paul Eckert, in Allegheny City, a rendezvous for anarchists; that the anarchist circulars distributed at Homestead were printed at Eckert's and taken to Homestead by Bauer and Knold, and that the two defendants had counseled and guided Berkman in his assault on the Carnegie chairman. Berkman was brought in from the penitentiary to testify, but proved a recalcitrant witness. The solitary sensational feature of the trial was a speech delivered by Colonel W. D. Moore, counsel for the defense, in which he lauded the doctrine of anarchy and traced its origin back to the Redeemer of Mankind. Judge Slagle, in his charge to the jury, expressed profound regret at the enunciation of such objectionable views by a member of the legal profession. Bauer and Knold were found guilty on both indictments and sentenced five years to the penitentiary. At the same time the rioters arrested at Duquesne during the strike at that place were sentenced to the workhouse for terms ranging from two to six months.

CONCLUSION.

ALTHOUGH ignobly routed in the courts, the Carnegie Company lost not a foot of the ground gained at Homestead. On the contrary, it has since doubly re-inforced itself, for not only is the spirit of unionism stamped out among the employees of the firm, but fully three-fourths of the former union men are now working, most of them at their old jobs, without exhibiting a trace of the independence which was once their pride, or making any pretensions to a voice in the determination of their wages.

The re-employment of so many of the old hands was one of the fruits of the substitution of Mr. Schwab for Mr. Potter as general superintendent. Mr. Potter, having received the non-union men who came in during the strike and guaranteed them permanent work, would have become a stumbling-block when the time arrived for treating with the defeated union men and was, therefore, removed just before the crisis came. Mr. Schwab was bound by no pledges of his own and refused to recognize those made by his predecessor. Hence but a short time elapsed after the collapse of the strike until most of the green hands were discharged and their places filled by ex-strikers, whose experience rendered their services almost indispensable.

The active leaders of the strike were, of course, excluded from the amnesty, and few of them have since been able to secure employment at their trade. They are the victims of a form of ostracism; blacklisted as dangerous agitators in every steel and iron mill in the country.

Hugh O'Donnell left Homestead to travel as manager of a concert company and subsequently became connected with a weekly journal published in Chicago.

Honest John McLuckie tried his hand in sundry small ventures, lectured a little, took the stump in the campaign of November, '93, and otherwise managed to keep his head above water, but always under the handicap of a lost cause and the diversion of energy from the familiar pursuits of a lifetime into new and untried fields.

William T. Roberts turned his attention exclusively to speechmaking and politics.

Thomas Crawford worked for a time for the Uniontown Steel Company, and on the suspension of that firm, went into business with Jack Clifford alternately as politician and book agent.

David Lynch obtained a position as agent for a liquor firm.

Hugh Ross visited his birth-place in Scotland and has been idle since his return.

William H. Gaches carried on a successful business enterprise in Chicago during the World's Fair, but has since been idle.

Eddie Burke, known as "Rioter Burke," was stricken with an affection of the eyes which prevented his working even if he could have found a place. The Amalgamated Association, at the '93 convention, voted an appropriation sufficient to pay for his treatment at an eastern hospital.

Of the Amalgamated lodges in Homestead nothing remains but the charters which have never been surren-

dered, and under which a reorganization may be effected
if the men should hereafter find themselves in a condition
to return to union principles and practice. There is, however, nothing to indicate a future revival of the old-time
order of things. If there are grievances to be suffered
the men must simply be contented to suffer them in
silence rather than invite a repetition of the calamitous
consequences of their first and only encounter with
Chairman Frick.

Of the rates of wages now paid, no more is known by
outsiders than that they are even lower than was contemplated by the firm when the lock-out was ordered and
that they promise to fall lower still. The firm refuses to
publish its scale rates on the pretext that, by so doing,
it would be playing into the hands of competitors.
Rival manufacturers have endeavored to secure the
Homestead schedules and so, too, has the Amalgamated
Association, but without success. The Amalgamated
officials made their last fruitless effort in this direction
during the scale-making period in June, 1893.

As an additional protection against surprises of any
description, the fortifications of the Homestead mills
have been strengthened and no one can enter otherwise
than through the offices, from which a bridge leads to
the workshops. Mr. Frick is evidently determined to be
always ready, hereafter, for battles, sieges or stolen
marches.

There is one means of defense, however, which, having weighed it in the balance and found it wanting, the
Carnegie chairman is not likely to try a second time.
He will never again undertake to capture his own territory with a posse of Pinkerton Guards.

The original publishers of *Homestead* decided to set apart 5 percent of the net profits from the sale of the book to start a fund to purchase a monument in honor of the workers who were killed in the strike. This drawing of the proposed monument appeared in the original edition. It is assumed that this monument was never erected.

A monument was erected in 1941 by Local 1397 "in memory of the Iron and Steel Workers who were killed in Homestead, Pa., on July 6, 1892, while striking against the Carnegie Steel Company in defense of their American rights." (Vernon L. Gay)

AFTERWORD

In March 1937 U.S. Steel capitulated and recognized the Steel Workers Organizing Committee—an "industrial" union that gathered all steelworkers, regardless of specific crafts, into a single bargaining unit. Newly formed, SWOC grew out of the successful efforts of the Committee for Industrial Organization to win rights for workers in America's mass-production industries. A key element had been the New Deal's Wagner Act of 1935 that gave workers the rights to bargain collectively and to choose their own representatives, without company interference.

In its central clauses the 1937 contract called for a "$5-a-day wage; . . . a 40-hour week with time-and-a-half for overtime; a paid vacation system granting one week's vacation to all employees with five years of service."[1]

U.S. Steel was the pacesetter for the industry, as it had been since 1901, when it was created by a merger in which the Carnegie Steel Company was the major component. The 1937 recognition of SWOC set the pattern for other companies, forecasting a new era in which most of the industry would eventually go union. (Most independent companies finally came to terms with the union but only after violent strikes in the late thirties.)

By modern standards the terms of the contract were meager. Five dollars a day in 1937 is the rough equivalent of $23 a day in late seventies money. But for steelworkers the 1937 contract was the first step in a gradual climb toward middle-class income—up from the depths of nearly a half-century's depression of wages below subsistence levels.

The members of SWOC could date the long, bad years in steel from 1892, when Carnegie Steel broke the Amalgamated Association in Homestead. A monument erected in 1941 by Local 1397 remembered that historic defeat: "In memory of the Iron and Steel Workers who were killed in Homestead, Pa., on July 6, 1892, while striking against the Carnegie Steel Company in defense of their American rights."

301

I

Two lurid events are associated in popular memory with the Homestead Strike of 1892—the bloody clash between the steel-workers and the Pinkerton Detectives along the shore of the Monongahela and the attempted assassination of Henry Clay Frick by the Russian anarchist, Alexander Berkman.

Arthur Burgoyne's account—the work of an on-the-scene Pittsburgh journalist—is not lurid. It tells the story of the strike from beginning to end, from the confidence with which the union approached discussions with management early in 1892 to its bitter defeat in the late days of November. Burgoyne's narrative is, in fact, the best contemporary source of detail about the strike. (Another book-length account, Myron R. Stowell's *"Fort Frick" or the Siege of Homestead,* was published in 1893, but it contains less information.)

The early chapters of Burgoyne's book present the struggle as a confrontation between the "stronghold of capitalism" and the hopeful claims to power of craft unions. Each of the antagonists could claim preeminence. By 1892 Carnegie Steel was already the industry's leader, renowned for its innovative automation of the steel process, for its year-by-year leaps in productivity and income. The Amalgamated Association of Iron and Steel Workers was, as 1892 started, one of the largest and richest of the craft unions that made up the American Federation of Labor. It was an organization of skilled workers whose well-learned experience—its members felt—was indispensable to the production of quality steel.

Burgoyne's account fills in the details, large and small. He shows how a conflict, at first apparently about minimum wages, gradually revealed itself as a company determination to break the union—so that the first overt hostility, late in June, was a company lockout, not a strike. He portrays the famous shoot-out with the Pinkertons as a tactical victory for the union, perhaps, but also as a strategic blunder, because it opened the way for an occupation of Home-stead by the state militia. By the end of July, a war of attrition had set in; scabs were being employed at the mill. Burgoyne follows the action to its end—the legal harrassment of union leaders, brought to trial on unprovable charges; the tiredness and hunger of the people of Homestead; and the vote, finally, to return to work and the dissolution of the union.

Burgoyne presents details that a historian writing years later might miss. In the weeks before the strike, for example, Frick had a fence built around the mill. Since there had never been one before, the workers read its meaning: a declaration of war that gave the Homestead Works a new name—"Fort Frick." In another detail Burgoyne shows the political bias of the state militia by dwelling graphically on the fate of Private Iams—ordered hung by the thumbs for having shouted "three cheers for the man who shot Frick."

Burgoyne sees events from the perspective of Homestead, through the eyes of the union men. Homestead was, in his phrase, a "mushroom town," exploding in population from less than 600 in 1880 (before the mill was built) to 12,000 in 1892. In this era the citizenry and work force were made up dominantly of Scots, Irish, German; probably mostly Protestants. Burgoyne gives some leading names: "Honest" John McLuckie, Hugh O'Donnell, William Roberts, Isaac Critchlow, Jack Clifford, Silas Wain, William Foy. The union men were active citizens, proud of their work, proud of their community. Homestead was totally dependent on the mill, but it was energized by an atmosphere of confidence and economic opportunity.

Why did the strike fail? Burgoyne gives answers. The passage of nearly 100 years supplies the benefit of hindsight.

II

Burgoyne's theme is political, and it grows directly from the immediate situation. The men of the Amalgamated Association are his subject—the union tactics they adopt and (perhaps even more important) their deportment as citizens of Homestead and as Americans. He shows no inclination to philosophize about alternative forms of unionism—the justice or injustice, the efficacy or inefficacy, in a mass-employment industry of a craft unionism that officially excluded the unskilled workers. In Homestead the unskilled workers struck in sympathy with the skilled men, and in the immediate event it was irrelevant that the Amalgamated had no vision of an industrywide "industrial" unionism. (In steel, that alternative would begin to evolve in 1919 and be brought to fruition in the mid-1930s by the CIO.)

In Burgoyne's account the Homestead members of the Amalgamated were conservatives. Good citizens, they were concerned with the coming U.S. presidential election; they were active in town government; they celebrated the Fourth of July and prepared to welcome the National Guard. Republicans and Democrats all, they were anything but "Anarchists, aching for a chance to strike a blow at 'Capital' " (p. 82). The positions the Amalgamated laid out to Carnegie Steel were reasoned, presented according to agreed schedules, and open to negotiation. To Burgoyne, the lodges of Homestead represented unionism at its best.

In the opening chapters he sets down the assumptions held, quite plausibly, by the unionists. They knew they were skilled—they were proud; they thought they were indispensable. They assumed they could bargain with the company as equals. They not only worked in the mill, but lived in the town that surrounded it. They were governing citizens. After the strike began, they closed the saloons and patrolled the streets; they meant not only to picket but to "protect" the mill. Vis-à-vis the Works, they had "the feeling of ownership" (p. 13); "the men and the firm were practically in partnership" (p. 17). With the irony of hindsight, Burgoyne summarizes the workers' attitude: "It was clearly impossible that men of substance, heads of families, solid citizens of a prosperous municipality could be rooted up, as it were, out of the soil in which they were so firmly planted and beaten to earth by the creature of their labor" (pp. 13–14).

Partnership, ownership, citizenship. It was those assumptions that, according to Burgoyne, explained the men's reaction to Frick's fence. It was "a huge threat—a challenge—an insult" (p. 23) because it usurped what partly belonged to them, by the claim of their labor. In the logic of Burgoyne's account, similar responses seem in some measure to explain the repeated attempts to annihilate the Pinkertons. At the end of the book the lawyers describe the Pinkertons as "armed men [who] invade[d] Homestead 'within two days of the anniversary of the signing of the Declaration of Independence' " (p. 247) and attacked the "peaceable citizens of Homestead" (p. 248).

In sum, Burgoyne's account argues that the unionists were motivated by a vision of American democracy that involved participation in workplace decisions, as well as in local government—assertions that seemed to follow naturally from American ideals. According to the Strike Advisory Committee, "both the public and the employes . . . [had] equitable rights and interests" in the mill.[2] Burgoyne quotes John McLuckie's statement, "The constitution of this country guarantees all men the right to live" (p. 24).

The workers expressed an ideal. Burgoyne shows that the strike was lost because that ideal actually had little basis in American law.

The simple fact is that the strikers of 1892 had few rights. The Bill of Rights was designed to protect people only from governmental interference (even in the late 1970s, it is not clear what protections it affords against abuses by a private employer). No constitutional rights and, in 1892, no tradition of law assured that workers could organize, establish a bargaining unit, or picket or assemble in any way that might be construed as interference with a private business. By law the strikers had no right to invade Carnegie's property and attack the Pinkertons. By law they had no right to interfere with company efforts to bring in scab labor.

By constitutional and legal tradition, property rights were inviolate. Not only could Carnegie Steel hire and lock out as it chose, it could defend its property by whatever means it deemed necessary—by Pinkertons or its own company mercenaries. *Ownership* was emphatically defined by capital investment, as it typically still is in the American tradition. Work created no entitlement, no partnership.

Again, for Burgoyne, the Frick fence is a key symbol. It declared that the workers were, under no circumstances, partners in the mill, but aliens serving at company convenience—that a state of war with the workers would be more profitable than bargained agreements. When the soldiers arrived and took over Homestead, the citizenry became aliens even in their own community. Unprotected by the American legal system, the unionists were, in fact, treated like outlaws.

Writing when he did, Burgoyne was able to dramatize an important transition in the evolution of labor-management relations in America. The mass-employment industries that arose after the Civil War, railroads and steel in the vanguard, were creating a new system of labor relations. In 1892 the top policymakers were remote from the workplace—Frick in Pittsburgh, Carnegie in New York (or Europe). Their trips to a place like Homestead were magisterial, ceremonial; their relations with their work force, impersonal, contractual. The workers were conveniently construed as digits on the account sheets, to be manipulated by automated cost-cutting and a continuing supply of cheap labor. The new corporations were working out, on their own terms, a system of management that enabled them to handle thousands of workers efficiently and profitably.

The law lagged behind these changes. In 1892 legislatures were not yet persuaded that new legal problems, affecting whole towns, were created by property owners like Carnegie Steel, and that both the general citizenry and the labor force needed the protection of new laws. (After the strike the Pennsylvania legislature did outlaw employment of the Pinkertons within the state, and in 1906 it created the state police as a mobile troubleshooting force that could serve in labor disputes. The "Coal-and-Iron" police—company mercenaries—remained legal until the early 1930s.)

Up against the pragmatic power of the corporation, the initial assumptions of the men of the Amalgamated, sharply drawn by Burgoyne, seemed to look back to an era of smaller, more localized business. The "American rights" of the industrial workers would have to wait until the 1930s to be legislated into the American system.

III

Burgoyne focuses on the political issues, particularly on the fact that democratic worker participation in workplace decisions was one of the ideals directly attacked by the new corporations. Other factors less apparent to a journalist covering a strike followed from the nature of mass-employment industries. The antiunion policy was effective in 1892 and remained so for the next two generations, not only because of the state of the law but because the steel industry was implementing a policy of production efficiency and drawing on an apparently endless supply of cheap labor.

Carnegie Steel was the premier example of a philosophy of cost-cutting. Part of its strategy was to gain cheap access to raw materials. In the early 1880s, for example, the company had established its coke supply by a merger with H. C. Frick & Co. In the mid-1890s it leased huge tracts of the Mesabi Range to ensure cheap iron ore. Then it built its own railroads, the Bessemer and Lake Erie and the Union, in order to control transportation costs.

Inside the mills, the industry from the start was America's foremost example of mechanization. Many of the giant machines that moved and shaped hot metal were innovated by Carnegie Steel—the "Jones mixer" that handled molten iron, "charging machines" that loaded the openhearth furnaces, "manipulators" that turned ingots and blooms during the rolling process, the "skip hoist" and "bell" system that charged blast furnaces. Carnegie Steel became a marvel of productivity, increasing the tonnage produced per hour and decreasing the number of workers.

Mechanization was the key to cost-cutting. Machines reduced the number of workers required, particularly the number of *skilled* workers—the kind of workers who could claim their knowledge was indispensable and could enforce their demands by joining a craft union. Burgoyne's account suggests that, already by 1892, the skilled workers were not as important to Carnegie Steel as they thought they were. A continuing emphasis on mechanization throughout the nineties put the company in the happy position of increasing production while cutting back on the high-priced men and—without a union to contend with—setting wages as it wished.

Looking back to 1892, John A. Fitch summed up the effect of automation in his 1910 book *The Steel Workers:*

The question of improved machinery and its bearing upon the labor situation is of great importance everywhere, but nowhere more than in the steel industry. . . . No change has been overlooked that would put a machine at work in place of a man; thousands of men have been displaced this way since 1892. . . . Fifteen or twenty years ago a large proportion of the employes in any steel plant were skilled men. The percentage of highly skilled has steadily grown less; and the percentage of the unskilled has as steadily increased.[3]

The companies were also able to exploit an abundant labor market. To fill its low-skill jobs, the steel industry increasingly hired, during the nineties, the new immigrants from eastern and southern Europe. By the turn of the century, or shortly after, towns like Homestead and Braddock had majority populations of Slovaks, Poles, Italians, and Ukrainians. For the time being, these people were willing to accept the industry's low wages; there was still more opportunity than at home, and single men (perhaps 50 percent of the immigrants) could even save enough to return to the Old Country with a nest egg. The low wages and the influx of "foreigners" drove native-born Americans away from the mills. It was not until 1919 that the immigrants, many of them citizens by that time, would strike on their own behalf.

The men of the Amalgamated may have made tactical blunders at Homestead. But the state of the law, the evolving steel technology, and the availability of cheap labor combined to make union success unlikely in 1892, or in the foreseeable years ahead.

IV

Burgoyne shows that the initial disagreement in 1892 was economic—a question of wages. Writing in the months immediately following the strike, he could not know the full bleakness of the future that lay ahead for steel labor.

After the strike union power disappeared; pay was cut, especially for the high-priced workers; and the twelve-hour day became the rule. In 1893–94 typical wages appear to have ranged from $1.20 to $2.00 for a twelve-hour day (equivalent to $10 to $16.00 in late 1970s dollars). The pay of the skilled workers was leveled down, declining in some categories as much as 40 percent from the 1892 rate, even though the work day was longer. Detailed studies done in the Pittsburgh district in 1907–08 show that about 60 percent of the steelworkers earned less than $2.00 per day (1970s equivalent, less than $15).[4]

In 1919 a survey conducted by the Interchurch World Movement of North America summed up the plight of the steelworkers in the preunion era. It measured wages against government standards for families of five for (1) minimum subsistence level (defined as "*animal well-being,* with little or no attention to the comforts or social demands of human beings") and (2) minimum comfort level (defined as providing for "health and decency, but very few comforts"). Even accepting, for the sake of argument, company-supplied wage figures, the study showed the following wages for 1918:

Workers	Yearly Salary	Government Standards for Living Requirement for Family of Five
Skilled	$2,373	
		Minimum comfort, $1,760
Semiskilled	1,683	
		Minimum subsistence, $1,386[5]
Unskilled	1,265	

The unskilled and semiskilled together made up about 70 percent of the work force. Moreover, up until the early twenties, wages for most steelworkers were based on the twelve-hour day, seven-day week.

What did the Homestead Strike mean? Carnegie Steel was the bellwether of the industry. When the union was broken at Homestead, companies throughout the industry were able to declare their own wage policies until the mid-1930s, without bargaining collectively with their workers. The historical record is an unambiguous statement of the result.

The low-wage policy had a high social cost. It was a major factor in creating the blighted living conditions in the mill towns of the Pittsburgh district. True, the steel companies assumed certain civic responsibilities in the steel towns—paying for street paving, supporting public buildings (including libraries), sponsoring athletic leagues. But such devices failed to address living conditions of the sort described by Margaret Byington in *Homestead: The Households of a Milltown* (1910).

From the cinder path beside one of the railroads that crosses the level part of Homestead, you enter an alley, bordered on one side by stables and on the other by a row of shabby two-story frame houses. The doors of the houses are closed, but dishpans and old clothes decorating their exterior mark them as inhabited. Turning from the alley through a narrow passageway you find yourself in a small court, on three sides of which are smoke-grimed houses, and on the fourth, low stables. The open space teems with life and movement. Children, dogs and hens make it lively under foot; overhead long lines of flapping clothes must be dodged. A group of women stand gossiping in one corner, awaiting their turn at the pump,—which is one of the two sources of water supply for the 20 families who live here. Another woman dumps the contents of her washtubs upon the paved ground, and the greasy, soapy water runs into an open drain a few feet from the pump. In the center a circular wooden building with ten compartments opening into one vault, flushed only by this waste water, constitutes the toilet accommodations for over one hundred people. Twenty-seven children find this crowded brick-paved space their only playground; for the 63 rooms in the houses about the court shelter a group of 20 families, Polish, Slavic and Hungarian, Jewish, Negro. The men are unskilled workers in the mills.

This court is one of many such in Homestead; one of hundreds of similar courts in the mill towns of the [river valleys].[6]

V

Democratic citizenship, Burgoyne's central theme, can be traced through the years that followed the failure of the strike. Burgoyne's book argues that citizens who are active in a political democracy will also expect democratic rights in the workplace. A reverse of that proposition, present by implication in Burgoyne, is that workers denied rights in the workplace will be less-effective political citizens.

If the accounts of various writers can be believed, the political tone of Homestead changed after 1892. As an up-against-the-mill town, it would have always been unbeautiful and rough-and-ready. But an attitude changed.

The city directories in the nineties make the point. Those of 1890 and 1891 open with a fanfare, a boostering history of the town: "The past and the present are known and the record fills every Homesteader with pride. What of the future? It is full of promise" (1890). The 1891 directory devotes a section specifically to the harmony of Homestead's labor-management relations:

The thorough organization maintained by the company, through a capable superintendent and competent heads of every department, is equaled by the complete organization of the two thousand wage workers in the eight lodges of the Amalgamated Association of Iron and Steel Workers of the United States. In these mills the value of organized labor and arbitration as a means of fixing wages is clearly and forcibly exemplified. Under this system, both labor and capital make concessions, and under a "sliding scale" the wages are regulated by the condition of the market. Proper committees and representatives from the company and the lodges confer and adjust all differences arising and protect each other's interests.

In the years following the strike, the city directories printed *no* town history, as though the editors were dumbfounded. Something vital had changed in Homestead.

In the generation after the strike, writers who interviewed steel-workers found fear and apathy. Workers were afraid to criticize labor conditions and company policy, and they had become apathetic about citizen participation in a town whose politics were dominated by the mill, even refusing to patronize the library Carnegie had provided for them. Company spies were a familiar threat. Articulate union sympathizers were subject to instant firing and then blackballed from future jobs in the industry, even outside of the Pittsburgh area.

Fitch in his 1910 *Steel Workers* sums up what he found in Homestead:

I doubt whether you could find a more suspicious body of men than the employes of the United States Steel Corporation. They are suspicious of one another, of their neighbors, of their friends. I was repeatedly suspected of being an agent of the Corporation, sent out to sound the men with regard to their attitude toward the Corporation and toward unionism. The fact is, the steel workers do not dare openly express their convictions. They do not dare assemble and talk over their affairs pertaining to their welfare as mill men. . . .

[The] skilled steel workers are very much like other Americans. They are neither less nor more intelligent, courageous, and reliant than the average citizen. Their extreme caution, the constant state of apprehension in which they live, can have but one cause. . . . They have learned the cost of defiance.[7]

As Fitch points out, this attitude in the skilled workers was not a direct result of a single event, the loss of the 1892 strike. It was the effect of company repression enforced for many years.

From Burgoyne's account, it might have been expected that men denied self-expression and participation in the politics of the workplace would be apathetic and cynical about citizen politics away from the job. But the company took specific measures to ensure its control of the town. Fitch notes that in Homestead there was little discussion of politics, because "that, too, could easily bring a man into dangerous waters." He quotes, anonymously, a local politician:

"There is not such a perfect political organization in the country as the steel trust. They aim to control the politics of every borough and town where their works are located, and usually they do control. They plan their campaigns far in advance; they are laying their wires now to control the borough council three years ahead. You ought to see the way they line up their men at the polls and vote them by thousands. What does a secret ballot amount to? . . . These men have been so long dominated by the Corporation that they dare not disobey. They have a sort of superstitious feeling that somehow the boss will know if they vote wrong."[8]

The antiunion policy of the steel companies meant an idea of American citizenship starkly different from Burgoyne's picture of the activist, vocal men of the Amalgamated.

Again, the city directories tell the story. Before the strike glowing accounts were given of *both* the mill and the union; it is as though the author of the directory was asserting a partnership among labor, management, and the town. When the town history was finally resumed in 1927, the company was described; there was no mention of unionism, not even a reference to the 1892 strike. Even after the recognition by U.S. Steel of the Steel Workers Organizing Committee in the late thirties, the directories (which were published through 1945) avoided mentioning unionism.

Burgoyne equated good citizenship with good unionism, political democracy with industrial democracy. In the long years of company domination and nonunionism that followed, the publishers of the Homestead directories had perhaps learned a different truth: that the cause of labor was to be regarded as subversive and separate from the accepted version of politics in America.

VI

Burgoyne's "heroes," Hugh O'Donnell and "Honest" John McLuckie, have disappeared into history. Blacklisted from jobs in the steel industry, they both left the Homestead area. In 1894 O'Donnell wrote to a political scientist doing an article about the strike, "I am now shunned by both labor and capital, a modern Ishmael, doomed to wander in the desert of ingratitude"[9]

Some years after the strike, McLuckie was living in Mexico, working as a miner. When Carnegie learned where he was, he offered him money. McLuckie refused, with the statement— according to Carnegie's autobiography—"Well, that was damned white of Andy, wasn't it?"[10]

History remembers Frick and Carnegie. Intervening years have not altered the picture of the former: an effective manager consistently committed to cost-effectiveness and a lifelong opponent of unionism. Frick stuck to a clear principle, the profitability of the corporation. The forcefulness of his character is indicated in the statement he issued shortly after being shot by Berkman: "I do not think I shall die, but whether I do or not, the Company will pursue the same policy and it will win."[11]

Because of his complexities, Carnegie remains the more interesting of the two men. With his rags-to-riches background, including his family's identification with reformist politics in Scotland, Carnegie could never resist declarations that showed a sympathy for working people. Burgoyne details Carnegie's statement in 1886 that "the right of the workingmen to combine and to form trades unions is no less sacred than the right of the manufacturer to enter into association and conference with his fellows, and it must sooner or later be conceded" (pp. 19–20). This view was climaxed by Carnegie's declaration against importing scabs to break a strike: "There is an unwritten law among the best workmen: 'Thou shalt not take thy neighbor's job.' "[12]

The violence in Homestead and the resulting attacks on him in the international press deeply disturbed Carnegie. The strike made him appear a hypocrite. Why was he off in Scotland? Was this sympathizer-with-labor condoning (perhaps even contriving) the use of the Pinkertons against his work force, and then the employment of scab labor? For the rest of his life, Carnegie was pained by the contradictions publicly exposed in him by the Homestead Strike and his conflicting roles of corporate manager ' and social philosopher.

No evidence exists that links Carnegie directly to the Pinkertons (though the company had hired them in earlier years). What does seem clear, from evidence unknown to Burgoyne in 1893, is that not only was Carnegie as fully determined as Frick to break the union, but the private instructions he sent back to Pittsburgh were at variance with the image of remote beneficence that he tried to maintain.

In late July, for example, Hugh O'Donnell asked high-placed Republicans in the East to contact Carnegie with the proposal that the Amalgamated would be satisfied with recognition of the union, regardless of wages. Reached in Europe, Carnegie gave the impression that he would see that the proposition was considered and at first so cabled Frick. He quickly followed with another message to his manager: "Probably the proposition is not worthy of consideration. Useful showing distress of Amalgamated Association. Use your own discretion about terms and starting. George Lauder, Henry Phipps, Jr., Andrew Carnegie solid. H. C. Frick forever!"[13] When the Republican party intermediaries talked to Frick in Pittsburgh, they found him adamant: "I will fight this thing to the bitter end. I will never recognize the Union, never, never!"[14]

Frick and Carnegie may have had different styles, but nothing has been shown in the historic record to alter the impression that at Homestead, Frick enforced a policy that had the full support of Carnegie. And nothing has emerged that changes the judgment that, of the two men, Carnegie had the greater concern—a passionate concern—for his public image, which he was willing to maintain through duplicity, if necessary.

Despite his prolabor talk, Carnegie's antiunion policy had, in fact, been in the making for several years. The union had been broken in Braddock in 1888, and when Carnegie gave his workers there a library in 1889, he looked forward to Homestead in his dedicatory remarks:

I should like to see a Library [in Homestead] . . . [but] our men there are not partners. They are not interested with us. On the contrary, an Amalgamated Association has for years compelled us to pay one-third more in the principal department of our work [there].[15]

Homestead got its library in 1898.

VII

Arthur Gordon Burgoyne (1863–1914) was born and raised in Ireland, came to Pittsburgh in the early eighties, and for some thirty years was one of the area's leading journalists. He worked for the *Pittsburgh Leader* until 1906, when he joined the *Gazette-Times*; in 1907 he moved to the *Chronicle-Telegraph*.

His regional renown seems to have been less connected with his story of the Homestead Strike than with the daily poems on local topics he wrote during most of his career. Articles written about him admire him as a master of many arts—"poet, composer, musician, editorial writer, linguist, author, historian, teacher."[16] He apparently lectured for a time at Carnegie Institute of Technology on music history and aesthetics and, at his home in Verona, hosted a circle of intellectuals and artists.

A 1911 article announcing a lecture by Burgoyne indicates his local reputation:

Burgoyne's experiences in thirty years of Pittsburg journalism have been varied, at times humorous, again exciting and bristling with adventure. His reminiscences of public men and events in the city and State could fill volumes. Some of the anecdotes he tells and experiences he has passed through are very funny, and as only he can tell them, with a true Irish appreciation of all their ridiculous features, they are side-splitting. It is on account of these experiences and anecdotes that he has been at last persuaded to emerge from the seclusion of his den and favor the Pittsburg public with a lecture, which has been arranged for Friday night, April 7, in the Carnegie Music Hall. A committee of newspaper men is looking after the details and there has been such an insistent demand for tickets that some concern is now felt as to whether Carnegie Music Hall is large enough to hold the crowd. Many of the musical set who have known the delights of Burgoyne's musical soirees have demanded permission to appear on the program with him and furnish music for his lecture and arrangements have been made to admit of this. The details of the musical part of the program will be announced later, and it is safe to predict that Pittsburgers never before had a chance to take in such a delightful evening as this particular Friday night will be.[17]

Burgoyne published several collections of verse from his newspaper columns. His poetry is light and witty, skillfully varied in rhythms and rhymes. He wrote about topics of the day as they caught his fancy: sports, weather, women's fashions, Pittsburgh personalities. While none of his poems deals with labor-management relations, he did write about politics, throwing barbs especially at the political bosses of his era.

In an unusually doggerel vein, he wrote about Andrew Carnegie:

> Bow down, ye folks whose worldly store
>   Is miserably slim;
> In abject reverence before
>   This dignitary grim;
> That plenipotential beard of his
>   And stony British stare,
> Betoken clearly that he is
>   A multi-millionaire . . .
>
> On public libraries he spent
>   Of shekels not a few;
> A goodly slice to Pittsburg went,
>   And to Allegheny, too;
> But still the loss he doesn't feel,
>   It cannot hurt his health,
> For his mills keep on with endless zeal
>   A-piling up the wealth.
>
> Since he became a prince sublime,
>   This burg for him's too small;
> New York upon his royal time
>   And interest has the call;
> His courtiers puff him to his face,
>   As the starry-spangled Scot,
> But he can't go back on this good place,
>   Which gave him all he's got.[18]

—David P. Demarest, Jr.

Carnegie-Mellon University
Pittsburgh, Pa.

NOTES

1. *Then and Now: The Story of the United Steelworkers of America*, p. 53.

2. Quoted from the *Pittsburgh Post*, July 23, 1892, by J. Bernard Hogg in "The Homestead Strike of 1892," p. 183. Burgoyne's account does not cite the statement, but it typifies the point he makes.

3. Pp. 140–41.

4. Fitch discusses the evolution of wages in steel in his chapter "Wages and Cost of Living," pp. 150–65. Rough translations into 1970s buying power can be made by consulting such a source as *Historical Statistics of the United States*.

5. Interchurch World Movement of North America, *Report on the Steel Strike of 1919*, p. 97.

6. P. 131.

7. Pp. 214, 216.

8. Pp. 230–31.

9. Joseph Frazier Wall, *Andrew Carnegie*, p. 567.

10. *Autobiography of Andrew Carnegie*, 1st ed., p. 237.

11. Wall, p. 563.

12. Wall, p. 525.

13. Wall, p. 566.

14. Wall p. 566.

15. Andrew Carnegie, *Dedication of the Carnegie Library at the Edgar Thomson Steel Rail Works, Braddocks* [sic]: *Address to the Workmen*, pamphlet in the Margaret Barclay Wilson Collection of Carnegiana, vol. 4, Carnegie Library of Pittsburgh, p. 13.

16. George Swetnam, "Arthur Burgoyne," *The Pittsburgh Press*, January 14, 1962, Family Magazine.

17. *Pittsburg Bulletin*, April 1, 1911, p. 12.

18. Arthur Burgoyne, *All Sorts of Pittsburgers, Sketched in Prose and Verse* (Pittsburgh: The Leader of All Sorts Co., 1892), p. 5.

ACKNOWLEDGMENTS

I wish especially to acknowledge the help of Bill Gaughan, Senior Designer, Operations Planning and Control, at the Homestead Works, who probably knows more than any other single person about the history of the mill. He was generous in providing "archaeological" tours of the facility and in sharing information. I also wish to thank Randy Harris of Homestead, who identified and processed some of the graphic materials, and Ann Hart and Evelyn Patterson of the Carnegie Free Library of Homestead, who take an active interest in all projects dealing with the town.

—DD

TEXTUAL NOTE

Homestead: A Complete History of the Struggle of July, 1892, between the Carnegie Steel Company, Limited, and the Amalgamated Association of Iron and Steel Workers, by Arthur G. Burgoyne, was published in Pittsburgh, Pennsylvania, in 1893 by the Rawsthorne Engraving and Printing Co. Although it was read widely within the Pittsburgh area when it was first published, it has not been available in a popular edition for many years, and extant copies are difficult to locate.

This new edition, published by the University of Pittsburgh Press, is not a facsimile, although the complete text has been reproduced by photo offset. We have changed the title from *Homestead* to *The Homestead Strike of 1892* to avoid confusion with Margaret Byington's *Homestead: The Households of a Mill Town.* We have also given this edition a new cover design.

Most of the grouped illustrations did not appear in the original edition. The sources of the new illustrations follow the captions.

OTHER READINGS ABOUT STEEL

History and Sociology

Bodnar, John. *Immigration and Industrialization: Ethnicity in an American Mill Town, 1870–1940*. Pittsburgh: University of Pittsburgh Press, 1977.

Bridge, James Howard. *The Inside History of the Carnegie Steel Company*. Aldine Book Company, 1903. Reprint, New York: Arno Press, 1972.

Brody, David. *Labor in Crisis: The Steel Strike of 1919*. Philadelphia: Lippincott, 1965.

———. *Steelworkers in America: The Nonunion Era*. Cambridge, Mass.: Harvard University Press, 1960. Reprints, New York: Harper & Row, 1969; New York: Russell & Russell, 1970.

Byington, Margaret. *Homestead: The Households of a Mill Town*. New York: Charities Publication Committee, 1910. Reprints, New York: Arno Press, 1969; Pittsburgh: University Center for International Studies, 1974.

Fitch, John A. *The Steel Workers*. New York: Charities Publication Committee, 1910. Reprint, New York: Arno Press, 1969.

Hogg, J. Bernard. "The Homestead Strike of 1892." Ph.D. dissertation, University of Chicago, 1943.

Interchurch World Movement of North America. *Public Opinion and the Steel Strike; Supplementary Reports of the Investigators to the Commission of Inquiry, Interchurch World Movement*. New York: Harcourt Brace and Company, 1921. Reprint, New York: Da Capo Press, 1970.

———. *Report on the Steel Strike of 1919, by the Commission of Inquiry, Interchurch World Movement*. New York: Harcourt Brace and Howe, 1920.

O'Connor, Harvey. *Steel-Dictator*. New York: The John Day Company, 1935.

Powers, George. *Cradle of Steel Unionism: Monongahela Valley, Pa*. East Chicago, Ind.: Figueroa Printers, 1972.

Stowell, Myron R. *"Fort Frick," or The Siege of Homestead*. Pittsburgh: Pittsburg Printing Co., 1893.

Then and Now: The Story of the United Steelworkers of America. Pittsburgh: United Steelworkers of America Education Department, 1974.

Wolff, Leon. *Lockout, the Story of the Homestead Strike of 1892*. New York: Harper & Row, 1965.

Memoirs and Biographies

Autobiography of Andrew Carnegie. Boston and New York: Houghton Mifflin, 1920. Reprint, Boston: Houghton Mifflin, 1948.

Foster, William Z. *The Great Steel Strike and Its Lessons.* New York: B. W. Huebsch, Inc., 1920. Reprints, New York: Arno Press, 1969; New York: Da Capo Press, 1971.

Harvey, George. *Henry Clay Frick, The Man.* New York and London: Charles Scribner's Sons, 1928.

Hessen, Robert. *Steel Titan: The Life of Charles M. Schwab.* New York: Oxford University Press, 1975.

Livesay, Harold C. *Andrew Carnegie and the Rise of Big Business.* Boston: Little, Brown and Company, 1975.

Vorse, Mary Heaton. *Men and Steel.* New York: Boni and Liveright 1920.

Wall, Joseph Frazier. *Andrew Carnegie.* New York: Oxford University Press, 1970.

Novels

Attaway, William. *Blood on the Forge.* Doubleday, Doran & Co., 1941. Reprints, Chatham, N.J.: Chatham Bookseller, 1969; New York: Collier Books, 1970.

Bell, Thomas. *Out of This Furnace.* Boston: Little, Brown and Company, 1941. Reprints, New York: Liberty Book Club, 1950; Pittsburgh: University of Pittsburgh Press, 1976.

Bonosky, Phillip. *The Magic Fern.* New York: International Publishers, 1961.

Davenport, Marcia. *The Valley of Decision.* New York: Charles Scribner's Sons, 1942. Reprints, New York: Popular Library, 1969; Cambridge, Mass.: R. Bentley, 1979.